Mussar in Recovery

A Jewish Spiritual Path to Serenity & Joy

Hannah L.

with Rabbi Harvey Winokur

Ben Yehuda Press
Teaneck, New Jersey

Mussar in Recovery ©2025 Hannah L. All rights reserved. No part of this book may be used or reproduced in any manner whatsoever without written permission except in the case of brief quotations embodied in critical articles and reviews.

Published by Ben Yehuda Press
122 Ayers Court #1B
Teaneck, NJ 07666
BenYehudaPress.com

To subscribe to our monthly book club and support independent Jewish publishing, visit Patreon.com/BenYehudaPress

Ben Yehuda Press books may be purchased at a discount by synagogues, book clubs, and other institutions buying in bulk.
For information, please email markets@BenYehudaPress.com

ISBN13 978-1-963475-35-7 paper; 978-1-963475-36-4 paper
978-1-963475-37-12 epub

25 26 27 / 10 9 8 7 6 5 4 3   20250909

Recent books from *Ben Yehuda Press*

Burning Psalms: Confronting Adonai after Auschwitz by Menachem Rosensaft. "It's amazing that Menachem Z. Rosensaft's *Burning Psalms: Confronting Adonai after Auschwitz* doesn't burst into flames. This book of poetry — every poem in it a response or counterpoint to every one of the psalms in the biblical book — written by the son of Holocaust survivors and the brother of a murdered sibling he never knew, is composed with fire, fueled by a combination of rage, love, and despite-it-all faith that sears your eyes as you read it." —*New Jersey Jewish Standard*

Weaving Prayer: An Analytical and Spiritual Commentary on the Jewish Prayer Book by Rabbi Jeffrey Hoffman. "This engaging and erudite volume transforms the prayer experience. Not only is it of considerable intellectual interest to learn the history of prayers—how, when, and why they were composed—but this new knowledge will significantly help a person pray with intention (*kavanah*). I plan to keep this volume right next to my siddur." —Rabbi Judith Hauptman, author of *Rereading the Rabbis: A Woman's Voice*.

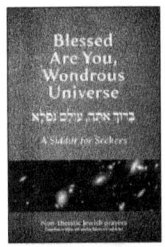

Blessed Are You, Wondrous Universe: A Siddur for Seekers. Non-theistic Jewish prayers by Herbert J. Levine. "Herb Levine has fashioned a sparkling collection of prayers for a thinking, feeling modern person who wants to express gratitude for the wonder of existence." —Daniel Matt, author, *The Essential Kabbalah*. "An exercise in holy audacity." —Dr. Shaul Magid, author, *The Necessity of Exile*

Siddur HaKohanot: A Hebrew Priestess Prayerbook by Jill Hammer and Taya Shere. Creative and traditional Jewish rituals and prayers that explore an earth-honoring, feminine-honoring spirituality with deep roots in Jewish tradition. "Far more than a prayerbook, this is a paradigm-shifting guidebook that radically expands our religious language, empowering us to reclaim what our souls have known for centuries: how to cook, season, and feast on our love of life, Spirit, and each other." —Rabbi Tirzah Firestone, author, *The Receiving: Reclaiming Jewish Women's Wisdom*

Eternal Questions by Rabbi Josh Feigelson. These essays on the weekly Torah portion guide readers on a journey that weaves together Torah, Talmud, Hasidic masters, and a diverse array of writers, poets, musicians, and thinkers. Each essay includes questions for reflection and suggestions for practices to help turn study into more mindful, intentional living. "This is the wisdom that we always need—but maybe particularly now, more than ever, during these turbulent times." —Rabbi Danya Ruttenberg, author, *On Repentance and Repair*.

Mussar in Recovery: A Jewish Spiritual Path to Serenity & Joy by Hannah L. with Rabbi Harvey Winokur. "A process of recovery that is physically healing, morally redemptive, and spiritually transformative." —Rabbi Rami Shapiro, author of *Recovery: The Twelve Steps as Spiritual Practice*. "A lucid and practical guidebook to recovery." —Dr. Alan Morinis, author, *Everyday Holiness: The Jewish Spiritual Path of Mussar*.

Other Covenants: Alternate Histories of the Jewish People by Rabbi Andrea D. Lobel & Mark Shainblum. In *Other Covenants*, you'll meet Israeli astronauts trying to save a doomed space shuttle, a Jewish community's faith challenged by the unstoppable return of their own undead, a Jewish science fiction writer in a world of Zeppelins and magic, an adult Anne Frank, an entire genre of Jewish martial arts movies, a Nazi dystopia where Judaism refuses to die, and many more. Nominated for two Sidewise Awards for Alternate History.

Recent books from *Ben Yehuda Press*

Just Jewish: How to Engage Millennials and Build a Vibrant Jewish Future by Rabbi Dan Horwitz. Drawing on his experience launching The Well, an inclusive Jewish community for young adults in Metro Detroit, Rabbi Horwitz shares proven techniques ready to be adopted by the Jewish world's myriad organizations, touching on everything from branding to fundraising to programmatic approaches to relationship development, and more. "This book will shape the conversation as to how we think about the Jewish future." —Rabbi Elliot Cosgrove, editor, *Jewish Theology in Our Time*..

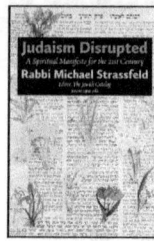

Judaism Disrupted: A Spiritual Manifesto for the 21st Century by Rabbi Michael Strassfeld. "I can't remember the last time I felt pulled to underline a book constantly as I was reading it, but *Judaism Disrupted* is exactly that intellectual, spiritual and personal adventure. You will find yourself nodding, wrestling, and hoping to hold on to so many of its ideas and challenges. Rabbi Strassfeld reframes a Torah that demands breakage, reimagination, and ownership." —Abigail Pogrebin, author, *My Jewish Year: 18 Holidays, One Wondering Jew*

A Passionate Pacifist: Essential Writings of Aaron Samuel Tamares. Translated and edited by Rabbi Everett Gendler. Rabbi Aaron Samuel Tamares (1869-1931) addresses the timeless issues of ethics, morality, communal morale, and Judaism in relation to the world at large in these essays and sermons, written in Hebrew between 1904 and 1931. "For those who seek a Torah of compassion and pacifism, a Judaism not tied to 19th century political nationalism, and a vision of Jewish spirituality outside of political thinking this book will be essential." —Rabbi Dr. Alan Brill, author, *Thinking God: The Mysticism of Rabbi Zadok of Lublin*.

Seeking the Hiding God: A Personal Theological Essay by Arnold Eisen. "This generation's preeminent scholar of contemporary Jewry, Arnold Eisen has devoted his career to studying the spiritual strivings within the Jewish soul. In *Seeking the Hiding God*, Eisen provides a personal window into his own theological vision. Eisen's explorations will inspire readers to ask today's urgent questions of meaning and faith." —Rabbi Dr. Elliot Cosgrove, author of *For Such a Time as This: On Being Jewish Today*.

Embracing Auschwitz: Forging a Vibrant, Life-Affirming Judaism that Takes the Holocaust Seriously by Rabbi Joshua Hammerman. The Judaism of Sinai and the Judaism of Auschwitz are merging, resulting in new visions of Judaism that are only beginning to take shape. "Should be read by every Jew who cares about Judaism." —Rabbi Dr. Irving "Yitz" Greenberg

Put Your Money Where Your Soul Is: Jewish Wisdom to Transform Your Investments for Good by Rabbi Jacob Siegel. "An intellectual delight. It offers a cornucopia of good ideas, institutions, and advisers. These can ease the transition for institutions and individuals from pure profit nature investing to deploying one's capital to repair the world, lift up the poor, and aid the needy and vulnerable. The sources alone—ranging from the Bible, Talmud, and codes to contemporary economics and sophisticated financial reporting—are worth the price of admission." —Rabbi Irving "Yitz" Greenberg.

The Way of Torah and the Path of Dharma: Intersections between Judaism and the Religions of India by Rabbi Daniel Polish. "A whirlwind religious tourist visit to the diversity of Indian religions: Sikh, Jain, Buddhist, and Hindu, led by an experienced congregational rabbi with much experience in interfaith and in teaching world religions." —Rabbi Alan Brill, author of *Rabbi on the Ganges: A Jewish Hindu-Encounter*.

About the Authors

Hannah L. is a student and facilitator of the Mussar tradition who draws on 10+ years of living the Twelve Steps and learning Mussar to reveal the transformative power of these synergistic paths for personal growth. A scientist, inventor, innovator, and explorer, she blends curiosity and creativity with heartfelt faith. As a mother and grandmother, friend and mentor, Hannah lives with purpose—guided by the twin blueprints of Mussar and recovery. Her journey is one of seeking and finding serenity, joy, and daily renewal—becoming her best self in a world full of the unpredictable. Through courageous storytelling rooted in personal experience and spiritual insight, Hannah offers readers practical wisdom, an actionable toolkit, and a guided pathway to their own healing and wholeness.

Rabbi Harvey J. Winokur was ordained by the Hebrew Union College (Cincinnati) and is Rabbi Emeritus of Temple Kehillat Chaim (Georgia). He continues to serve the Jewish community as a certified Spiritual Director and a Trainer-Facilitator for The Mussar Institute. He and Hannah met over a decade ago—she a new Mussar student on a personal spiritual journey and he a new facilitator—exploring the practice of the Mussar tradition together. Now, after their shared study and growth in the Mussar tradition, Rabbi Winokur joins Hannah to bring this Jewish wisdom to the spiritual path of fulfilling our potential for greatness in the face of life's great challenges.

Arden, Trisha Ilene, Iris, Diane, Pat, Andrea), giving me the confidence to write *Mussar in Recovery*.

DT and ST, thank you for putting up with my obsessive writing schedule, cancelled play dates, missed dinners and random calls looking for just the right word.

My immediate family, JP, MA, ES, PG, EM, and MJ, thank you for your unconditional love, your ongoing willingness to forgive me, for inspiring me to be my best self and for this amazing life we get to share.

Last, and surely not least, are my beloved clergy at Central Synagogue in New York City who rekindled my faith and love of Judaism. Your vision, wisdom and love inspire and guide me in recovering my best self so I can be of service one day at a time. Thank you.

You all made this adventure of my life more joyful and fulfilling than I could ever have imagined.

Thank you all for journeying with me. May you be blessed.

—*Hannah L.*

Acknowledgements

There are so many to thank for the love and support that enabled this book.

I must start with Alan Morinis, the teacher who brought Mussar wisdom to life for me, first on the printed page and then through his teaching and leadership of The Mussar Institute. Alan, you have illuminated my path; your light shines bright. Your generosity, love of the Tradition and insights inspire me. Thank you.

Rabbi Harvey Winokur, you introduced me to Mussar 12+ years ago. Over subsequent years of study and discussion, you helped me find spiritual purpose in this blueprint for living laid out by our Sages. Quite simply, this work together changed me and my life. Collaborating on *Mussar in Recovery* is a dream come true. Thank you.

Larry Yudelson at Ben Yehuda Press, thank you for taking me on as a new author and supporting this project to serve the Jewish community.

Laura Logan, my editor, thank you for your patience and guidance. Knowing that you believed in the value of this project fueled me through the rewrites and revisions. You worked your magic on my words, vastly improved the manuscript and helped make *Mussar in Recovery* clear and readable. Thank you.

Diane, Stan, Ann, Faye, Michael, Rabbi Sasha Baken, and Rabbi Nicole Auerbach, thank you for taking your precious time to read early drafts, give me feedback and keep me honest, humble and focused.

My Program sponsor, fellows and community, thank you for sharing your experience, strength and hope and carrying me through my darkness to a life filled with serenity and joy.

My *chevruta* partners, Jeff, Dan, and Susan, thank you for believing in me and, in concert with my va'adim (Rayna, Barb, Annette, Ilene, Andrea, Lisa,

jewishaction.com/religion/inspiration/the_power_of_jewish_prayer.

[329] Rabbi Lord Jonathan Sacks, "Prayers from the past and present can shape our world of the future," The Rabbi Sacks Legacy, January 7, 2006, https://rabbisacks.org/archive/prayers-from-the-past-and-present-can-shape-our-world-of-the-future/.

[330] Rabbi David Wolpe, "Sukkot V—Why Do We Pray?," Sinai Temple, 2021, https://www.sinaitemple.org/worship/sermons/sukkot-v-why-do-we-pray/.

[331] Rabbi Steven Fisdel, *The Meditation Practice Within Kabbalah* (Katriel Press, 2014), 1.

[332] Rabbi Jeff Roth, *Jewish Meditation Practices For Everyday Life: Awakening Your Heart, Connecting With God* (Jewish Lights, 2009), 1.

[333] Rabbi Sam Feinsmith, "What Is Jewish Meditation?," My Jewish Learning, 2024, https://www.myjewishlearning.com/article/what-is-jewish-meditation/.

[334] Jay Michaelson, "Shabbat and Meditation: Just Be It—How mindfulness can deepen your Shabbat experience—and vice versa," My Jewish Learning, 2024, https://www.myjewishlearning.com/article/shabbat-and-meditation-just-be-it/.

[335] Morinis, *Everyday Holiness*, 100.

Chapter 16

[336] Bill W., *A.A. 12 & 12*, 106.

[337] Bill W., *A.A. 12 & 12*, 125.

[338] Sarah Kristenson, "Joy VS Happiness: 11 Important Differences Between Each," Happier Human, April 26, 2022, https://www.happierhuman.com/joy-vs-happiness/.

[339] Shapiro, *Recovery—The Sacred Art*, 68.

[340] "Step 12 – A blend of spiritual, awakening, carrying the message, and daily practice," Hazelden Betty Ford Foundation, January 3, 2019, https://www.hazeldenbettyford.org/articles/step-12.

[341] Al-Anon Family Groups, *One Day at a Time in Al-Anon* (Al-Anon Family Group Headquarters, 2000), 335.

[342] Leviticus 23:23.

[343] Talmud, Bava Batra 9a.

[344] Rabbi David Jaffe, "N'divut—Generosity: Giving Away, Bringing Close," in *The Mussar Torah Commentary*, 152.

[345] Rabbi Joseph B. Meszler, "N'divut—Generosity: Let A Generous Spirit Sustain Me," in *The Mussar Torah Commentary*, 119-120.

[346] Morinis, *Everyday Holiness*, 156.

[347] Alan Morinis, "Path Of The Soul #6. Giving From The Heart," Aish.com, https://aish.com/48907677/.

[348] Micah 6:8.

[349] *The Ways of the Tzaddikim*, 310.

[350] Morinis, *Everyday Holiness*, 151.

[351] *The Ways of the Tzaddikim*, 311.

[352] *The Ways of the Tzaddikim*, 317-319.

[353] Morinis, *Everyday Holiness: The Jewish Spiritual Path of Mussar*, 159.

[354] *The Ways Of The Tzaddikim*, 309-310.

[355] Talmud, Bava Batra 9b.

[356] Morinis, *Every Day, Holy Day*, 119.

[357] Genesis 12:1-3.

[358] Jaffe, "N'divut—"Generosity: Giving Away, Bringing Close," 152.

[359] Rabbi Avi Fertig and Alan Morinis, "Stinginess #3.3—The Chaburah Program," The Mussar Institute, 2012, 4.

[360] Dessler, *Strive For Truth*, v. 1, 119-120.

[361] Dessler, *Strive For Truth*, v. 1, 141-142.

[362] Fertig & Morinis, "Stinginess #3.3," 4.

[363] Fertig & Morinis, "Stinginess #3.3," 4.

[364] Morinis, *Everyday Holiness*, 12.

Chapter 17

[365] Rabbi Angela W. Buchdahl, "Breathing In The Endings—A Meditation," podcast, Central Synagogue, Aug. 24, 2021, https://www.centralsynagogue.org/adult-engagement/meditation/breathing-in-the-endings.

[366] Dachner Keltner, *Awe: The New Science of Everyday Wonder and How It Can Transform Your Life* (Penguin, 2023), 94-116.

[367] Keltner, *Awe*, 101.

[368] Keltner, *Awe*, 7.

[277] Morinis, *With Heart in Mind*, 200.
[278] Morinis, *Everyday Holiness,* 83; Morinis, *With Heart in Mind,* 202
[279] Morinis, *Everyday Holiness*, 84.
[280] *Sefer HaChinuch*, cited in *Everyday Holiness* (Morinis), 158.
[281] Luzzatto, *Path of the Just*, 45.
[282] Sara Kupor, "The Flow of Generosity: How Tzedakah Benefits Both the Receiver and the Giver," Building Jewish Bridges, 2019, https://buildingjewishbridges.org/High-Holidays/The-Flow-Of-Generosity-How-Tzedakah-Benefits-Both-The-Receiver-And-The-Giver/.
[283] Dessler, *Strive for Truth*, v. 1, 130.
[284] Morinis, *Everyday Holiness*, 80.
[285] Morinis, *Everyday Holiness*, 143-144.

Chapter 14

[286] Taub, *God of Our Understanding*, 91.
[287] Al-Anon Family Groups, *Hope For Today* (AFG, 2002), 173.
[288] Fred H. *Drop The Rock: The Ripple Effect* (Hazelden 2016), 4.
[289] Al-Anon, *Hope For Today,* 173.
[290] Bill W., *A.A. 12 & 12*, 88.
[291] *A.A. Big Book*, 84.
[292] Al-Anon, *Hope For Today,* 173.
[293] Jodi Picoult, *House Rules: A Novel* (Simon and Schuster, 2010), 162.
[294] Pirkei Avot 1:2. The act of kindness is subject to some variation in translation. https://www.jpost.com/judaism/torah-portion/article-827022.
[295] Alan Morinis, "Chesed/Lovingkindness—Mussar In Action Session #18," The Mussar Institute, 2011, 4.
[296] Rabbi Angela W. Buchdahl, sermon, "The World is Built on Kindness (Yom Kippur 5783)," Centralsynagogue, Oct. 4, 2022, https://www.Centralsynagogue.Org/Worship/Sermons/The-World-Is-Built-On-Kindness-Yom-Kippur-5783.
[297] Talmud, Avot D'Rabbi Natan 11a.
[298] Shapiro, *Recovery—The Sacred Art*,139.
[299] Buchdahl, "The World is Built on Kindness."
[300] Ruttenberg, *On Repentance and Repair*, 49.
[301] Ruttenberg, *On Repentance and Repair*, 175.
[302] Pirkei Avot 2:10.
[303] Talmud, Shabbat 153a.
[304] Rabbi Dr. Abraham J. Twerski, "Is the 12-Step Program Kosher," Aish, https://aish.com/judaism__the_12_steps/.
[305] Geffen, *Stairway to the Sky,* 165.
[306] Morinis, *Everyday Holiness*, 193.
[307] Talmud, Berachot 27b.

Chapter 15

[308] Al-Anon, *Courage to Change*, 182.
[309] Al-Anon, *Hope for Today*, 213.
[310] Justin Kunst, "Understanding And Practicing Step Eleven" Amethyst Recovery Center, 2023, https://www.amethystrecovery.org/understanding-practicing-step-eleven/.
[311] Al-Anon, *Courage To Change*, 129.
[312] Bill W., *A.A. 12 & 12*, 102.
[313] Dan Harris, 10% Happier: *How I Tamed the Voice in My Head, Reduced Stress Without Losing My Edge, and Found Self-Help That Actually Works—A True Story* (!Tbooks, 2014), cover flyleaf.
[314] Al-Anon Family Groups, *One Day at a Time in Al-Anon* (Al-Anon Family Group Headquarters, 2000), 291.
[315] Al-Anon Family Groups, *Reaching For Personal Freedom* (Al-Anon Family Group Headquarters, 2013), 58.
[316] Al-Anon, *Courage To Change*, 182.
[317] Al-Anon, *Hope For Today*, 341.
[318] *A.A. Big Book*, 86-88.
[319] Bill W., *A.A. 12 & 12*, 98.
[320] "Kedusha: Holiness—Unit 2. Classic Sources," The Mussar Institute, 2020.
[321] "Kedusha: Holiness—Unit 1. Introduction. What Is So Important About Holiness?," The Mussar Institute, 2020.
[322] David Siff, "What is Holiness?," Sefaria. https://www.sefaria.org/sheets/68206.
[323] Luzzatto, *Path of the Just*, 6.
[324] Rabbi Angela W. Buchdahl, "Get Shabbat Retreat" Centralsynagogue.org, 2023.
[325] Luzzatto, *Path of the Just*, 176.
[326] 1 Samuel 2:2.
[327] Paquda, *Duties of the Heart*, v. 1, 229.
[328] Rabbi Lord Jonathan Sacks, "The Power Of Jewish Prayer," *Jewish Action*, 2009, https://

[232] Al-Anon Family Groups, *How Al-Anon Works—for Families And Friends Of Alcoholics* (Al-Anon Family Group Headquarters, 2008), 57.
[233] Rabbi Danya Ruttenberg, *On Repentance and Repair: Making Amends in an Unapologetic World* (Beacon, 2022), 19.
[234] Ruttenberg, *On Repentance and Repair*, 28.
[235] Lew, *This Is Real*, 85.
[236] Rabbi Berel Wein, "Accountability: Parashas Vayakhel Pekudei," Torah.org., March 15, 2012, 5772, https://torah.org/torah-portion/rabbiwein-5772-vayakhel/.
[237] Rabbi Peter B. Schaktman, "Acharayut—Responsibility: The Personal and the Communal," in *The Mussar Torah Commentary*, 179-185.
[238] Ruth Schapira, "The Hidden Meaning of Responsibility," Inner Judaism, March 23, 2022, https://www.innerjudaism.com/post/the-hidden-meaning-of-responsibility.
[239] Talmud, Shevuot 39a.
[240] Talmud, Bava Kamma 2:6.
[241] Talmud, Shabbos 54b.
[242] Rabbi Chaim Walkin, *The World Within: Contemporary Mussar Essays* (Targum, 2000), 117-122.
[243] Rabbi Rachel Gurevitz, "Acharayut—Responsibility: Responsibility to the Other," in *The Mussar Torah Commentary*, 261.
[244] Dessler, *Strive for Truth*, v2, part 3, 130.
[245] Ruttenberg, *On Repentance and Repair*, 58-59.
[246] Morinis, *Everyday Holiness*, 199.
[247] Rabbi Angela W. Buchdahl, "Hanukah's Leap Of Faith Miracle – A Meditation," Centralsynagogue.org., Dec. 12, 2023, https://www.centralsynagogue.org/adult-engagement/meditations.
[248] Ecclesiastes 10:18.
[249] *The Ways of the Tzaddikim*, 295.
[250] Proverbs 24:30-31.
[251] *The Ways of the Tzaddikim*, 295.
[252] Pirkei Avot 2:21.
[253] Micah 6:8.
[254] "Tikkun Olam: Repairing the World," My Jewish Learning, 2023, https://Gevurah.myjewishlearning.com/article/tikkun-olam-repairing-the-world/.
[255] Rabbi Lori Shapiro, "Clergy Leadership Incubator—Can Mussar Help Us Repair the World?," Clergy Leadership Incubator, 2021, https://www.cliforum.org/2021/04/can-mussar-help-us-repair-the-world/.
[256] Rabbi Michael Farbman, "Seder—Order," Temple Emanuel of Greater New Haven, 2015, https://tegnh.org/2015/08/25/seder-order/.
[257] Walkin, *The World Within*, 122.
[258] Rabbi Yehuda Geffen, *Stairway to the Sky: A Step-By-Step Guide to Achieving a Torah Life,* adapted from the original Hebrew by Avi Fertig (Feldheim, 2012), 75-76.
[259] Pirkei Avot 4:1.
[260] "Gevurah—Count the Omer Week Two," The Mussar Institute, 5782.

Chapter 13

[261] Rabbi Ilan Glazer, *And God Created Recovery: Jewish Wisdom to Help You Break Free From Your Addiction, Heal Your Wounds, and Unleash Your Inner Freedom* (Maddix, 2019), 114.
[262] "Making Amends in Addiction Recovery," Hazelden Betty Ford Foundation, 2020, https://www.hazeldenbettyford.org/articles/making-amends-addiction-recovery/.
[263] Bill W., *A.A. 12 & 12*, 84.
[264] Bill W., *A.A. 12 & 12*, 87.
[265] Bill W., *A.A. 12 & 12*, 84.
[266] Ruttenberg, *On Repentance and Repair*, 12.
[267] Rabbi Paul Steinberg, *Recovery, the 12 Steps and Jewish Spirituality: Reclaiming Hope, Courage and Wholeness* (Jewish Lights, 2014), 86; Glazer, *And God Created Recovery*, 119-126; *Tanya, The Masterpiece of Hasidic Wisdom*, trans. and annotated by Rabbi Rami Shapiro (Skylight Paths & Jewish Lights, 2014), 100.
[268] Lew, *This Is Real*, 189.
[269] Luzzatto, *Path of the Just*, 105.
[270] Paquda, *Duties of the Heart*, v. 2, 605-663.
[271] Olitzky & Copans, *Twelve Jewish Steps to Recovery*, 69.
[272] Shapiro, *Recovery—The Sacred Art*, 136.
[273] Shapiro, *Recovery—The Sacred Art*, 134.
[274] Ruttenberg, *On Repentance and Repair*, 174.
[275] Shapiro, *Recovery—The Sacred Art*, 130.
[276] Morinis, *Everyday Holiness*, 79-82.

[173] John Assaraf, "Are you interested or are you committed," *Medium*, May 21, 2020. https://medium.com/@kumarprasanjitshaw/are-you-interested-or-are-you-committed-by-john-assaraf-efdebc806b5b.
[174] Bill P. et al., *Drop the Rock*, 18.
[175] Justin Kunst, "The Origins of Willingness," Amethyst Recovery Center, 2023, https://www.amethystrecovery.org/the-origins-of-willingness/.
[176] "On Self-Respect: Joan Didion's 1961 Essay from the Pages of Vogue." *Vogue*, Dec. 23, 2021. https://www.vogue.com/article/joan-didion-self-respect-essay-1961.
[177] Morinis, *Every Day, Holy Day*, 190.
[178] Exodus 12:8.
[179] Morinis, *Everyday Holiness*, 127.
[180] *The Ways of the Tzaddikim*, 285-287.
[181] Morinis, *Everyday Holiness*, 127.
[182] Morinis, *Everyday Holiness*, 126.
[183] Isabel Rose, Hannah Story. https://www.youtube.com/watch?v=1AZ3KJLBhis.
[184] Bamidbar Rabbah 13:5.
[185] Levin, *Cheshbon HaNefesh*, 137.
[186] Deuteronomy 29:14-30:19.
[187] *The Ways of the Tzaddikim*, 283.
[188] Pirkei Avot 5:23.
[189] Twerski, *Teshuvah Through Recovery*, 91.
[190] Shapiro, *This Is the Path*, 45-48.
[191] Lew, *This Is Real*, 60.
[192] Morinis, *Everyday Holiness*, 128.
[193] *The Ways of the Tzaddikim*, 291.
[194] Rabbi Elizabeth Bahar, "Z'rizut—Alacrity: With Joy In His Heart," in *The Mussar Torah Commentary*, 135-140.
[195] *The Ways of the Tzaddikim*, 293.
[196] Luzzatto, *Path of the Just*, 52.
[197] *The Ways of the Tzaddikim*, 293.
[198] Helaine Sheias, PhD and Nancy Weiss, "Tapestry, Lesson 1," The Mussar Institute, 2022.

Chapter 11

[199] Al-Anon Family Groups, *Al-Anon's Twelve Steps and Twelve Traditions*. (Al-Anon Family Group Headquarters, 2005), 45. Also called *Al-Anon 12 & 12*.
[200] *A.A. Big Book*, 59.
[201] Bill W. et al., *Drop the Rock*, 57.
[202] Dr. Edith Eva Eger, *The Choice—Embrace The Possible* (Scribner, 2017), 34.
[203] Eger, *The Choice*, 237.
[204] Marisa Crane, "Step 7 of AA: Ask Him to Remove Your Shortcomings," Sober.com, https://sober.com/step-7-of-aa/.
[205] Paquda, *Duties of the Heart*, 589.
[206] Morinis, *Everyday Holiness*, 53-54.
[207] Luzzatto, *Path of the Just*, 152-162.
[208] Paquda, *Duties of the Heart*, 549-603.
[209] Shapiro, *This is the Path*, 51-52.
[210] Morinis, *Everyday Holiness*, 46.
[211] Rabbi Abraham J. Twerski, *Lights Along The Way—Timeless Lessons for Today from Rabbi Moshe Chaim Luzzatto's Mesillas Yesharim* (Mesorah, 1995), 291.
[212] Luzzatto, *Path of the Just*, 152.
[213] Talmud, Sanhedrin 43b.
[214] Deuteronomy 26:17.
[215] Luzzatto, *Path of the Just*, 152.
[216] Luzzatto, *Path of the Just*, 163.
[217] Luzzatto, *Path of the Just*, 163.
[218] Paquda, *Duties of the Heart*, 591.
[219] Twerski, *Lights Along The Way*, 291-292.
[220] Olitzky and Copans, *Twelve Jewish Steps to Recovery*, 54.
[221] Shapiro, *Recovery—The Sacred Art*, 103.
[222] Morinis, *Everyday Holiness*, 47.
[223] Rabbi Abraham Isaak Kook as cited by Morinis, *Everyday Holiness*, 46.
[224] Morinis, *Everyday Holiness*, 107.
[225] Morinis, *Everyday Holiness*, 109.
[226] Rabbi Lord Jonathan Sacks, "Greatness is Humility—Shoftim 5772," The Rabbi Sacks Legacy Trust, 2024, https://www.rabbisacks.org/covenant-conversation/shoftim/greatness-is-humility/.
[227] Kurtz and Ketcham, *The Spirituality of Imperfection*, 187.
[228] Pirkei Avot 4:1.
[229] Pirkei Avot 2:10.
[230] *The Ways of the Tzaddikim*, 97-103.
[231] Kurtz and Ketcham, *Spirituality of Imperfection*, 185.

Chapter 12

54.

[130] Rabbi Chaim Ephraim Zaitchik, *Sparks of Mussar: A Treasury of the Words and Deeds of the Mussar Greats*, retold from Hebrew by Ester van Handel (Pisgah Foundation, 1985).

[131] Rabbi Yeruchem Levovitz, by attribution of Alan Morinis in *Every Day, Holy Day: 365 Days Of Teachings And Practices From The Jewish Tradition Of Mussar*, (Feldheim, 2010), 25.

[132] Rabbi Adin Steinsaltz, *Change And Renewal: The Essence Of The Jewish Holidays, Festivals, And Days Of Remembrance*, trans. Daniel Haberman (Maggid Books, 2011), 29.

[133] Benjamin Franklin, "Plan for Attaining Moral Perfection," 1790, https://www.gutenberg.org/cache/epub/20203/pg20203-images.html#IX.

[134] Levin, *Cheshbon HaNefesh*, 44.

[135] Morinis, *Everyday Holiness*, 30.

[136] I refer you to the Institute for Jewish Spirituality Program "Awareness in Action."

[137] Dessler, *Strive For Truth*, v1, part 2, 77.

[138] Dessler, *Strive For Truth*, v1, part 2, 76.

[139] Deuteronomy 31:7.

[140] Rabbi Marc Margolius, "Mindful Torah For Our Time: Mindful Forgetting—Nitzavim—Deuteronomy 29:9-30:20," Institute for Jewish Spirituality, n.d.

Chapter 9

[141] Shapiro, *Recovery: The Sacred Art*, 78.

[142] Paquda, *Duties of the Heart*, 775; Luzzatto, *Path of the Just*, 14.

[143] Luzzatto, *Path of the Just*, 19.

[144] Paquda, *Duties of the Heart*, 775.

[145] Rabbi Marc Margolius, "Vayera, Bechira/Choice Points: Imagining Another Way," Institute for Jewish Spirituality.

[146] Martin Buber, *The Way of Man—According to the Teaching of Hasidism* (Citadel, 1966), 16, https://lib.tcu.edu/staff/bellinger/rel-sec/Buber.pdf.

[147] Psalms 128:1.

[148] Lew, *This Is Real*, 45-46.

[149] Paquda, *Duties of the Heart*, 717.

[150] Lew, *This Is Real*, 41.

[151] Numbers 5:1-7.

[152] Rabbi Joseph Soloveitchik, "Yom Kippur: The Dimensions of Repentence," My Jewish Learning, 2024, https://www.myjewishlearning.com/article/the-dimensions-of-repentance/.

[153] Twerski, *Teshuvah Through Recovery*, 90.

[154] Genesis 32:11-33:10.

[155] Numbers 20:11.

[156] Morinis, *Everyday Holiness*, 265.

[157] Genesis 2:25.

[158] *Ways of the Tzaddikim*, 81-95.

[159] Rabbi Samuel J. Rose, "Bushah—Shame: The Soul Trait of Shame" in *The Mussar Torah Commentary*, (CCAR, 2020), 176.

[160] Berachos 12b and Avot 5:20 are cited in *The Ways of the Tzaddikim*, 81-95.

[161] Margolius, "Mindful Forgetting," Institute for Jewish Spirituality.

[162] Paquda, *Duties of the Heart*, 201.

[163] Pirkei Avot 2:5.

[164] *The Ways of the Tzaddikim*, 95.

[165] Dessler, *Strive for Truth*, v2, p. 106.

[166] Luzzatto, *Path of the Just*, 21.

[167] Alan Morinis, "Awareness/Zehirut—Being Careful Not To Fall Into A Spiritual Pit," Mussar Program Class #17, Jewish Pathways, 2007, https://avivwithinsidewithoutside.files.wordpress.com/2013/12/awareness.pdf.

Chapter 10

[168] "Verbatim." *Science & Spirit* 17, no. 4 (2006): 5. *Gale Academic OneFile.* https://link.gale.com/apps/doc/A171141094/AONE?u=mwy&sid=bookmark-AONE&xid=35f92d5e. https://link.gale.com/apps/doc/A171141094/AONE?u=mwy&sid=bookmark-AONE&xid=35f92d5e.

[169] Bill W., *A.A. 12 & 12*, 66-67.

[170] Bill P., Todd W., and Sara, S., *Drop The Rock: Removing Character Defects*, (Hazeldon, 2005), 4-5.

[171] Bill P. et al., *Drop the Rock*, 12.

[172] Keith Harrell, "Why Your Attitude Is Everything," Success.com, May 11, 2023, https://www.success.com/why-your-attitude-

[92] Rabbi Avi Fertig, *Bridging the Gap* (Feldheim, 2007), cited by Alan Morinis in *A Season of Mussar* Unit 12, "*Emunah*/Faith for *chevrutah*," (The Mussar Institute, 2014).
[93] Morinis, *Everyday Holiness*, 221.
[94] Deuteronomy 31:6.
[95] Proverbs 28:14.
[96] This is an adaptation of the poem which was published in its entirety in *The Penguin Book Of Hebrew Verse*, T. Carmi, Ed. & Trans. (Penguin Books, 1981), 338, http://heskaamuna.org/wp-content/uploads/Where-Lord-will-I-Find-You.pdf.
[97] Dessler, *Strive for Truth*, v2, part 3, 116.
[98] Luzzatto, *Path of the Just*, 11-13.
[99] Bava Batra 14b.
[100] Morinis, *Everyday Holiness*, 14.
[101] Deuteronomy 10:16.
[102] Dessler, *Strive for Truth*, v2, part. 3, 116.

Chapter 7

[103] Nachmanides (aka Ramban) was a medieval Spanish rabbi (ca. 1194-1270). His name is easily confused with that of another Spanish rabbi, Maimonides (aka Rambam), who lived 1138-1204.
[104] Morinis, *Everyday Holiness*, 220.
[105] *Introduction to Judaism: A Sourcebook*, compiled and edited by Stephen J. Einstein, et al. (UAHC Press, 1998 Rev. Edition), 188-189.
[106] The stars of this show were Rabbi Mark Golub z"l, President of the Jewish Broadcasting Service and Rabbi Angela Warnock Buchdahl, Senior Rabbi of Central Synagogue, New York, NY. You can listen to the interview at https://www.youtube.com/watch?v=Dw0M2GUh3TY.
[107] Paquda, "The Gate of Trust in God," in *Duties of The Heart*, v1, 349-465.
[108] Jeremiah 17:5.
[109] Job 5:13.
[110] Paquda, *Duties of The Heart*, v1, 361.
[111] Jeremiah 17:7.
[112] Rabbi Cantor Alison Wissot, "Bitachon—Trusting the Path," in *The Mussar Torah Commentary*, ed. Rabbi Barry H. Block (CCAR Press, 2020), 101-106.
[113] Leviticus 26:11.
[114] The Mussar Institute, "Bitachon/Trust—Alter of Novardok," from *Middah of the Month* (The Mussar Institute, January 2017), 5.
[115] Proverbs 3:6.
[116] Psalms 32:10.
[117] *Ways of the Tzaddikim*, 287.
[118] Pirkei Avot 2:4.
[119] A traditional charm in the shape of a hand to ward off the evil eye.

Chapter 8

[120] Howard Sovronsky, "The Importance of Remembering," Jewish Federation of Greater Hartford, Feb. 3, 2017, https://www.jewishhartford.org/blog/the-importance-of-remembering.
[121] Al-Anon Family Groups, *One Day At A Time In Alanon*, (Al-Anon Family Group Headquarters, 2000), 328.
[122] A variety of Step 4 Inventory tools are available. We are not recommending any in particular. For examples, check out *Fourth Step Guide: Journey Into Growth* from Hazelden Publishing; *Blueprint for Progress* from Al-Anon Family Groups.
[123] Rabbi Angela W. Buchdahl, "Forgetting to Remember—A Meditation," Centralsynagogue.org., May 3, 2022, https://www.centralsynagogue.org/adult-engagement/meditation/forgetting-to-remember.
[124] *A.A. Big Book*, 84.
[125] Rabbi Alan Lew, *This Is Real And You Are Completely Unprepared* (Little Brown, 2003), 67.
[126] Paquda, "The Gate of Self Accounting – On Making a Personal Accounting before God," in *Duties of The Heart*, v2., 665-783.
[127] Luzzatto, *Path of the Just*, 14.
[128] Paquda, "Gate of Self Accounting," *Duties of the Heart*, 777.
[129] Rabbi Menachem Mendel Levin of Satanov, *Cheshbon HaNefesh: A Guide to Self Improvement and Character Refinement,* trans. Rabbi Shraga Silverstein (Feldheim, 1995),

52 Proverbs 14:23.
53 Pirkei Avot 2:21. Translated as *Ethics of our Fathers*, Pirkei Avot is a collection of writings that are part of the Mishnah (ca. 200 CE) where Jewish oral law was codified.
54 Morinis, *Everyday Holiness*, 3.
55 Pirkei Avot 1:14.

Chapter 4

56 Morinis, *Everyday Holiness*, 30.
57 Morinis, *Everyday Holiness*, 249-285.

Chapter 5

58 Center For Professional Recovery, "What Does It Mean To Be Allergic To Alcohol? Alcoholism Q&A," 2018, https://www.centerforprofessionalrecovery.com/what-does-it-mean-to-be-allergic-to-alcohol/.
59 *A.A. Big Book*, 62.
60 Pirkei Avot 1:18.
61 Rabbi Yisrael Salanter (as cited by Alan Morinis in *With Heart in Mind*, (Trumpeter, 2014), 213.
62 Rabbi Eliyahu E. Dessler, as cited by Alan Morinis in "Tiferet (Truth)," The Mussar Institute, 5782, https://mussarinstitute.org/wp-content/uploads/2022/04/Tiferet-Omer-Week-3-2022.pdf.
63 Shlomo Wolbe, *Alei Shur* v2, 520-521, cited in "Falsehood #9.3," (The Chaburah Program of The Mussar Institute, 2013).
64 Exodus 23:7.
65 Rabbi Moshe Chaim Luzzatto, *Path Of The Just*, trans. Yosef Leibler (Feldheim, 2004), 74.
66 Talmud, Chagigah 11b.
67 Talmud, Chullin 94a.
68 Dessler, *Strive for Truth*, v1, part 1, 267-272.
69 *Cheshbon HaNefesh* is translated as accounting or inventory of the soul.
70 Rabbi Menachem Mendel Levin, *Cheshbon HaNefesh. A Guide to Self Improvement and Character Refinement*, trans. Shraga Silverstein (Feldheim, 1995), 173.
71 Rambam is the nickname of Moses ben Maimon (1138–1204), a scholar also commonly known as Maimonides.
72 Alan Morinis and Avi Fertig, "Falsehood #9.1," The Chaburah Program, The Mussar Institute, 2013.
73 Luzzatto, *Path of the Just*, 53-91.
74 Psalms 24:3-4.
75 Luzzatto, *Path of the Just*, 56.
76 "The Gate of Falsehood," in *Ways of the Tzaddikim: On Refining Character Traits And Maintaining Balance In All Matters*, ed. Rabbi Gavriel Zaloshinsky and trans. Rabbi Shraga Silverstein (Feldheim, 1995), 383.
77 Levin, *Cheshbon HaNefesh*, 173.
78 Sanhedrin 97A.
79 Luzzatto, *Path of the Just*, 82.

Chapter 6

80 The Twelve Steps of A.A. were adapted to create the 12 Steps of Al-Anon. The point of difference is in Step 12. A.A. calls for carrying the message to alcoholics; Al-Anon's 12th step says carry the message to others.
81 Maimonides' Mishnah Commentary, *Thirteen Principles of Faith* (ca. 12th century CE).
82 Writing about 800 years after Maimonides, Levovitz was a prominent Mussar teacher known as the Mashgiach or spiritual leader of the Mir Yeshiva in Poland.
83 Dessler, *Strive For Truth*, v1, part 2, 224.
84 Pesachim 50, Sanhedrin 105.
85 Alan Morinis, "Faith/Emunah—Mussar in Action, Session 23," The Mussar Institute, 2011, 1.
86 Morinis, "Faith/Emunah—Mussar in Action, Session 22," The Mussar Institute, 2011, 4.
87 Genesis 15:5.
88 Morinis, *Everyday Holiness*, 227.
89 Midrash Temurah 5, trans. Chabad.org, 2023, https://www.chabad.org/112059.
90 Fred Claar, "Israel Means To Struggle With God. It is possible to be a good Jew and have questions about God," My Jewish Learning, 2023, https://www.myjewishlearning.com/article/israel-means-to-struggle-with-god/.
91 Morinis, *Everyday Holiness*, 225.

[13] Rabbi John L. Rosove, "Do You Have To Believe In God To Be A Jew?", Reformjudaism.org., January 18, 2018, https://blogs.rj.org/blog/do-you-have-believe-god-be-jew.
[14] Pew Research Center, "Jewish Americans in 2020."
[15] *The "God" Word. Agnostic and Atheist Members in A.A.* (Alcoholics Anonymous World Services, Inc., 2018), 5.
[16] Rabbi Rami Shapiro, *Recovery—The Sacred Art: The Twelve Steps As Spiritual Practice* (Skylight Paths, 2009), ix.
[17] Exodus 33:19-20.
[18] Rabbi Abraham J. Twerski, "Correspondence," in *I Am I* (Shaar, 1993), 209.
[19] Twerski, *Teshuvah Through Recovery—Experience The Transformative Power Of The Twelve Steps* (Mekor, 2016), 57.
[20] Rabbi Rami Shapiro, *This is the Path—Twelve Step Programs In A Jewish Context* (EnR Wordsmiths, 1989), 17.
[21] Rabbi Sarah Berman, Shabbat Service, Centralsynagogue.org, December 22, 2023, https://www.youtube.com/watch?v=CWHTG-oM3j8.
[22] Alan Morinis, *Everyday Holiness: The Jewish Spiritual Path Of Mussar* (Trumpeter/Shambala, 2007), 17.
[23] Morinis, *Everyday Holiness*, 11.
[24] Morinis, *Everyday Holiness*, 289.

Chapter 3

[25] *A.A. Big Book,* 17.
[26] Proverbs 12:25.
[27] Leviticus 19:10.
[28] Rabbi Jill Jacobs, "The Importance of the Community (*Kehilla*) in Judaism," My Jewish Learning, 2024, https://www.myjewishlearning.com/article/community-focused/.
[29] Pirkei Avot 1:14.
[30] Psalms 89:3.
[31] Rabbi Moshe Cordovero is considered to be a Mussar Master. He wrote the classic text *Tomer Devorah* (Palm Tree of Deborah) in the 16th century.
[32] *The Elucidated Tomer Devorah: Learning Compassion Through Hashem's 13 Attributes of Mercy*, adapted by Rabbi Shmuel Meir Riachi, trans. Rabbi Daniel Worenklein (Feldheim, 2015), 198-213.
[33] Talmud, Ta'anit 7A.
[34] Greg Marcus, "What is Mussar?" My Jewish Learning, 2024, https://www.myjewishlearning.com/article/the-mussar-movement.
[35] Rabbi Salanter is another Mussar master. He is credited with launching the Mussar movement in Europe during the 1800s.
[36] Alan Morinis, *Climbing Jacob's Ladder: One Man's Journey To Rediscover A Jewish Spiritual Tradition* (Trumpeter/Shambala, 2007).
[37] Al-Anon Family Groups. *Courage to Change: One Day at a Time in Al-Anon II* (Al-Anon Family Group Headquarters, Inc., 1992), 92.
[38] Morinis, *Everyday Holiness*, 253-259.
[39] Ernest Kurtz, and Katherine Ketcham, *The Spirituality of Imperfection—Storytelling and the Search for Meaning* (Bantam, 1992), 19.
[40] Ruchi Koval, *Soul Construction: Shape Your Character Using 8 Steps from the Timeless Jewish Practice of Mussar* (Lifecodex, 2021), 46-60.
[41] Alcoholics Anonymous, "Origin Of the Serenity Prayer: A Historical Paper," (Alcoholics Anonymous General Service Office, 2009), https://www.aa.org/sites/default/files/literature/assets/smf-129_en.pdf.
[42] "50 inspiring Maya Angelou quotes to improve your outlook on life," Today.com, Dec. 18, 2023, https://www.today.com/life/inspiration/maya-angelou-quotes-rcna126821.
[43] Genesis 2:7.
[44] Genesis 1:27.
[45] Morinis, *Everyday Holiness,* 19-20.
[46] Tanya, Chapter 31. Tanya is the foundational book of Chasidic philosophy written by Rabbi Zalman, founder of the movement.
[47] Leviticus 11:44.
[48] Morinis, *Everyday Holiness,* 20.
[49] Morinis, *Everyday Holiness,* 253-259.
[50] Rabbi Eliyahu E. Dessler, *Strive for Truth,* trans. Rabbi Aryeh Carmell (Feldheim, 1985), v1, 53.
[51] Psalms 34:15.

Endnotes

Chapter 1

[1] Substance Abuse and Mental Health Services Administration, *Key Substance Use and Mental Health Indicators in the United States: Results from the 2022 National Survey on Drug Use and Health* (HHS Publication No. PEP23-07-01-006, NSDUH Series H-58), 2023, https://www.samhsa.gov/data/report/2022-nsduh-annual-national-report.

[2] Brian J. Grim and Melissa E. Grim, "Belief, Behavior, And Belonging: How Faith Is Indispensable In Preventing And Recovering From Substance Abuse," *Journal of Religion and Health*, 58, (October 2019): 1713-1750, https://doi.org/10.1007/s10943-019-00876-w; Ofir Livne, Tovia Wengrower, Daniel Feingold, Dvora Shmulewitz, Deborah S. Hasin, and Shaul Lev-Ran, "Religiosity And Substance Use In U.S. Adults: Findings From A Large-Scale National Survey," *Drug And Alcohol Dependence* (Aug. 2021): 225:108796, https://doi.org/10.1016/j.drugalcdep.2021.108796; Rabbi David R. Hodge, Paul Cardenas, and Harry Montoya, "Substance Use: Spirituality And Religious Participation As Protective Factors Among Rural Youths," *Social Work Research*, 25 (2001): 153-161, https://doi.org/10.1093/swr/25.3.153; Amy M. Burdette, Noah S. Webb, Terrence T. Hill, Stacey Hoskins Haynes, and Jason A. Ford, "Religious Involvement And Marijuana For Medical And Recreational Purposes," *Journal of Drug Issues*, 48 (2018): 421–434, https://doi.org/10.1177/0022042618770393.

[3] Pew Research Center, *Jewish Americans in 2020*, https://www.pewresearch.org/religion/2021/05/11/jewish-americans-in-2020/.

[4] Melanie Baruch, Abraham Benarroch, and Gary E. Rockman, "Alcohol And Substance Use In The Jewish Community: A Pilot Study." *Journal of Addiction* (2015): 763930, doi: 10.1155/2015/763930. Epub 2015 Jun 16. PMID: 26161279; PMCID: PMC4487707.

[5] Addiction Center, "Jewish Beliefs on Drug and Alcohol Addiction and Rehab," 2023, https://www.addictioncenter.com/treatment/faith-based-drug-and-alcohol-rehab/jewish-drug-and-alcohol-rehab.

[6] Rabbi Rami Shapiro, *Recovery – The Sacred Art. The Twelve Steps As Spiritual Practice* (Skylight Paths, 2009).

[7] Paulo Coelho, "Inner beauty is not enough," *Stories and Reflections*, https://paulocoelhoblog.com/2018/01/#:~:text=The%20eyes%20are%20the%20mirror,the%20person%20looking%20into%20them.

[8] Genesis 1:26.

Chapter 2

[9] Carol Glass, "Addiction And Recovery Through Jewish Eyes." in *Addiction And Spirituality: A Multidisciplinary Approach*, ed. Oliver J. Morgan and Merle Jordan (Chalice Press, 1999), 235-247; Craig Nakken, *The Addictive Personality* (Hazelden, 1996), 288; Kerry M. Olitzky and Stuart A. Copans, M.D., *Twelve Jewish Steps to Recovery: A Personal Guide to Turning From Alcoholism and Other Addictions—Drugs, Food, Gambling, Sex* (Jewish Lights, 2009); Rabbi Shais Taub, *God of Our Understanding: Jewish Spirituality and Recovery from Addiction* (Ktav, 2011), 18.

[10] My Jewish Learning, "Ask the Expert: Jews in Church," My Jewish Learning, 2024, https://myjewishlearning.com/article/ask-the-expert-jews-in-church/.

[11] Dr. Eliyahu Lizorkin-Eyzenberg, "Does The Lord's Prayer Have Jewish Liturgical Roots?," Israel Bible Center, June 9, 2022, https://weekly.israelbiblecenter.com/lords-prayer-jewish-liturgy.

[12] A.A.W.S., *Alcoholics Anonymous: The Story of How Many Thousands of Men and Women have Recovered from Alcoholism*, 4th ed. (Alcoholics Anonymous World Services, Inc., 2001), 562. *This big blue book is commonly called the *A.A. Big Book*.

Sponsor: One person in the Program who works with a member as a confidant and personal resource, to help them understand and work the steps of a Program.

Stinking thinking: A pattern of illogical and irrational thinking that has us believe we alone can control our addiction and are failures who are shameful, guilty, and unattractive—generally *less than* anyone else.

Tools [of recovery]: These include the 12 Steps, 12 Traditions and 12 Concepts of Service, 12 Step meetings, sponsorship, conference-approved literature (books and pamphlets), prayer, meditation and fellowship.

Denial: Failure to see objective reality as it is.

Dis-ease: Not an official term, it conveys the inner discomfort and turmoil that is a consequence of our addiction.

Disease: Acknowledges that addiction is an involuntary disorder of the body and mind/spirit, and that it is not something we can control.

Distorted thinking: See Stinking thinking.

Fellows/fellowship: Those who gather at meetings to share their experience, strength and hope, and who support one another in seeking their best selves. Together, the fellowship is a community to which we belong once we enter the Rooms of recovery.

Higher Power: Some entity in/of the universe that has more power than we do.

Program: Refers collectively to the components of a 12 Step recovery program—generally literature, prayer, meetings, sponsorship and fellowship.

Qualifier: Not an official term. This is used to refer to the individual who caused us to seek recovery. We can be our own qualifier or it can be someone we love/care about.

Recovery: Shorthand for the process of uncovering/recovering our inherent beauty and goodness, lifting the veils that cover our inner light so we can live as our best selves.

Rock bottom/Hitting bottom: The point where the life of an addict is at its lowest—physically, financially, emotionally and/or spiritually depleted. It is the point at which we see truth about our lives, stop the descent and seek help to create something better. Sometimes hitting bottom delivers the gift of desperation.

Rooms [of recovery]: Shorthand reference to places where fellows gather, where we learn how to apply the 12 Steps to the problems of living, where we can meet others like ourselves and we can find help. A starting place for new beginnings.

Sobriety: Free of intoxicants—whatever we use to change or numb our feelings. Here, it refers to a pattern of living that includes making positive changes in our way of life and patterns of thinking.

Recovery Terminology used in *Mussar in Recovery*

12 Steps (Twelve Steps): Refers to the 12 Steps that originated in Alcoholics Anonymous and became the foundation of the sister program, Al-Anon. The 12 Steps of A.A. have been adapted to support derivative programs such as Narcotics Anonymous (NA), Adult Children of Alcoholics (ACOA) and Overeaters Anonymous (OA). *Mussar in Recovery* reflects the 12 Steps of A.A. and Al-Anon.

Addict: Biologically, an addict has a physical dependence on a substance. Distorted thinking is a concurrent and perhaps an underlying aspect of their disease. For our purposes, the addict is an individual who makes choices that defy logic to satisfy an uncontrollable craving that makes their lives unmanageable.

Al-Anon: A 12 Step Program for those who love alcoholics or others who habitually make choices that disturb us. Our compulsive focus on that other entity (people, places or things) makes our lives unmanageable.

Alcoholics Anonymous: A 12 Step program for alcoholics. A.A. spawned programs related to other obsessive behaviors—food, narcotics, gambling, cocaine, adult children of alcoholics.

Conference Approved Literature (CAL): Books, pamphlets or other materials published and distributed by the bodies that govern a 12 Step program globally. The centralized control assures that everything in the literature is in accord with the principles, steps, traditions and concepts of service of a Program.

Crazy/insane: This is an easily understood shorthand among addicts that lovingly conveys the chaos, turmoil, illogical thinking and actions that addiction brings to those who suffer when their disease has the upper hand.

Patience: See *Savlanut*.

Rachamim (Compassion): Feeling the pain of another.

Responsibility (*Acharayut*): Being accountable for others and what comes after.

Sages: Legendary teachers (of eras past) who are notably wise about the human condition.

Savlanut (Patience): Sitting with the pain.

Seder (Order): Everything in its place. Doing first (most important) things first.

Shtikah (Silence): Controlling harmful speech. Savoring pauses.

Tikkun middot: Repair of our soul traits.

Trust (*Bitachon*): Letting go of control and leaning on the power of the universe.

Truth (*Emet*): Being honest with ourselves and others about objective reality.

Tzedakah (Charity): In common practice, an obligation to give to help others. Lit. righteousness, justice.

Va'ad: A Jewish study group in which we unpack text to extract wisdom, wrestle with ideas together and see how they apply to life.

Vidui: Confession to God of our wrongdoings, most commonly recited on Yom Kippur.

Yetzer Hara: An idea of talmudic Rabbis to explain the human inclination to be self-focused, sometimes referred to as the evil inclination.

Yetzer Hatov: An idea of talmudic Rabbis to explain the human inclination to do good, to serve the needs of others and God.

Zehirut: Illuminated awareness.

Zerizut (Alacrity): Enthusiasm; brisk willingness.

Yirah (Awe): Fear and reverence of God.

Faith (*Emunah*): Concretized belief that there is a power of the universe that is bigger than we are.

Gevurah: Strength, discipline, staying on task to do what needs doing—the right thing.

Gratitude (*Hakarat Hatov*): Recognize the good.

Hakarat Hatov (Gratitude): Recognize the good.

Hitbodedut: Quiet reflection.

Hitbonenut: Meditation.

Hitlamdut: The ongoing process of contemplation and learning how to learn. Nonjudgmental curiosity.

Holiness (*Kedushah*): Living in alignment with God's will.

Honor (*Kavod*): Looking for the good in everyone. Everyone has a holy soul.

Humility (*Anavah*): Rightsizing ourselves. Taking up no more or less than our rightful space.

Kabbalot: Intentions; refers to steps we will take to refine a *middah*.

Kavod (Honor): Looking for the good in everyone. Everyone has a holy soul.

Kedushah (Holiness): Living in alignment with God's will.

Menuchat HaNefesh (Equanimity): Balanced disposition.

Middah: A soul trait/force that drives our thinking and chosen actions. Plural, *middot*.

Mitzvot: Duties and commandments defined in the Hebrew Bible. Singular, *mitzvah*.

Mussar: Centuries-old school of Jewish thought about refining the inner forces that animate us so we are our best selves. *Mussar* practice includes activities that reinforce a spiritual attitude for living. The goal is to connect the head and the heart in the actions of living.

Nedivut HaLev (Generosity/Heart Willingness): A compulsion of the heart to benefit others.

Nekudot Bechira: An inflection point, a point of choice.

Ometz Lev (Courage): Courage from the heart.

Order (*Seder*): Everything in its place. Doing first (most important) things first.

Mussar Glossary

Acharayut (Responsibility): Having responsibility for others and what comes after.

Alacrity (*Zerizut*): Enthusiasm; brisk willingness.

Anavah (Humility): Rightsizing ourselves. Taking up no more or less than our rightful space.

Awe (*Yirah*): Fear and reverence of God.

Bitachon (Trust [in God]): Letting go of control and leaning on the power of the universe.

Bushah (Shame): Self-deprecating belief that we are not fulfilling our purpose.

Charitzut v'bechira: Decisive choice making.

Chesed (Loving-kindness): Loving-kindness; a heart-driven desire to serve/benefit others with nothing expected in return.

Cheshbon HaNefesh: An inventory of our soul (soul traits).

Chevruta: A study partner with whom, one-on-one, we get honest and think deeply about the meaning of text.

Compassion: (*Chesed*) Loving-kindness; a heart-driven desire to serve/benefit others with nothing expected in return.

Continuum: A way to think about where we are in relation to each *middah*. Aiming for a balanced place in the center, we can experience too much or too little of the trait.

Courage (*Ometz Lev*): Courage from the heart.

Discipline (*Gevurah*): Strength to do what's right.

Emet (Truth): Being honest with ourselves and others about objective reality.

Emunah (Faith): Concretized belief that there is a power of the universe that is bigger than we are.

being inflicted on you, this orientation originates in owning what we can do to ourselves and others when we become complacent in our commitments to living right as outlined by the sages, ignoring the guidance of your moral compass. But you can draw inspiration and energy when you acknowledge the wisdom of the Program, the support of fellows, and show deep gratitude for the goodness that flows to you in your life.

The actions of gratitude include awakening to the good in our lives and giving thanks. On the simplest level, awareness of our bodies and breath, of cycles of light and dark and relationships and opportunities cultivates the humility that fosters awe in its fullest glory.

When harnessed, *yirah* fuels the ongoing work to protect and honor the gifts of healing and growth that we can enjoy in recovery. Awe of the Program and the lives we see rebuilt fuels our efforts to keep the disease at bay, to stay the course and serve as role models of living in recovery and lighting up the world. We don't want to disappoint. Indeed, trying our best to live principled, responsible lives of service (being a mensch) makes us beacons of hope for those who continue to suffer. *Yirah* is essential for long-term recovery on a personal level and for the survival of the Program itself. Interestingly, whatever the stimulus, the experience of awe inevitably reminds us to be grateful; feeling grateful heightens the experience.

Final Notes

These five concepts are essential for the life you are seeking. Make no mistake—progress on the journey of healing and happiness is not a matter of chance, it is a matter of choice. The mental posture or attitudes that course through your thoughts as you navigate each day are critical to your experience of this journey. Your spiritual condition can drag you down or lift you up. You have all the tools and resources you need to reach new heights. To send you off on your journey, let me share a final nugget of experience, strength, and hope from a wise Program fellow, Diane T. Looking for the good, the God and the gifts in each encounter is a surefire approach to assure that your days are filled with serenity and joy. You are never done. You are never alone. The choice is yours and your time is now.

On one hand, *yirah* means awe or wonder. This aspect of *yirah* refers to that uplifting feeling that can be sparked by experiences of life and the world that transcend your understanding.[368] I've heard fellows describe experiencing awe when they discover the timelessness of ancient or sacred wisdom such as that found in the Bible, the Twelve Steps, or Mussar wisdom that was nearly lost. Others are awed by their spiritual awakening; it may come from standing atop a mountain, viewing a sunset or sunrise, tapping into the energy of a group (such as their home group) or praying and singing with fellow congregants at their synagogue. For others, becoming immersed in a piece of music, holding a new baby, or viewing the aftermath of a natural disaster and considering the power that wreaked havoc juxtaposed with the kindness of survivors to one another evokes awe.

For some, their personal journey through powerlessness, surrender and a relationship with a Higher Power that came from working the Twelve Steps opens them to awe. This aspect of *yirah* relates to something within the universe that we can neither explain nor control. While we cannot comprehend it, it can lift us up and it creates a flood of gratitude for our bounty. It is my experience that there is an inherent paradox here. While feeling small in relation to the majestic forces at work, when in this state of awe, I feel that I am in touch with the wonder at its source. Listening to others who describe their experience, it has a deep impact on those who are awake and open to it.

Yirah also encompasses the aspect of human experience that we can call respect or reverence. As I am sure you understand, reverence can morph into fear. Think about our reverence of a bald eagle or Siberian tiger. They are beautiful creatures in their majesty but fearsome predators to be avoided for our personal safety. Those who believe in a judging, punishing God live mostly in the fear dimension of *yirah* as if the tiger or eagle of life is stalking them as prey. We need not bait or poke the tiger; with safe conduct (living with a moral compass) we can enjoy its beauty and the journey on which to see it in its habitat. In this domain we can enjoy gratitude for our safety and wellbeing in the face of fragility.

The fear of falling short is a way to look at this second dimension of *yirah*, making it productive. Rather than an aversion to judgment or punishment

and forgiving is a trap set by our trickster, the yetzer hara, seeking the easy way and protecting itself. An attitude of victimhood and pain, guilt, shame and blame leaves no room for connections with others. In isolation, we lose vitality and a sense of value and purpose for living. It is said that holding resentments about such past experiences is like taking a poison pill and hoping the other person will die. The reality is that we die.

Stinking thinking tells us that we are entitled to things being better for us and that others need to be held accountable and punished. Indeed, focus on judgment and revenge foster the ego-based self-righteous delusion that you alone know what's right, that someone put you in charge, or that you are entitled to have someone else change so you can feel better. Such thinking keeps you in the prison of the past. You become the cause of your own isolation and related pain, robbing yourself of the joy of loving and being loved.

Embracing forgiveness involves giving up your delusions and the hope that the past will change. Forgiveness creates freedom for all involved. The housecleaning Steps (4-9) focus on forgiving ourselves and those who hurt us. Rest assured that forgiveness is not to be confused with condoning unacceptable behavior. Healing does not delete memory; with an orientation of humility and forgiveness you can learn to reframe hurtful experience by finding meaning in it. Making peace with the past is essential to staying present in today. It is here in the present where you learn and practice living in recovery, one day at a time, free of fear about the future.

Forgiving is not simple or easy. A forgiving mindset promotes choosing to be happy over being right. Conscious choice in this area unclutters the space in your heart and soul for deeper connection with self, others, and a power greater than you. It is liberating to stop letting anyone else, including that voice in your head, rob you of your chance at joy.

FIVE: Embrace *Yirah*—Practice Gratitude (*Hakarat Hatov*)

Yirah is a Hebrew word and like many Hebrew words, it eludes simple translation. There are two meanings embedded in this one word: awe and fear (or reverence.) Both are important to unlocking gratitude that is an essential attitude for living with serenity and joy.

THREE: Embrace Community—Practice Compassion (*Rachamim*)

Isolation fuels stinking thinking, including the self-perpetuating delusions, ridicule and the silent monologue that we are alone, unworthy, unlovable and unloved. Being part of community, knowing that others understand us, is the secret sauce of recovery and Judaism. Recovery is a *we* program. This runs through every Step, beginning expressly with the first word of Step 1 and continuing as the unspoken focus in each of the remaining 11 Steps. The unconditional support and understanding that is the invisible thread of compassion derived from shared experiences within community has the power to open hardened hearts…if you let it.

In community, we learn that we are not unique or alone and, in the safety of fellows, we can begin to receive and share empathy and compassion with others. Community simultaneously teaches you, loves you and holds you accountable for your actions by encouraging and supporting you as you navigate the challenges of living according to your moral compass. In the safety zone of community, where you feel and share acceptance, you can enjoy learning and growth with serenity that opens you to joy and lights the way for others.

The power of the group is its "collective effervescence."[366] It is within community that we learn to give and to receive with grace, humility and gratitude. This is likely a radical change from the focus on self with which you started your journey. Psychologist Dacher Keltner observes that over time, "…shared understanding leads to goodwill, cooperation, and a transformed sense of self as part of community."[367] These experiences are transformative to our sense of self and our place in the universe. Practicing an orientation of community membership and mutual understanding is a key part of healing and transformation.

FOUR: Embrace Forgiveness—Practice Humility (*Anavah*)

Forgiveness is the process of letting go of feelings of resentment and anger that lock us in the past. These may be directed at ourselves for damage we have done, at another whose actions have hurt us, or at God for the condition of our lives. A focus on judging rather than learning, discerning

knowing that experiences are not good or bad. They can all offer help and hope that we may need.

Without open eyes, you may not see what's right in front of you; without an open heart you cannot receive help and beauty when it arrives. It's amazing what appears when you are looking. Being open to the possibility that the Program can help is a critical starting point. Almost every Step tests our openness in one way or another. Many Steps require that we be open to directed actions. Look at the calls to action: *admit* (Steps 1, 5 & 10); *turn* (Step 3); *make* (Steps 4 & 8); *ask* (Step 7); *take* (Step 10); *carry* (Step 12); *pray* and *meditate* (Step 11). A greater challenge than doing (which is a high hurdle) is being open to believing. Belief that there is, and trusting in, a Higher Power is a pillar of the Program and the foundation of Steps 2, 3, 6, 7 and 11. Without personal openness there can be no Program miracle.

The mindset that life is our curriculum and we are here to learn allows us to see each day as a new opportunity. To discover your full self and find meaning in your life journey, it's essential that you be open to new experiences and perspectives (even surprises), seek knowledge, and cultivate an attitude of continuous learning through life's ups and downs. Taking a God's-eye view, we can appreciate that there is no such thing as failure. Seemingly negative outcomes, which are inevitable, can help you appreciate life's complexity and the depth of your resilience. They foster gratitude, which you can use to bolster your openness as each new day dawns.

Remember that you don't know the ending of your story yet. Self-refinement and recovery are continuous processes. Every experience has the potential to shape how we will evolve to become a better version of ourselves. Being curious, adaptable and receptive to life's teachings are key to making the journey enriching and fulfilling. Which middot relate? They all do—especially humility, trust, courage, alacrity, responsibility, compassion and generosity. Seriously, recovery is a spiritual journey, so it makes sense that all of these intersect with the path. They are not achieved by leaps—unless, of course, we're talking about leaps of faith, which are made possible by openness.

sonal growth and beginning anew. Judaism is grounded in the idea that we have the capacity to change; the concept of change is central to the Mussar tradition. In regard to our addictions, change is essential to break destructive habits of action and thought, to foster resilience and build lives that are productive, fulfilling and joyful. Although the need may be obvious, undertaking change requires great strength. There is no comfort in the growth zone and no growth in the comfort zone. You have what it takes; nurture your emotional, mental and spiritual domains to be sustained in the journey. Please do not be deterred by the discomfort of losing what's familiar as you grapple with a natural resistance to accepting and integrating what's new. Patience with yourself and your HP, supported by courage, faith and trust feed the orientation toward change.

In the context of ending and beginning, Step 1 brings a significant change in self-perception. Step 3 encourages a shift in thinking and behavior. Steps 6 and 7 are about the willingness to change your patterns. Steps 10 and 12 relate to actualizing new behavior. Mussar wisdom provides goals to aim for and tools to sustain you on the path. You will inevitably be tested; that is the nature of our spiritual curriculum. Collectively, the work is the basis for re-creating ourselves. The wisdom of the 12 Steps and Mussar practice provides a runway for growth. The refinements you make need not be earth-shattering; in fact, they should be small steps. The journey is about progress, not perfection. Oh, yes. A word of caution: Do not confuse activity with progress. Remember to get off your rocking chair—while it moves a lot, you will go nowhere.

TWO: Embrace Openness—
Practice Non-judgmental Curiosity (*Hitlamdut*)

A learning orientation refers to staying curious, open-minded and open-hearted—no matter what. Remembering that life can test us; an attitude of receptivity opens space for new possibilities, even amid what's hard. I think of flowers that grow in cracked pavement. Yes, some experiences are welcome and some not. Often, assumptions that reflect fear, discomfort and impatience cause us to assume the worst and divert before we discover the miracle that was hidden. Openness allows us to engage,

on it. It is no coincidence that the Hebrew words for past (*kedem*) and future/ahead (*kadima*) share the same root word. For many, the process of uncovering our inner light is arduous, perhaps painful. Pain is not to be wasted; our human capacity to learn through such lessons transforms them into gifts.

While you can't go back and change the beginning of your story, you can change the ending by persistently integrating what you have experienced and learned into your choices from this moment on. Continued growth and healing require that you step into each successive moment on your life path with zeal, with enthusiasm, with cheerful briskness. This is made easier by focusing on one day at a time, seeing each day and each experience as full of potential beginnings that offer you ongoing opportunity. Carpe diem—seize the day!

Days can flow into weeks, weeks into months, and months into years of recovery despite the uncertainty and imperfection that is inherent in each day. This is the essence of understanding life backwards and living life on life's terms going forward. The 12 Steps and Mussar wisdom provide structure and insight for this radical new way of thinking and living. We can each continuously look inward to better understand, accept, and love ourselves, looking out toward the horizon and engaging with life—informed and committed to make meaningful connections.

Getting beyond what we realize is visible in the universe to what is hidden is an important aspect of the journey of recovering—uncovering the light of our best selves. Hidden within the middot and Steps that we have explored together are five insights that can fuel your journey to *kadima*, a future in which you live with intention as your best self, and with the potential to enjoy all that life offers. As you embark on the new beginnings ahead, you are encouraged to weave these ideas into your choices and your way of living. Engaging with a welcoming attitude will result in life experience that fills your treasure chest with fulfillment, serenity, and joy.

ONE: Embrace Change—Practice Strength (*Gevurah*)

Insanity is repeatedly doing the same thing and expecting a different outcome. Change, while uncomfortable, is a fundamental aspect of per-

Mussar lives here, helping the parts that are revealed function harmoniously for the benefit of the whole.

In our human design, our specimen has two key control centers. Reconciling which is in charge can present unique challenges and opportunities. Our brain wants to be in charge, or have us think so. Our heart is an engine. Biologically, the human heart can live without the brain, but not vice versa. So, which is in charge? A car can't decide where to go or how to get there without a driver. Our brain maps out the path; our heart provides the power to drive to our destination; our personal attributes determine how we get there. Activate humility to help you stay in your lane, modulate the shame thruster to navigate the curves, add patience while stuck in traffic, adjust your alacrity and flip the compassion switch to create space for travelers around you. You can refer to your GPS and trust that it will show you how to get back on track if you hit a construction detour or make an unexpected stop to add a special destination to your itinerary. Some stops on our journeys help us see how our patterns of living can be harmful to ourselves; other stops allow us to learn or practice corrective maneuvers.

Mussar wisdom offers tools to probe deeply, especially important in the self-exploration of Step 4 and everything that flows from it. This excavation of our essence is complemented by action-based supportive practices that are intended to enhance the efficacy of our work. Purposeful journaling, setting and reinforcing intentions, and using messages to ourselves as quick reminders are tools that we can use when intentionally engaging with components of our spirit that are revealed with both coarse and fine focus. Doing so has been integrated into the work of recovery and adapted here to be in sync with the rhythm of Twelve Step work.

Having completed this journey through the Steps, it's important to remember that "the way we meet an ending shapes the way the next moment arises."[365] This juncture is important both as an ending and a beginning. There is value in making time to recognize the distance you have travelled, all you have experienced along your route, and especially all that you have accomplished in the many domains of your life—financial, physical, emotional, and spiritual. Ending a journey and forgetting the past can doom us to repeat it; for this reason, it is important that we not shut the door

Chapter 17

New Beginnings

One Day At a Time.
—*Seneca*

Mussar in Recovery was written to introduce you to Jewish wisdom that enriches the journey of recovery. While the circumstances may vary, given our common human nature, both Mussar and 12 Step recovery work have similar focus—addressing the brokenness which is inherent to the human condition and learning how to be a decent human being (a mensch). Both recognize that the path to mensch-hood is paved by understanding ourselves and cultivating our patterns of thought, choice, and our innermost personal traits. Whether this is your first time or some multiple to walk through the Twelve Steps, you now have a model for the ongoing integration of the Jewish pathway of Mussar practice into your work of being a light in the world.

The ideas behind all of the Twelve Steps can be found embedded within Jewish wisdom and observance. Mussar offers us structure and practices that personalize the attitudes and actions that fuel human decency. It's fair to say, I believe, that the Twelve Steps, Jewish wisdom, and Mussar work in tandem.

Have you ever used a microscope? Most microscopes have two knobs for focus—coarse and fine. The knob for coarse focus functions to rapidly bring a specimen into view. Perhaps you can think of the Twelve Steps and the whole of Jewish wisdom as the coarse focus, directing us toward recovery and our best selves. The fine focus works in tandem with the coarse. It helps the investigator achieve clarity and detail. Turning the fine focus knob reveals details within a structure that would otherwise remain hidden.

SECTION III. THE TREASURE FOUND

Prompts for journaling or study with your *chevruta*/sponsor
- What is driving your generosity—your heart or mind?
- What middot are at the base of your resistance to generosity?
- What middot do you need to strengthen to enhance generosity?
- Do you agree that generosity comes from joy?
- Describe how it feels to be heart-willing. What is your internal narrative?
- Describe the relationship between addiction, selfishness, spiritual consciousness, love, gratitude, and generosity.

Playlist
- "Try A Little Kindness"—Glen Campbell
- "With A Little Help From My Friends"—Joe Cocker
- "I Saw God today"—George Strait
- "Heart of Gold"—Neil Young
- "Change of Heart"—Cyndi Lauper
- "Give A Little Bit"—Supertramp
- "Give to Liv"—Sami Hager

Daily reminders to help work Step 12

Following are some phrases that you might use as your daily reminders. Feel free to choose one, or create your own.

- We are born to give.
- Generosity is for fun and for free.
- Am I a giver or a taker?
- Give from a place of joy and get joy from giving.
- Don't wait to be asked.
- External action is the route of inner transformation.

Kabbalot to cultivate generosity (*nedivut halev*) as you take Step 12

If you lean toward excessive generosity you might try:

- Practice giving yourself small treats every day.
- Work with someone else and explore your motives for giving so excessively.
- Make of list of who you are giving to. Where are you on the list? Move yourself up on the list.
- Meditate on your generosity to increase awareness.
- Make a budget and increase saving by reducing what you give away.

If you lean toward sagging generosity (stinginess/taking) you might try:

- When you attend meetings, put something extra in the basket for donations to the Program.
- For a week, plan to give tzedakah three times a day. Notice when it gets uncomfortable.
- Write *joy* on the palm of your hand. Set a timer to look at it every hour during the day.
- Wear a loose rubber band on your wrist to remind yourself to loosen your grip.
- Throw away selfish motivations.

…when our minds, emotions, desires, and actions are all in sync, we experience joy, because nothing is obstructing the radiance of holiness that resides within our innermost souls from shining brightly into our lives. And then we are in a state of joy, our pure soul flows freely to our hearts and animates our behavior. The result is pure generosity.[363]

Trust the process

As you close this leg of your journey, it's useful to look through a God's-eye view and appreciate the miracle of what you have built with the Twelve Steps and Mussar tradition as blueprints for your life.

Starting as individuals who were sick and suffering from distorted thinking about the world and our place in it, most started this journey consumed by selfishness, dishonesty and isolation. You had a crumbling foundation and no moral compass or zest for the project of living.

Through the gift of desperation, you sought love and wisdom in the Rooms where you found the starting materials for building a life of usefulness. The building blocks that you put into your inventory were spiritual consciousness and unconditional love. Your honesty, openness and willingness opened the door to the impossible.

You did the hard work of confronting your demons and became able to lift the veils that shrouded the light of your spirit and learned how to be in healthy, caring relationship with yourself and others.

With newfound connectedness to the God of your understanding and fellows you experienced feeling complete, grateful, and joyful. Perhaps the ultimate paradox is that accepting your imperfection freed you to thrive as an individual, fulfilling your spiritual purpose and living an extraordinary ordinary life, one day at a time.[364]

It works if you work it. You're worth it, so work it—one day at a time. Wishing you blessings as you journey on.

ourselves generously to others is self-reinforcing. It is for this reason that Rabbi Salanter taught that another person's material needs are my spiritual responsibility.[356] This idea has expansive potential, like sharing the flame of a candle. The light of a candle does not diminish when you share it; it grows. Our Twelve Step work reveals our light. Carrying the message and serving others by applying these Mussar principles in all our affairs is how we can be generous, cultivate generosity, and brighten the world. The act of serving the Program or fellows leaves an imprint on our hearts and in our lives and fosters the middah so as agents of *tikkun olam* we fulfill the charge to be a blessing.[357]

Secondary middot

Focusing on the physical and psychological well-being of another to whom we want to be generous raises up thoughts about the middot of loving-kindness, honor, humility and compassion, all of which are dimensions of how we care for others.[358] And, thinking about what's necessary for our own state of mind and heart in order that we can practice heart-willingness raises thoughts of gratitude for our bounty, courage to be uncomfortable, and faith and trust that our needs will be met. Our sages weave these ideas together with the thread of joy/*simcha*. "Joy is at the root of *nedivut ha'lev*."[359]

Starting with the idea that we were created in the image of the Divine, Rabbi Dessler examined our tendencies as givers and takers. He viewed taking, which stems from egotism or selfishness, as the opposite of giving and "the root of all evils in the world."[360] He concluded that feeling complete is associated with the faculty of giving.[361] This is an important nugget, because the healing that comes from working the Steps is associated with our feeling complete—that we are enough, have enough, and do enough. So, solid recovery is essential to generosity. Beyond that, Rabbi Dessler is cited as teaching, "the force of giving rests only within one who is joyful," referring to being satisfied with one's portion. "We experience joy through feeling complete, accomplished, and especially when we are connected with others, and to Hashem."[362] Again, the connectedness and sense of having what we need are important aspects of recovery. Alan Morinis brings this together:

Our hearts follow our deeds. To become more generous, be generous. This is another arena in which faking it does pave the way to making it so.

A great place to start is with tzedakah, being guided by our sponsors or spiritual advisors. Making coffee, greeting newcomers, and listening at meetings are starting points for "…compulsory giving as an opportunity to engage with the resistance, so you can loosen its grip on your heart and move closer to becoming more loving and generous as you have the potential to be."[353] These practices frequently precede sharing our experience, strength, and hope via telling our stories. At whatever pace we take on the work, we need to keep our motives clean; generosity can be a mask for egotism.

"The trait [*nedivut*] resides in habit; we are not truly magnanimous until we are accustomed to giving as much as we can at all times."[354] Recalling that generosity can be in the form of wisdom and support for others, the Talmud says the one who gives even a small coin to a poor person is blessed with six blessings, but one who kindly offers words of comfort to a needy person as well as a coin is blessed with 11 blessings.[355] In regard to recovery, we are not generally dispersing coins; we are sharing from our hearts—our experience, strength and hope …and love. Doing so with brisk willingness and respect for our fellows is essential to cultivating the middah.

Blessings

In the context of Step 12 especially, it's helpful to practice generosity as love for our fellow travelers. The acronym LOVE—letting others voluntarily evolve—is useful for me as it reminds me to leave space for another. Everyone has something to offer and our practice of humility is critical to the well-being of all involved. I learn from newcomers as well as old-timers. Sponsorship is one domain in which this plays out. Being tasked to listen without passing judgment or offering advice is, in the end, a great honor.

Generosity is intended not only for the recipient, but for the giver, too. Our tradition is concerned for the material needs of the poor and the spiritual needs of the one who gives. The paradox is that we care for our hearts by caring for others. In *Parashah Terumah*, God asked the Israelites to contribute to the construction of the mishkan to open their hearts. Giving of

The human heart, having been created in the image of the Divine spirit (**G**ood **O**rderly **D**irection) is naturally inclined to be generous. The scars of our past life experiences and residual negative attitudes such as resentment, fear, shame, laziness, an attitude of scarcity, judgmentalism and the like might be barriers to generosity, especially for those early in recovery.

Putting armor around our hearts (being hard-hearted) may protect us from discomfort and unhappiness. But it also prevents us from experiencing happiness and joy. Our sages have observed that generosity is a trait that comes through joy, making this fertile ground for nurturing our spiritual practice. Take heed, don't quit—even those who are "poor" are encouraged to give what they can. As with so many middot, to become more generous we are urged to be generous. The action of generosity works to pry open the heart little by little.

Our yetzer hara (selfish inclination, ego) is the primary concern when thinking about barriers to generosity. Beyond being generous to grow in this middah, we must also be "… careful not to scatter wealth to indulge in our heart's desire in vain, and in pursuit of lust that lead to all manner of ills."[352] Our disease can be cunning. Thus, our sages warn that we must seek the truth in our motives and be sure not to confuse an honorable desire to help the poor with feeding our egos or hiding our malevolence. Constrained generosity reflects middot that are out of balance. Let's turn our attention to how to cultivate *nedivut halev*.

Cultivating generosity

Scarcity, fear and ingratitude might be at the root of our personal barriers to liberate generosity. We can focus on these or work on strengthening the positive correlates such as middot of gratitude, faith, or trust in a Higher Power. We might reframe our inner dialogue by cultivating a sense that what we do for others is actually a great gift to ourselves.

While this self-examination reveals domains of our spiritual curriculum on which to focus, on the topic of cultivating generosity, there is agreement among teachers across the generations that external action is a route to interior transformation. No matter how you slice it, the message is clear.

Twelfth Step call is all of these wrapped together. We know from personal experience that for many people, these direct points of contact are initially intimidating. Please persist. Gently.

Supporting the institutions that assure continued access to the Program and creating space for fellowship is an alternate kind of service and also important. For example, we can help clean and maintain clubhouses or meeting rooms, contribute financially via our meeting groups to the offices that coordinate activities, services and communication around the world and serve on committees that support the network of meetings in our communities. We can make coffee, greet newcomers, and support the emergency phone lines.

Early in recovery, our service is commonly more of the obligated type. Our sponsors tell us to do service, so we comply. When asked to tell our stories or lead a meeting we are discouraged from saying no. After a time, love of the Program and fellows-in-need move our hearts to carry the message in any way we can. There is an irresistible feeling that stirs within us. When you experience this, you have been touched by *nedivut halev*. Perpetuating the cycle of generosity is a path to a high that you can safely enjoy.

Barriers to generosity

Much of what is taught about generosity relates to its monetary aspect. Body and wisdom are other forms that generosity can take. Body includes supporting others through their hardships; wisdom includes sharing our knowledge and helping guide others in their spiritual growth. Fellows who need what we have suffer in mind and body with crazy thinking and the physical consequences of unhealthy and broken relationships and patterns of living. Seeing their pain may be too close to home for some. If you are triggered or repelled, it's an indication that you may need to return to earlier Steps. If we are ready to take Step 12, working with others gives us a healthy frame of reference in which to appreciate our recovery.

The phrase *a stopped-up heart* is used to describe the spiritual condition in which generosity of our heart does not flow. *Timtum halev* (blocked heart) reflects our disease; it is not our natural (God-given) state of being.

action you take, or the amount you give, but the energy of the response itself. "All is according to abundance of the deed."[349] This form of generosity (*nedivut halev*) is "spontaneous open, trusting, voluntary, inspired—an internal overflow that erupts from the inner depths in response to the needs of or love of another."[350]

Recalling our release from the prison of our own addiction, we arrive at Step 12 being keenly aware of the role that the Program and fellows had in helping us create a better life and loving relationships. When we ask *How can I thank you?* we are told to carry the message. Indeed, helping others is a mantra in the Rooms. Trust God, clean house, help others! That's the essence of the Program. Although we were broken and spiritually depleted, we were given limitless time, wisdom, and love. Now that we are well into our healing, it's our turn to pay it forward by transmitting it to others.

We know that we own no material object that can help another get sober or repair broken relationships. What we do possess is experience, strength, and hope. When shared with the spirit of generosity these can be the foundation of a beautiful new house—a new way of life for others like us. Filled with gratitude and humility, patience and compassion, faith and trust, Step 12 encourages us to share with no expectation of anything in return. It's important to note again that Step 12 is not asking us to get anyone else sober. That is between fellows and their Higher Power. The call to action is to share what we have from a place of abundance. Our sages teach that "one who gives 1,000 gold pieces to a deserving person at one time is not so magnanimous as one who gives out 1 gold piece a 1,000 times.[351] What do we have to share? Experience, strength, and hope, delivered with love. Spending time and sharing the bountiful harvest of our Twelve Step work with anyone who wants it is Step 12 in action.

How to keep it going

The tangible components of our Twelve Step programs are meetings, sponsorship, fellowship, literature, and our stories. Each of these has associated service opportunities. Showing up at meetings, making and taking phone calls, telling our stories, meeting for coffee, and helping others work through the Steps are all touch points at which we can carry the message. A

doing something good in someone's broken world. Being generous, giving gladly, is not merely a human virtue, but a divine attribute and doing so is a godly choice.[345] Alan Morinis teaches that giving to others, especially the needy, is an essential aspect of piety and as such, it's on our journey toward holiness/goodness.[346]

Nedivut halev, meaning generosity or heart-willingness, reflects giving because our heart is moved. We commonly ask in our Program work, what are your motives? As we've said, *tzedakah* relates to sharing with others out of obligation. Generosity as a soul trait goes far beyond giving from the head (what's obligated) to a heart-based "... movement of the soul that erupts when we are pierced by the recognition of our direct connection to another soul... Your need is my need, your suffering is my suffering. I feel one with you and respond freely, as if for myself.."[347] Practicing *tzedakah* and *nedivut halev* are clearly on the path of our biblical teaching that we are "to act justly, love kindness and walk humbly with your God."[348]

Meeting the needs of others in the spirit of *nedivut halev* comes from a place of wholeness—self acceptance and connection to the Divine and to others. In the Rooms, we hear about *giving for fun and for free*, meaning that we expect nothing in return. In our spiritual lives, we practice the middah of generosity when we share without expectation of anything in return; with a goal of rebalancing the distribution of wealth; and we do so gladly. It's useful to note that we are not simply sharing our excess or because we have more than enough. The foundation here is knowing that we have what we need and having the faith that we can both have enough when it's shared. And sharing gives us a sense of purpose.

Parashah Terumah is an important biblical source that relates to the middah of generosity. In it, the Israelites are asked to donate materials for the construction of the Mishkan, the portable sanctuary. The commentaries explain that the rationale for asking was that the act of giving would open the hearts of the givers and invite God into their midst. When we act with *nedivut* to help others, we elevate ourselves—closing the gap between us and the individual we help as well as closing the gap between us and God. The closeness is a form of intimacy—a deep human connection that is the opposite of addiction. This sort of generosity is not defined by the kind of

Generosity (*Nedivut HaLev*): A Mussar perspective on Step 12

> *All is according to abundance of the deed (not the greatness).*
> —*Ways of the Tzaddikim*

Jewish wisdom is rich with teachings that relate to meeting the needs of others and it's useful to explore how they can enrich our understanding of ourselves and the practice of Step 12. In Jewish thought and tradition, meeting the needs of others is commonly lumped into the bucket of charitable giving and captured in the word *tzedakah*. Harkening back to the messages we got in religious school and congregational and community fundraising events and the like, we are taught that sharing from our bounty to support those in need is not a matter of choice; it is a Jewish obligation.

Feeding the hungry by leaving a corner of our fields for the poor and the stranger is a well-known Jewish mitzvah—it's actually a biblical commandment that is an example of meeting the obligation of *tzedakah*.[342] In modern times, we think about donating money, canned food and clothes to satisfy this obligation. Regrettably, the intended spiritual purity can get lost because the action is not relational. A seasonal ritual of cleaning out discards that we no longer want or need accompanied by little consideration for those receiving our donation may be a self-righteous truth in our contemporary practices.

Beyond the simple meaning of giving to charity that we learned as children, *tzedakah* can be interpreted as justice or righteous behavior. The idea that we are fostering justice or are righteous when sharing our bounty puts a different spin on it. The importance of these obligations is also reflected in the Talmudic declaration that "*tzedakah* is equally important as all the other mitzvot put together."[343] Along this line of thinking, scholars argue that a portion of our wealth does not belong to us at all, but is intended to be the rightful property of those in need.[344] One might imagine this as a spiritual test (or opportunity)—whether we will rise to the occasion of

so gives us purpose and gives our life meaning; it is self-reinforcing. It has been my experience that being of service is a source of boundless joy and gratitude, all the while stoking my humility and the desire to keep growing in my own recovery. I could not have done this alone. The experience of serving others has, honestly, become my *life of choice*. Serving others draws me closer to my HP, a source of courage and support that is plentiful. I am, by virtue of this journey, compelled to share these life-changing gifts with those looking to me for inspiration and support.

Making it personal—in all our affairs

It's critical to note that ours is a program of mutual aid. Selflessly serving others as fellows did for us is essential to sustain the Program. Thus, we hear at most meetings, "When anyone, anywhere reaches out for help, let the hand always be there…" Our gratitude drives us to do what we can to assure that meetings are available to others. We take phone calls and work with new members as sponsors because we often hear something we needed to—perhaps even hearing our own words from a new perspective. Doing this service challenges us to continue working our own program. Our gratitude and humility grow as we are reminded how far we have come and see how far we have yet to travel. This is the birth of the idea that *to keep it, we have to give it away*. It is in this way that Step 12 ushers in a new beginning that lasts for the rest of our lives, one day at a time.

The future action called for in Step 12 is to practice these principles on all our affairs. It is a statement of intention. Focusing on the actions to be taken teaches us how we are to live our lives going forward. In addition to the service described above, we practice love and service via our daily efforts to be honest, own our actions, make amends as needed, and humbly admit when we are wrong. Living principled lives is a sure path to healthy relationships and can help in the healing of those we damaged. While it's natural to start with family and friends here, the principles apply equally in business and community. Our best message is to be a good example of recovery; we draw people into relationship with us by our own example. This is truly a case where your actions will speak more loudly than your words.

seats, sharing at meetings, greeting newcomers, sponsorship, and simple fellowship over coffee are all important forms of service. A Twelfth Step Call is another example of carrying the message as suggested by the Twelfth Step. Being non-judgmental and non-threatening, a fellowship member reaches out to speak or meet with somebody who is suffering from their addiction to try to help them choose recovering. The message is simple:

> I was where you are. There is a solution. The Program worked to help me get sober and helps me stay sober because I work it. You can have what I have if you do as I did.

We let them decide if the message resonates. Speaking from personal experience, we can attest to our truth that what we found in working the Steps opened the door to our recovering our best selves. Do you remember reading earlier that connection is the opposite of addiction? Connection is an opportunity for someone suffering to break free of isolation and welcome the same love and support that we received flowing through us. Can you think of a more powerful message to carry to someone still suffering?

The affirmation in Step 12 says we tried to carry the message of healing to others. It does not require that we fix anyone or convince them that our way of thinking is best. Since we do not know what is right for anyone else, our role is to contribute what we can—our experience, strength, and hope. Keeping in mind that the Program teaches us that our goal is attraction rather than promotion, our most powerful tool is being an example of how it works. Proof positive is showing up through good and bad; by doing that we demonstrate that continued spiritual development and practicing the principles of the Program in all our affairs allows us to take life in stride.

Making it personal—practice the principles

Having seen the life-changing and life-saving power of the Program firsthand, helping others whose pain we know from deep inside ourselves is essential to our continued growth. The generosity of our spirit for this work grows out of gratitude for our lives. It is our turn to give back with no expected reward. It is common to hear from fellows that sharing with others fills them up. In fact, we help ourselves by helping others. Doing

but I can say that I've experienced compassion for my Ex. And, as if by magic, the hatred that ate me up from the inside and I worked so hard to bury has disappeared and my compulsion went along with it. That experience, as unexplainable as it is, woke me up to the power of something intangible that I can reach for when I need help.

What we have here is the imprecision of language. Questioning the path to a spiritual awakening is just a distraction. What is important is that while working all the Steps, we change the way we see ourselves and the world. This is the essential message. Through working the Steps, we learn that we are not in charge, not in control, and not alone. Rather, there is a source of goodness and strength into which we can tap. Holding onto the controlling, judgmental, impatient, self-serving mindset that we brought with us into the Rooms is a choice and it keeps us stuck in our disease. The spiritual awakening that comes from our work opens a channel of connectivity that is essential to finding and living in recovery.

Making it personal—carrying the message

It is here at the Twelfth Step where the focus of our efforts shifts somewhat. Perhaps it's better to say that it expands. We can't take the focus off our recovery; false pride and complacency lead to trouble. That said, individuals who have worked all twelve Steps are encouraged to share their experience, strength and hope with others, especially those who still struggle in their disease. This is a constant call to action in the Rooms of recovery. In fact, the chapter on the Twelfth Step in the *Big Book* is entitled "Working with Others." Our lived experience allows us to bring love and tolerance, humility, gratitude and authenticity to our efforts of helping other addicts. We must always be "…ready to help another person in trouble—someone new, who may not yet have heard that Al-Anon can help them when there is alcoholism in a family"[341] and their lives.

It is an unwritten practice that we should never say no to an opportunity to help another who is seeking recovery. The slogan *let it begin with me* serves as a reminder to serve with generosity. Our service can take many forms, depending on the state of maturity of our own recovery—taking our

gram. The premise is that "discovering our powerlessness and the hope that lies in the Higher Power (whatever that means for us) sets us on the road to recovery."[339] The Step goes on to connect our awakening with the other actions it directs us to take (having had it, we tried and now are to practice this…). Structured as it is, Step 12 conveys that recovering through the Steps is grounded in the connection to something bigger than ourselves. We know from our work that that something is of our personal understanding—it may be the spirit of your group, the spirit of the universe, or an entity that you call God. By extension, this Step reminds us that we cannot get and stay healthy (sober) by ourselves. In this regard, the spiritual awakening is described as discovering a previously unknown source of strength beyond our own and that we never imagined possible. As is the case with the spiritual curriculum that we discovered and embrace in our Mussar practice, our awakening manifests in a degree of honesty, tolerance, unselfishness, peace of mind, and love beyond what we thought we were capable of.

At this point, let's be as clear as we can regarding references to spiritual awakening. Our literature sometimes refers separately to having a spiritual experience and a spiritual awakening. For some, these may be one and the same; for others, they are not. For Bill W., the co-founder of A.A., his spiritual awakening was a sudden, dramatic and life-changing event. In his autobiography, Bill recalled that "he was bathed in light and seized by an ecstasy beyond words."[340] One person in my home group believed that stopping drinking was a spiritual experience and that awakened him to a Higher Power early in his Program. The Higher Power was a perspective that permeated his worldview. In contrast, another fellow shared:

> … I tried everything I knew to do, over and over again, to stop using before coming into the Program. Nothing stuck. Working Step 4 and 5 helped me see that I was a prisoner of resenting my Ex, and it fed my stinking thinking and poor choices. My sponsor told me to pray "bless them, change me." Over time, my hollow words became heartfelt yearning. I can't say that I've mastered forgiveness

the Step refers to them in the past might be taken to imply that as we take Step 12, we are finished with these elements of our work and can graduate from the Program. Such an inference is a mistake. The open-ended closing phrase of Step 12 reflects the fact that this is a lifelong program; our work of personal growth and principled living, which includes being in relationship with something greater than we are and helping others, continues indefinitely. We cannot take our foot off the pedal. Pulling these together, I submit that the introductory clauses in the Step refer to experiences and a mindset that we need to keep in the forefront, to inform and fuel us in our work to live usefully.

Offering a very different perspective, Bill W. wrote that "The joy of living is the theme of A.A.'s Twelfth Step, and action is its key word."[336] He viewed living usefully as moving through life with humble gratitude and envisioned this to include helping fellows who are still in distress, extending ourselves in the spirit of love and service (without expected reward) and embracing the principles of the Program in our daily lives so that our relationships are healthy. Bringing this back to joy, Bill wrote that "Understanding is the key to right principles and attitudes, and right action is the key to good living; therefore, the joy of good living is the theme of A.A.'s Twelfth Step."[337] His view that joy is a payoff of serving others is very consistent with some current thinking. For example, joy can be a selfless feeling of contentment and peace that arises when we help others become more content.[338] In this light, Step 12 draws our attention to the beautiful rewards of our work—the benefit to us personally and to the fellowship, whose sustainability depends on our continued growth and success. The key to taking Step 12 is knowing, with humble gratitude, that we have been given a lifesaving gift and we cannot risk being complacent. It is only through the practice of these Twelve Steps in all our affairs that we can maintain the resilience to live life on life's terms with the equanimity that comes with recovery.

It's all about the spiritual awakening

Let's start with the language of the Step itself. It starts by referring to the experience of spiritual awakening as the result of the Steps. In other words, this awakening is the single intended outcome of working the Pro-

Chapter 16

Step 12: Generosity/Heart-Willingness

Step 12. Having had a spiritual awakening as the result of the steps, we tried to carry this message to others, and practice these principles in all our affairs.

Too Little		Too Much
Miserly Takers	Tight-Fisted Scarcity-Based	Service-Focused Inspired Givers	Wasteful Self-Harming

"To keep it, you've got to give it away."
—*12 Step fellowship wisdom*

Generosity: A recovery perspective

Much of our 12-Step journey together has been focused on discovering and fixing what was out of balance in ourselves and our lives. Most of us entered the Rooms thinking that our goal was to somehow kick our habitual compulsive choices and thereby get sober—to stop our crazy behaviors. In Steps 1 through 11 we did the work to understand our disease, to find healthier patterns for living and embrace resources that could sustain us. Dr. Bob summed up the essence of the Program as trusting God, cleaning house, and helping others. Over time, listening to those who got here before us, we came to see the potential for so much more—not just surviving, but thriving.

Step 12 can be interpreted in many ways. On the surface, it seems to be just another set of directions. In a positive light, the reference to a spiritual awakening and trying to help others reflects achievements. The fact that

- How does equanimity relate to seeking holiness for you in taking Step 11?
- Write briefly about other middot we have studied together that are important in taking Step 11 and climbing your ladder toward holiness.

PLAYLIST
- "God's Will"—Martina McBride
- "The Other Side"—SZA and Justin Timberlake
- "Best is Yet To Come"—LuvBug
- "Try Everything"—Shakira
- "Live Your Story"—Tina Parol

- Wear a bracelet and move it to the other wrist when you do something that honors yourself. Practice "I" sentences when sharing what you need.
- Get a meditation app and try it every day, adding one minute each day.

If you lean toward a sagging *kedushah* (you tend to be self-serving) you might try:
- Create a God box and practice making one deposit a day that reflects gratitude or need.
- Wear a bracelet and move it to the other wrist when you take an action to serve the needs of another over your own desires.
- PAUSE before acting and practice asking yourself how an action would be different if you focused on another's needs rather than your own desires.
- Get a meditation app and try it every day, adding one minute each day.
- Practice asking *What would you like?* to others in your life.

Prompts for journaling or study with your *chevruta*/sponsor
- What does it mean to pray for God's will? How can you distinguish between God's will and your will?
- What do you need to have the power to carry out God's will for you? Which middot can you strengthen to help make this so?
- What holds you back from prayer and meditation?
- How do you interpret the text "You shall be holy because I, the Lord, am holy"?
- How might you bring holiness into your recovery program?
- Give an example of your holiness in action.
- Can you think of a time when you experienced holiness through separation?
- Can you think of a time when you experienced holiness through connection?
- What experience have you had with prayer changing you?

contact with the God of our understanding is our center of gravity, helping us keep our balance, following our moral compass.

Prayer and meditation are integral to calmness of the soul. Jewish wisdom encourages the practice of *hitbodedut*, isolating yourself with God and speaking in your own words. It may be yelling or writing or rapping—whatever allows us to feel seen and heard releases us to go about our business. *Hitbonenut*, the practice of meditation, helps us open a space in which we are not entangled by our whirling minds. An image I find helpful in maintaining my equanimity is a bungee cord from my center to HP. It allows for some motion for us to be ourselves but provides stability at the same time. Maintaining the connection through prayer and meditation allows us to separate ourselves from the ups and downs that can pull us off balance. In this way, equanimity powers our journey toward holiness and a life of recovery.

Daily reminders to help work Step 11

Following are some phrases that you might use as your daily reminders. Feel free to choose one, or create your own.

- Prayer asks, meditation listens.
- God's will, not mine.
- Make time to connect.
- The answer is in following **G**ood **O**rderly **D**irection.
- Whatever it may look like.

Kabbalot to cultivate holiness (*kedushah*) as you take Step 11

If you lean toward excessive *kedushah* (you are self-sacrificing) you might try:

- Include at least one action of self-care/joy-making on your daily agenda.
- Do a humility review with someone else to see where you might take up more space.
- Create a daily kedushah list—list 3-5 things that reflect your holiness.

3 by telling us to intentionally awaken to the message and messengers, as did our ancestors.

Like prayer, meditation can take many forms. The library and the internet are filled with teachings on different techniques of Jewish meditation that you can bring to your recovery. Perhaps knowing that meditation is an ancient Jewish spiritual practice will help you be more open to the idea. Our Mussar sages included meditation in addition to daily reminders and journaling as essential to an effective Mussar practice. These are many different modalities for conscious contact. None is intended to be onerous; together they create a rhythm in our days that enhances the value of our practice. Whatever the tool, their essence is to see clearly into the truth of what is.[334] Journaling, walking in nature, silence, and isolation can all be meditative practices. Prayer can also be meditative. I encourage you to try these approaches as if they are a tasting menu. Mix it up to maximize what you come to know of yourself and your HP. Because we get only a daily reprieve, make a commitment to your practice. Finding freedom in habit will break you free. Please don't let your mind just say *yeah, sure*. Do it! Through meditation, you can change how you relate to every dimension of your life. Filling up with wonder, joy, yearning and gratitude will power you to share your energy by serving others. Step 11 is critical to sustain your holiness through action.

Secondary middot

Humility, faith and trust are foundational middot for authentic *kedushah*. Openness to seeking, accepting and acting on guidance from outside ourselves is not possible without any of these middot. Another middah that intersects with *kedushah* is equanimity (*menuchat hanefesh*). This is translated as calmness of the soul, referring to a sense of inner balance. This is a form of separating from the turmoil of our ever-changing and challenging world. Alan Morinis describes *menuchat hanefesh* in terms of becoming more skilled at the process of living.[335] In the Program we'd call it living life on life's terms. An image that may help you understand the core idea is riding a surfboard. We do not calm the waves in the ocean; by keeping our balance we can ride them. The tests of life are the waves and our conscious

and in others it's indirect, through Moses (Exodus 3) and other prophets (2 Kings 21). Although with our current knowledge we cannot explain the mechanics, the fact is that our tradition teaches that tuning our mind's ear to the right channel can be lifesaving and life-changing.

Fast forward to today. We are no different than the Israelites of old. Their bondage was imposed by Egyptians; ours is the bondage of self, of booze or drugs, of workaholism or self-doubt, shame, regret, and the speed of life. We are blinded by doing, doing, doing. Our version of the flood is the wreckage we create that destroys our world and our desert is the isolation of our disease. And we race through our days to take care of everyone and everything on the to-do list and arrive at the end of the day exhausted and sapped. There's no time to smell the roses—we are busy pulling weeds, oblivious of the beauty around us.

Have you heard news stories of art conservators discovering an image in a painting that was concealed when the artist painted over it? Often it is discovered via an X-ray. Meditation, which can take many forms, is our mental power to X-ray, a means to awaken and uncover what's hidden under the barrage of messages and images that fill our lives and minds in this contemporary world. Rabbi Jeff Roth likens the benefits of meditation to awakening—awakening the spiritual side of Judaism within our own hearts and empowering us to respond with wisdom, kindness, and compassion to life challenges. In other words, meditation helps us recover our holiness.[332]

As it relates to recovery and our Mussar work, meditation is a tool for "finding a degree of inner spaciousness and freedom from habit that keeps us tripping over our own mind."[333] Using the example of meditation practice that involves concentration and awareness, Roth describes becoming aware of the thoughts that take up space and time. "At the moment of coming back to your object of focus, you can notice where your thoughts took you." Looking at this can create clarity about what has happened, for example how our yetzer hara lured us away from our holiness. We can also choose not to follow that stream of thought but to intentionally expand our awareness to discover the hidden image below the surface with its messages for us. It is my interpretation of Step 11 that it extends the effort of Step

Making it personal

Another Hebrew word often associated with prayer is *tefilah*, which is interpreted to connote thinking, judgment, and pleading. *Tefilah* is translated as introspection and self-judgment—but not in a disapproving way. Think of it as reflecting on what you need in order to be of service to others (including the God of your understanding). We take Step 11, starting with humility and looking outside ourselves for help in making life choices; what applies here is the oft heard advice that we do not think less of ourselves, we think of ourselves less. At this point in our recovery, we dig below the surface to identify what we need in the physical, emotional and spiritual domains and focus on it in our prayer.

Think of standing in a crowded room wanting to convey a message or request to someone. Would you rather shout it into the din or get closer to deliver it personally? For me the choice is easy. Stories that I have heard in the sanctuary of meeting rooms and prayer spaces convince me that someone is listening. While we can't be sure, I know two things for sure. First, you are unlikely to get what you don't ask for. Also, the God of my understanding has, over time, become the God of my experience. When I pray on something I always get an answer. I may not like it, but that's not the deal; I do get an answer. I don't know where I comes from and I don't care. Since I did not know what actions to take, the guidance I get opens me up. I would not go to a doctor and choose to ignore a prescription I was given. Nor do I ignore this guidance; it always works out, in my experience.

Cultivating holiness through meditation

Meditation (*hitbonenut*) is also called out in Step 11 as a tool for improving our conscious contact with the Divine. Please keep in mind that the general idea in relation to our recovery work is that meditation complements prayer—meditation is how we listen for guidance. There is a sense of knowing that comes from meditation and this is, in fact, a core purpose of Jewish meditation practice.[331] Viewed this way, there is a long history of meditation in Jewish tradition. We have many stories of prophets using it to connect with the Divine and other ancestors receiving direction. In some instances, the contact is direct from God (Genesis 22, Exodus 20)

I want to suggest that the prayer referred to in Step 11 is not scripted; it is the natural longing-based expression of what's in an individual's heart. Done with sincerity and intentionality (also called *kavanah*) it is our primary means of conscious contact with the God of our understanding. Whether directed to the power of the universe, Mother Nature, the sea, the Program, your home group, or God *as you understand*, prayer is the act of communicating about our dreams, gratitude, frustrations, anger and yearnings. "Prayer is the act of turning ourselves into a vehicle for the Divine."[328]

What does this have to do with our Mussar practice and recovery? The answer is in the fact that prayer changes the pray-er. Rabbi Lord Jonathan Sacks wrote:

> …regular prayer works on us in ways not immediately apparent….prayer gradually wears away the jagged edges of our character, turning it into a work of devotional art…. We begin to see the beauty of the created world. We locate ourselves as part of the story of our people. Slowly we come to think less of "I", more of we.[329]

This thinking captures the essence of recovery. Our work within the Twelve Step program and our Mussar practice is ultimately focused on the very benefit that Sacks notes: refining ourselves, thinking of ourselves less (not thinking less of ourselves) so that we can do God's will and be of service to others. Prayer gives us the strength and courage to change by bringing us closer to the source of power in the universe. In a sermon on why we pray, Rabbi David Wolpe shared a powerful message that prayer brings us closer to God. We are not, he said, pulling God down closer to us; rather, we are raising ourselves up to be closer to God.[330]

Some people think of God as beyond the limits of our physical world, and others as deeply within us. Prayer is reflexive; hence the verb for prayer, *l'hitpallel*, is a reflexive verb. It bridges us to the spiritual domain in which we uncover where we need to grow as we continue up the ladder to holiness and service. Rest assured that the specifics of your prayer practice are not at issue here. That you have a prayer practice at all is what's important.

instincts. This is us in our addiction. The *beinoni* is intermediate; she has wicked thoughts and chooses to take a path that is righteous/holy. This is us in recovery. The *beinoni* has a more challenging and, I argue, more rewarding journey.

Acknowledging this reality of our human struggle in his writings on the virtue of holiness, Rabbi Luzzatto says it is "…impossible for a person to achieve this state [the height of holiness/*tzeddek*] on his own, for it is beyond his capacity (since he is, after all, corporeal, and [made] of flesh and blood)…"[325] There is "none Holy like the Lord."[326] While we cannot expect to achieve perfection, we can strive to act in godly ways for which we, the Israelite family, were chosen.

Step 11 says, in essence, that we are to use prayer and meditation to discover how to be holy. Knowing that HP wants us to be holy is a perfect North Star. Frequently, the next right thing is clear. However, the challenges of everyday life seen through the lens of our own self-serving instincts (*yetzer hara*) may require that we confront choices that necessitate more detailed guidance. In this scenario, the *mitzvot* give us the traffic laws: stop at red lights; yield to pedestrians; pass in the left lane only. We are stymied when we do not know which roads to take. A dialogue of questions and answers is needed. Prayer and meditation are tools through which we get clarity, both in terms of our questions and the answers. Our virtual phone line has HP on one side and our inner realm on the other. Our prayer may be as simple as *help*. And somehow, from somewhere, the solution appears. I call out to God, and he answers me.[327]

Cultivating holiness through prayer

Our tradition does suggest a structure and content for prayer, called *keva*. This aspect of prayer is captured in our prayer books and worship services. This communal prayer connects us to one another; the mutuality we share can be an important component of recovery. The knowledge that we are part of a chain with a 5,000-year history connects us to something much bigger than us. It is my experience that this fills my heart and spirit. It allows me to bring humility and the power of hopefulness to the work of self-judgment and refinement which is integral to prayer.

ing it as separation from sinful thoughts and actions.[322] Relating this to Step 11, God's will is that we clean up our lives and motives, abstain from self-serving choices, and separate from our distorted thinking so we can connect with and serve others.

Mussar wisdom explains the conditions necessary for the perfection of our Divine service as including the ordered acquisition of vigilance, alacrity, cleanliness, abstinence, purity, piety, humility, and holiness.[323] Holiness, the final step of self-refinement identified by Luzzatto, is clearly a high goal for a Mussar student to pursue. Through this lens, our journey through the Twelve Steps is scaling a ladder toward holiness. To me, that feels pretty good.

Holiness (*kedushah*) is not about perfection

Contrary to the images evoked by the words *holy* and *holiness*, *kedushah* does not refer to purity or perfection. It's important that this idea of striving for holiness fits with the reality of our human imperfection. *Kedushah* is translated to mean that something is set apart for a specific purpose. Let's take, for example, a kiddish cup. It is any cup that is set aside for use on Shabbat or other sacred days as the vessel in which the wine is blessed. If we use it on Monday for wine with dinner, its specialness is corrupted and it is no longer sanctified.[324]

Unlike a cup, our essence is multi-layered and includes all our middot and our free will. In the course of life, we exhibit the range of traits in our unique mix. And, in the course of our disease, we addicts often err on the side of using our life force to make some unwise choices. We use our vessel for non-sacred purposes. Think of it as throwing some dirt on our inner light. In our work of recovery, *tikkun middot* and *teshuvah*, we turn from these patterns and re-sanctify/purify ourselves by striving for clean motives and actions, cleaning the dirt off. The path is not a straight line and you can take comfort in knowing that you are not unique in your struggle to stay on a good path. Humans have been described in Jewish wisdom as having three archetypes: *tzaddik, rasha,* and *beinoni*. The *tzaddik* is righteous and does not have bad thoughts. I envision Mother Teresa in this way. In contrast, the *rasha* is the individual who succumbs to his animal

commanding or punishing God, so let's keep looking. We might interpret it as referring to an attribute that is a default condition of humanity. Because the text does not say you *are* holy, (and generally such a tall order is something that would not be so easy to satisfy), I also do not think this is a plausible explanation.

The phrase *because I, the Lord, am holy* does, however, add an important element. Let's start with the idea that holiness is part of our essence. According to our tradition, God is holy, the breath of God is holy and as life was breathed into us (Genesis 2:7), we were given holiness in our essence. Judaism teaches that it is the source of our purity and it endows us with the capacity to do good, godly things—to make godly choices, drawn by an inner urge to do so.[320] The action-based phrase *You shall be holy* combined with the reason to believe (because I am holy) allows me to subscribe to the idea that this verse is a suggestion on how to use our endowment to live a fulfilling life (which is what God wants for us). It is aspirational but also empowering because we are gifted with this potential. Going with the idea that we are bestowed this way resonates and that brings us to the middah of holiness (*kedushah*) to inform Step 11, leaning into prayer and meditation as our tools. Whatever holiness looks like, it's God's will for us, so let's proceed to clarify that together.

The nature of holiness—*kedushah*

We find the word *kedoshim* (holy ones) in the Hebrew text of this verse we are exploring (Lev. 19:2). The verse is found in *Parashah Kedoshim*, the Torah portion often referred to as containing the Holiness Code, instructions for striving to live with holiness. According to Torah, holiness comes from walking in God's ways—performing *mitzvot*.

Conceptually, holiness flows from the Divine into and through us, to be manifest in our actions. Luzzatto described the virtue of holiness like a reflexive verb. He wrote that it begins with effort and ends with a Divine gift. In other words, taking holy actions leads to our holiness.

The Hebrew word *kedoshim* is derived from a root that relates to purification, cleanliness, abstaining and separating.[321] Rashi and talmudic scholars clarify what holiness (*kedushah*) means for us humans, describ-

is my experience that this Program is a blueprint for living a life that exceeds anything I ever thought possible. My hope for you is that you keep up your weaving—it is a lifelong undertaking. You might not realize it yet, but the product of your efforts is a magic carpet that can take you to a beautiful life. As they say, don't leave before the miracle happens.

Holiness (*Kedusha*): A Mussar perspective on Step 11

> *I call out to God, and he answers me.*
> —*Duties of the Heart*

Step 11 challenges us to discern the will of the God of our understanding and our power to fulfill it. Judaism, through Torah, tell us that God says we shall be holy. Scholars have long debated how to interpret this and to define the goal. Insofar as the Program and living in recovery encourage us to focus on our relationship with the God of our understanding, it's helpful that Torah goes further to relate this ideal for us to our connection to the Divine. The full verse in Leviticus 19:2 says, "You shall be holy, because I, the Lord, am holy." Like so much in our sacred texts, there is a lot to explore and interpret in these few words.

The opening phrase, "You shall be holy," appears to be a strong, future-related statement. I say future-related considering that *shall* is synonymous with *will*, which refers to something in the future. Do you think it is a commandment or a piece of advice when you read this as *You will be holy*? Is it a promise that is conditional on something that we are to do or is it something that happens passively? Knowing that every word is important to our understanding, let's keep digging.

Indeed, one perspective on the statement *You shall be holy* is that it connotes that you *will* do this (because I told you to), i.e., it is a command. Personally, this triggers a question about consequences of noncompliance—whether it is my intentional resistance or simply just falling short. In my personal theology I do not subscribe to the idea of a threatening/

is important to verify with others that we're not simply closing our eyes and hearing what we want to hear.[316] There is danger in the voice of self-will and the deception it creates in the guise of a Divine source.

Sometimes, when in the midst of making a decision, it's not easy to know our Higher Power's will for us. Much of my dilemma comes from fear of making a wrong decision or getting guidance I don't like. Despite our wishes, rarely does it appear on a neon sign. We must actively invest personal energy and be discerning. Perhaps you will go to a meeting that you don't usually attend and hear a speaker say exactly what you needed to hear. The guidance may come from your conscience, Program literature, a fellow or a sponsor. I can simply say that it never has your voice. We might also find that our bodies give us signs. Whatever we do will be the right thing as long as we live in the spirit of seeking our Higher Power's will.[317]

Final notes

My prayers are in my conversational style—they are not filled with words like *king, father* or *thou doest*. Fostering an attitude of gratitude and living one day at a time, my prayer practice begins before my feet hit the floor in the morning; I give thanks for another day and all the opportunities to be my best self. Focused on the day ahead "…we ask God to direct our thinking, especially asking that it be divorced from self-pity, dishonest or self-seeking motives."[318] During the course of the day, I ask for courage, inspiration and guidance regarding decisions. Which course to take, how can I best serve? Let me show up in humility and stay on my side of the street.

We can ask the power greater than ourselves for wisdom, courage, inspiration, an intuitive thought, or right action. Our old friends honesty, openness, and willingness are essential. Patience is key while we wait for answers to become clear, as is acceptance of God's will and time. For many, the Serenity Prayer is the go-to in the Program, reminding us that we no longer run the show. To remind ourselves of our part in it all, we are encouraged to conclude our prayers with the affirmation, *thy will be done*.

I am sustained in my Step work by learning that "There is a direct link among self-examination, meditation, and prayer….when they are logically related and interwoven, the result is an unshakable foundation for life."[319] It

tool for this is meditation, a practice in which we create spaciousness and open the windows of possibility. My dear friend Dan (not Dan Harris), a teacher and practitioner of mindfulness, explains it this way:

> Meditation involves bringing the mind toward a focal point—for example, the breath, an image or a sound. Over time, the object drifts in and out of focus. During the "outtakes'" when we are diverted by other thoughts, images, scents, etc. we can say to ourselves," Oh yes, there's that …." With mindfulness, we let the diversion float away without getting entangled in a reaction or judgment and bring ourselves back to our resting point. Over time, we experience our mind as an open expanse. That space is where we have the freedom to connect to "knowing" beyond simple consciousness. It may be in a flashing thought or wave of an image, scent or sensation. The possibilities are infinite but one thing is for sure, it has the potential to invigorate us physically, emotionally and spiritually by releasing us from the prison of our minds.

Meditation in Step 11 refers to listening and discerning. Meditation practices are as varied and personal as prayer practices. The exact form does not matter. What is important is that we actively engage in opening ourselves to help and support. Whose voice is it that we hear? For us addicts, typically the voice in our heads is our own. Our will is broadcast at such high volume that it drowns out everyone and everything else. In the Rooms, meditation is described as listening for what God would have us do; it's the answer to our prayers. One of our daily readers teaches that "Meditation is the quiet and sustained application of the mind to the contemplation of a *spiritual truth*. Its purpose is to *deflect* our minds from the problem we are experiencing, to raise our thoughts above the grievances and discontent that color our thinking."[314] Commonly fellows who are able to get honest regarding meditation admit that "…one of my difficulties in listening was my anxiety about having the "right" response [answer]."[315] It

help me keep my hands off Josh, to leave room for you to work your plan, whatever that may look like." For me, the phrase at the end makes all the difference in separating myself from the solution. This is important because not only are we often wrong, but my experience is also that the range of solutions I can envision is tiny. Another way to up your game is to use a God box, a tool mentioned previously in the context of trusting God. Put worries, questions and fears on notes and deposit them in a God box. This is another form of letting go so we can get on with our day. When I clean out my God box, I can see that most of the situations I wrote about are resolved. My sponsor says, "One of two things will happen. Either it's going to work out or it's going to work out." I am reminded of a magnet my sponsor gave me that says "Hello, this is God. I will be handling all your problems today and won't be needing your help. So just relax and have a nice day." My prayers include remembering to take that advice.

The nature of meditation

The practice of meditation has a long history across time, cultures and geography. It has garnered recent attention as a way to enhance wellness and happiness. Meditation yields "emotional balance"[312] and scientific research has demonstrated that meditation can benefit our mood, stress, anxiety, and even high blood pressure. A well-known TV journalist, Dan Harris, shared his story of how meditation helped him unlock happiness by quieting the "incessant, insatiable voice in his head."[313]

Do you remember the committee in our head that we talked about in Chapter 9? The committee is meeting in our cranial conference room all day every day, beckoning us to follow its commands. Adding to the cacophony is advice and opinions of loved ones, social media influencers, and self-help gurus. Being locked in that conference room by our disease is like driving through the countryside with the windows rolled up and radio blaring. We can't hear the wind and birds unless we step into the quiet outside.

Step 11 directs us to turn down the volume of our inner voices so we can hear and tap into the signals that the universe and our HP have for us. The

outcomes—getting sober, avoiding jail, staying married, etc. We are told in the Rooms, "Do not pray that someone will do what you want them to do. Only pray that things will work out well for them."[310] When we go to meetings and talk to fellows we are reminded that things are the way they are supposed to be. "I [We] don't have to like reality, only to accept it for what it is."[311]

Consider this story from the Rooms.

> I remember an incident with my son, who was in full blown disease. What was I to do? I took him to a hotel across the street from a rehab center in the city where we live. Did I mention that he had been asked to leave this place a few months before? I told him that I would pay for one night at the hotel to give him a chance to decide whether he would walk across the street and ask for help or choose to live on the street. Would he be alive in the morning and make the right decision—to check himself in? My motives were selfish—I did not want him to die. A Program friend who sat with me that night brought me back to my spiritual reality. Going to rehab might have been the right answer to me, but it was not right for my son unless he wanted to get better. So, we prayed together that his Higher Power would take care of him and that I could find the strength to let him choose. It's been an arduous journey—suffice it to say he has 15 years now and I have 20. I thank my HP for the strength to let him go and that this brought him to the Rooms where he could find what I knew awaited him.

Permit me to share two key aspects of my personal practice. First is an extension of the slogan *Let go and let God*. I cap my prayers with the phrase "whatever that may look like." So, in practice I say (or write), "God, please keep Nicky under your wing, whatever that may look like." Or, "God,

others to a cloud, the Program, or a sponsor. It's important to clarify that praying to a sponsor or the Program does not imply that we view them as superhuman deities. Like praying to a theologically defined God, deferring to something beyond ourselves with humility and healthy self-esteem simply acknowledges that there is power and wisdom that we do not have.

Within the context of your Twelve Step work, I will suggest that you think about praying *to* rather than praying *for*. Considering that we struggle with a disease of isolation, praying *with* is also a powerful aspect of recovery. Next time you recite the Serenity or Lord's Prayer with your meeting group, try to feel the resonance of the voices in your body. Prayer is an outlet for practicing gratitude and trust; try to focus on what you have rather than what you lack or want. While our fellows and loved ones each have their own Higher Power, we can be of service to others by praying on their behalf, provided that we do not try to dictate outcomes. We are not to pray for things, rather for knowing and doing, for being of service and for receiving **G**ood **O**rderly **D**irection. It may be in regard to ourselves, or our prayers may relate to others.

We are advised to turn to prayer when we need to discern what is the next right thing to do. Personally, I ask the universe what is the *Godly* action, solution or approach to whatever I am pondering. You might direct your question to the universe in the course of a walk or to a sponsor or Program fellow with whom you check in to reason things out. Openness to the direction of the God of our understanding allows us to "set my [our] thoughts aside and take time to focus on His thoughts and how…" they might be expressed through me.[309]

Let's be honest, this can be really, really hard in the context of addiction, which dials up our desire to control and delivers thorny problems to solve and bitter pills to swallow. It is natural that when we or those we love are troubled or in doubt about what to do next, the hardest thing is to trust something over which we have no control. That is exactly what Step 11 demands. Whether we are praying for our benefit or for others, the Program teaches that we are to pray for what is right, not what we want. Subduing the "suggestions" we want to offer as part of our prayers is a challenge in the practice of Step 11. Our prayers are not to be used to request specific

answers come from or in what form they will arrive. We are simply asked to maintain close contact consciously and intentionally with our support system or network and willingly ask for guidance as we continue to develop our own power to make healthy choices and put positive energy back into the universe.

Some will resist the idea because once prayer is labelled as intentional it seems awkward or implies ceding control to something that they question or reject. The atheists and agnostics among us, who may rely on a sponsor or other spiritual advisor as their Higher Power, will say it's unnecessary to call this out. Others will embrace and engage with the ideas because they are "believers" or have surrendered their doubt and are not willing to take a chance of missing out on something helpful. To be 100% clear, the references to God, prayer and meditation do not have any religious or magical connotation. None of these perspectives violates Step 11 because, like the God of our understanding, prayer and meditation are according to your personal custom. As was the case in Step 3, these spiritual practices are as you understand the ideas of any Higher Power or force that is bigger than you. By now you know that; but a reminder of this important principle of the Twelve Steps is never out of order.

The nature of prayer

Praying as directed in Step 11 refers to talking to a power greater than us (which many refer to as God) about this Higher Power's will for us and asking for the capacity and capability to carry it out. Celebrities pray, presidents pray, as do athletes, soldiers, my doctor and my mother, to name just a few. Why not me? What could be bad? Actually, it seems there is more downside in not partaking.

Prayer is a very personal form of communication. We can pray by consciously thinking, writing, creating, feeling, and hoping. The spirit of prayer rather than its form is what matters. "God meets me where I am."[308] Our task is to be willing. Prayer practices vary widely—from traditional, organized religious rituals with recitation of text to unstructured personal compositions. Some people pray in public and some privately; some prayers are offered out loud and some silently. Some pray to a defined God and

human form, prayer and meditation are often spoken of as tools of spiritual mindfulness. In the context of our Twelve Step work and our recovery, prayer and meditation are described as means of talking to and listening to our HP, respectively.

Much more than simply being spiritually aware, Step 11 reflects the intentional action of engaging with this power that is greater than us. While we may be comfortable with ideas such as gravity, which is also intangible, the personal nature of a connection to a power that affects our own being or that of those we love is a challenging idea for some. Having come to value this HP as the source of wisdom, strength, and hope that brought us to this place in our recovery makes engagement a significant goal in our work. Reinforcing its importance is the teaching that our spiritual condition is fundamental to living in recovery, which we try to do one day at a time. This is a relationship that we grow to treasure; through it we sustain our ability to live by the spiritual principles of the Twelve Steps and navigate life on life's terms. The spiritual connection about which we are speaking allows us to freely share what's on our minds and in our hearts, know our HP's will for us, and find the power in ourselves to carry it out in all our affairs. Engaging in prayer and meditation involves quieting our minds and opening our hearts, creating the space to become aware of the vast array of possibilities available to us—many of which we may never have imagined were possible.

I venture that in the course of time since beginning the journey of recovering through the Twelve Steps, you have prayed and meditated, perhaps unknowingly. An example of prayer would be sharing your thoughts and questions about which path to take with the God of our understanding, the universe, or your sponsor, spiritual advisor, or fellows. So, too, is expressing gratitude for a new start, for the chance to earn back trust of a loved one or for the newfound beauty around us or in our lives. Calling out the actions as intentional in taking Step 11 is off-putting for many. For those looking for a reason to reject the Twelve Step way of life, labelling it prayer or meditation may provoke strong feelings and elicit images with religious or New Age connotations. Working a Twelve Step program does not require that we hold any particular theological or mystical belief relating to where

Hearing one another's stories in the Rooms and in fellowship surely supports the premise that living a spiritual life is at the core of our well-being. This sounds as simple as making choices guided by spiritual principles such as those we've examined together. Our human reality, however, is that while the Twelve Steps may be a simple Program, we are complicated, imperfect people and life is complicated, to say the least. Our nature, which is to worry and fear, to be self-serving and controlling, makes it easy to shift our Program practices into lower gear and even to glide in neutral. The slow drip, drip, drip of our deep-seated patterns of stinking thinking and reactions, mingled with the stress of everyday problems and the flood of feelings that are new to us, can easily divert us from our best intentions. For some of us, worry and fear actually feel productive, as if we are staving off inevitable problems. Embracing Step 11 by consciously nurturing our relationship with the force of the universe or other God of our understanding, who wants us to be happy and healthy, is the core of Step 11 and is key to maintaining our lives in recovery.

The concept of wellness is integral to this Step. Conventionally, we accept the idea that adopting practices of exercise and clean living are key to staying healthy, which plays out in our physical and emotional well-being. The same concept applies to our emotional and spiritual domains. Step 11 leverages practices of prayer and meditation to stay connected with the source of guidance, comfort and strength we tap to live morally principled, purposeful lives. Maintaining this connection with our Higher Power requires a commitment. Openness to the guidance we receive from the God of our understanding is integral to its effectiveness. Through this channel, the practices of prayer and meditation sustain and energize our physical and emotional well-being, providing support and guidance that we need to joyfully and serenely navigate life on life's terms.

The nature of spiritual connection

Undoubtedly, we each interpret the terms *prayer* and *meditation* differently. So too tuning into or connecting with something that is intangible and outside of our consciousness. Insofar as the target of prayer and meditation is not physically concrete and somehow manifests itself through our

Chapter 15

Step 11: Holiness

Step 11. [We] Sought through prayer and meditation to improve our conscious contact with God *as we understood Him*, praying only for the knowledge of His will for us and the power to carry that out.

Too Little ←——————————————→ *Too Much*

| Self-Serving | Seeking to Meet the Physical Needs of Others | Selfless Service to Community & Fellows, Fueled by God-Consciousness | Careless with Our Vessel |

Prayer asks the question. Meditation listens for the answer.
—*12 Step fellowship wisdom*

Holiness: A recovery perspective

Banter among fellows reflects that life itself has gotten easier for many and they are enjoying progress in building meaningful relationships. Through sharing their experience, strength and hope with one another, many also report that they have begun to joyfully give freely of themselves to help others. Explaining how their lives were transformed, many also gratefully marvel at the power greater than ourselves that has worked through them to bring us here.

- What does Rabbi Salanter mean by "the material needs of my neighbor are my spiritual need?"

Playlist
- "You've Got A Friend"—James Taylor/Carole King
- "Try A Little Kindness"—Tori Kelly
- "Treat People With Kindness"—Harry Styles
- "Try a Little Kindness"—Glen Campbell
- "Loving Kindness"—Ashana

- We attract what we give.
- The solution is in our actions.
- Be a conduit of *chesed*.
- The stranger is someone I have not helped [yet].

Kabbalot to cultivate loving-kindness (*chesed*) as you take Step 10

If you lean toward excessive loving-kindness (you are neglecting yourself)
- Do one self-indulgent thing each day. Allow someone to do something nice for you that you might otherwise resist.
- Examine your motives to be sure they are clean of doing for others to get something in return.
- Ask for something you need from another.
- In your daily inventory, identify 3 laudable acts you did each day.
- Strengthen your boundaries; where do you fit on your daily to-do list?
- Practice saying *no*. Use your rubber band to remind yourself not to say *yes* when you want to say *no*.

If you lean toward sagging loving-kindness (you are selfish)
- Feel your pulse 3 times a day; with every beat, imagine *chesed* pulsing through you.
- Use your toothbrushing time to imagine yourself as a conduit of loving-kindness to others.
- Make an effort to greet others by saying to them, "It's good to see you."
- Ask someone who is important to you what they need; provide it.
- Make a Program call, share in a meeting, or perform another active service every day this week.

Prompts for journaling or study with your *chevruta*/sponsor
- What distances you from others?
- What helps you cultivate loving connections?
- How are acts of loving-kindness different than charity?
- How might loving-kindness look in thought, speech, deed?

power greater than ourselves. I am not one to believe in magic, but somehow this magically can become a cycle that sustains itself and all involved.

Our Twelve Step programs depend on members' acts of chesed. Being vulnerable and sharing our stories, extending ourselves in sponsorship and practicing non-judgmental listening are examples of how we make loving loving-kindness a pillar of our world. Loving-kindness sparks trust, service to others, spiritual development, and loving connections among neighbors in our new world.

Secondary middot

By now you understand that the middot intertwine during our spiritual journeys and no one middah is a bullet train to recovery. Not surprising, Step 10 intersects with many middot. Order/*seder* is a priority if we are to make time for the work of the Step and practicing chesed. Our yetzer hara wants us to let things slip. Adam's story reminds us that we risk expulsion. Mussar teachings on responsibility/*acharayut,* alacrity/*zerizut* and humility/*anavah* clearly enrich our work in Step 10. We must commit to the difficult work of rightsizing our egos (humility) to inventory our days and admit our wrongs (responsibility) and promptly apologize (alacrity). Generosity/*nedivut* is a middah that we have not examined but which applies here as well. It guides our stretching to make apologies in the face of internal resistance. *Nedivut* is an example of the heart following the body; thus, it is said that opening the hand opens the heart.

Taking right actions in the present and planting positive seeds for the future are the best apologies for wrong actions of the past. Accessing chesed as we take Step 10 breaks the bonds of isolation and fosters the connections that bind people together—caring for and helping one another to live life on life's terms.

Daily reminders to help work Step 10

Following are some phrases that you might use as your daily reminders. Feel free to choose one or create your own.

- The world is built through *chesed.*
- Love what you do; do what you love.

lacked. How are we to conduct ourselves in this new world to enjoy loving connections? The idea that "the world is built on kindness" (Psalms 89:3) teaches that we must be trustworthy sources of loving-kindness. Program wisdom about living on life's terms and Jewish wisdom align 100 percent.

In life, overcoming our internal resistance to do generous, sustaining acts is a spiritual test.[306] Step 10 does not explicitly require that we love (enjoy) the work of recovery. In fact, it's commonly said in the Rooms that you don't have to like it, you just have to do it. Even so, we generally are very committed to things we love and I do believe the Program asks us to practice with commitment what is espoused in Jewish wisdom. Through this lens, I submit that Step 10, in every dimension, is spiritual work. Promptly admitting and apologizing when we have done wrong per Step 10 gives us a chance to fulfill all of the biblical imperatives to do justice (*tzedek*), love kindness (*chesed*) and walk humbly (*anavah*).

The aspect of promptness follows teachings of energetically seeking to be of service (*zerizut*). And, referring to Abraham soon after his circumcision (at age 99), our Sages speak to a willingness to suffer physically or spiritually to do chesed (Shabbat 104a). The prompt apology fits with these ideals. Finally, in the Rooms of recovery we talk about giving for fun and for free. The giving of an apology in the spirit of chesed similarly has no expected return; the focus is simply on sustaining the other selflessly (generosity). Practicing Mussar as we take Step 10 strengthens the loving connections among our neighbors in the new world we are creating.

As we have learned together, we can't be content with good acts alone. We strive to have our insides (heart) match our outsides (actions).[307] Since our heart follows our actions, Jewish wisdom teaches that we must practice the actions to cultivate a love of doing them. To repeat: If you want to be one whose heart loves doing acts of kindness, do acts of love and kindness. It's my experience that in time, your insides will match your outsides.

Whatever fills your heart with love, that's what to focus on to feed your practice. Humility (*anavah*) and gratitude (*hakarat hatov*) fuel my loving-kindness. So does performing mitzvot. The magic that we create from actions of loving-kindness is a heart or perhaps a soul connection with those we sustain. Supporting others connects us to our best selves and a

our own feelings associated with losing a loved one, we enter the space of compassion.

We get all the way to chesed (loving-kindness) by the combination of our actions and the orientation with which we take them. Stretching past our own discomfort because we care deeply about the mourner's suffering, listening with an open heart to "feel" the mourner's sadness, and taking an action that sustains the mourner (bringing a meal, helping them clean out clothes of the deceased) all without any expected return reflects chesed (loving-kindness) It is kind and we do it lovingly because we feel drawn to help.

In the realm of Step 10, I posit that when our action to address a wrong arises from a place of heartfelt gratitude for our blessings and love for the other, it begins to take on the attributes of chesed aka loving-kindness. Stretching beyond what's convenient or feels good for us by forcing ourselves to be honest and present with the person we wronged reflects the many dimensions of chesed. The key question is whether in doing the mitzvah your insides match your outsides. Through our hearts and actions, do we feel the pain of the other and respond selflessly—able to say/think/feel "I love you, love being here with you to comfort you and will do whatever I need to do to sustain you"?

It is certainly admirable to aspire to such in all connections with others. The bar is admittedly very high. This is one middah that is often in my spiritual curriculum. Speaking selfishly, in my fullest imperfection, I am comforted that "what we accomplished with our *mitzvos* and our Torah study is not the essential issue. What is important is how hard we've tried."[305] Just keep trying!

Cultivating *chesed*

Serenity Place and the Rooms of recovery are filled with individuals who are eager to enter into loving relationship so they can share their experience, strength and hope, and help one another build connections in our new community. With the risk that we might make unwise choices and get lost or expelled from the community, we are blessed that in our fellowships we have available to us resources that Adam, Eve, and Moses

we should be in repentance every day since we never know on which day we shall die.[303] More recently, Rabbi Wolbe suggested keeping track of daily occurrences of a moral/ethical nature and doing a nightly review to keep our slates clean.[304] I suggest that the energy required to be accountable daily, to admit and remedy our wrongs with promptness and resistance of the yetzer hara, elevates the actions of Step 10 to the stretching and generosity of chesed/loving-kindness.

As we close out our examination of this aspect of Step 10, it's important to note a seeming paradox. Conventionally, we tend to think of direct actions that we take to sustain one another. Giving clothes, money, or time are examples. With our Program fellows, what we may give is our trust in the wisdom of another fellow. Asking for help that draws on the gratitude, humility, generosity and experience of others in recovery can be an act of loving-kindness. The asking, usually done with our own humility, is often a sacrifice. The action of helping that sustains another fellow infuses the giver with a sense of value and purpose in serving the Program and God. Thus, asking for help can be a spiritual choice. Taking Step 10 with loving-kindness in mind will enhance the potential for the relationships to be loving connections.

Making it personal—loving-kindness (*chesed*) and compassion

Perhaps you are thinking that what I am describing as loving-kindness sounds a lot like compassion. Let's look at how these relate. Permit me to say that semantics aside, acting on any of these attributes (with the right motives) is a beautiful thing. Recognizing my limits as a scholar, this is only my perspective and I encourage you to delve inside yourself and consult your spiritual advisor, moral compass, and the wisdom of others to ferret out the perspective that drives serenity and joy for you.

As you will recall, compassion/*rachamim* asks us to get [so] close to another that we sense their feelings. We do not have to agree with them. We show compassion when we listen to others' stories without judgment and identify with their feelings and needs. Compassion is about our shared humanity. Let's again use a *shiva* call to illustrate. Most of us are fulfilling an obligation and not loving doing it. That's being kind. If the visit triggers

Loving-kindness is the path to rebuilding our world

Jewish wisdom teaches us that doing acts of loving-kindness is the blueprint for rebuilding the world.[296] Rabbi Angela Buchdahl teaches that the foundation for this idea was laid by our Sages when the Temple was destroyed and animal sacrifices were no longer possible. Acts of loving-kindness were identified as a path to communicate with God rather than animal sacrifices.[297] Fast forward to us and our move to Serenity Place. We are imperfect human beings in relationship with others like us in an imperfect world. That complex reality sets the stage for errors of judgment and action. Most are unintended. As with Adam and Moses, diverse forces can be at play.

Step 10 provides the path to address incidents of life that can derail us; Jewish wisdom enriches the solution of admitting our wrongs by teaching that acts of loving-kindness are a bridge to rebuilding. Through them, we construct connections that can weather such incidents and help us create a meaningful life in our new world. This is no easy task. "Working Step 10 requires great moral courage."[298] I encourage you to engage and to embrace the work; it fosters growth by highlighting our broken patterns and places so we can heal.

When we have to make an apology, as we are asked to do in practicing Step 10, we selfishly worry about the risk of being judged and rejected. After all, we came to claim our seats with a dubious track record. Will we still be loved and accepted if we need tolerance of our imperfections or even forgiveness? At the core, sustaining relationships with others requires that we accept being vulnerable at times. Remember though, that from the perspective of our tradition, our acts of loving-kindness/chesed take the place of sacrifices. "The awkwardness or inconvenience, even feeling the risk of rejection, is the sacrifice."[299]

Regarding repentance in personal relationships, we are challenged to cross that bridge to do the humbling, hard work of trying to make things right.[300] The apology in Step 10 "is to make things as right as can be with the victim, to attend to their needs…"[301] The idea of staying current with life (promptness) is found in numerous Jewish texts. Rabbi Eliezer taught that we should "repent one day before our death."[302] Talmud explains that

others as called for in this middah does not involve mindreading, fixing, curing or smothering others with our care.)

Abraham's infusion of caring for others with generosity and alacrity leads to him being recognized as an icon of loving-kindness. Along the lines of kindness, we are taught by Jewish wisdom to help meet the needs of others. Tuning into those needs can be hard work. The imperatives to feed the hungry and clothe the naked are often invoked as examples where we share our assets to help meet the needs of others. This is kind but does not necessarily rise to the level of chesed. Through a Mussar lens, to qualify as loving-kindness (chesed), the gesture must go beyond simply completing the action of giving resources. We are to be proactively kind to others (and the world), bringing generosity, refraining from judgment, and fostering the best for the other.

S-t-r-e-t-c-h-i-n-g into *chesed*

One important distinguishing aspect of chesed relative to lovingkindness is stretching ourselves in our sharing/sacrifice. We must proactively look for opportunities to serve and, when doing so, go beyond what is required or expected. It is for this reason that *I'm sorry* is not enough to meet the goal of Steps 9 and 10. So how much is enough? My rabbi/Mussar teacher describes the goal as getting to the point of feeling a little uncomfortable. Chesed through a Mussar lens is finding places where we can stretch beyond our comfort zone to share our bounty for the purpose of sustaining another and doing so with nothing expected in return. Essentially, we act in the image of the Divine who sustains us with loving-kindness.

When our actions to correct what we got wrong come from the heart, our practice of chesed reflects a spiritual alignment between our insides and our outsides. This merits a moment of reflection because it relates to the all-important goal in recovering our best selves and of keeping our motives clean. Are your insides aligned with your outsides? Are the physical actions you take in supporting another coming from a place of generosity and love—are they free of judgment and expected return no matter the outcome? Through this practice, we cultivate loving connections that can even help us avert problems before they crop up.

"I feel like a conduit. I think it's Divine love flowing." So, we show up in the Rooms and we take calls to be present for and allow another person to feel seen and loved. Being accountable for the hurts we cause is surely an action of lovingkindness and it helps us get started as valued neighbors in our communities.

Rising toward *chesed*—loving-kindness

At the highest rung on this ladder, the heart and body dimensions of our acts of lovingkindness are integrated and it's here that we are in the domain of chesed. Think of this middah as loving lovingkindness. And remember that love is both a noun and a verb.

In addition to meeting the needs of another, expecting nothing in return is an aspect of loving-kindness. If you are a dog or cat person, I am guessing that you can relate—this describes the feelings you have for your furry friend. You expect nothing in return but are inclined to smother it with touching, kisses, and treats. I am a dog person and look forward to returning to my home where my powder-puff Murphy awaits me and displays effusive happiness that I am there. The belly rubs, pile of dog toys, cabinet full of treats and gourmet holistic food reflect my loving-kindness for him. Murphy's greeting is almost as good as having my grandchild run to greet me when I visit, which makes me want to spoil her rotten. I am drawn to sustain them and make them happy without anything in return.

The gold standard would be God's feelings toward us; loving-kindness is often referenced as an attribute of God. Having been made *b'tzelem elohim* (in the image of God), loving-kindness reflects the orientation with which we do kind acts. The human attribute or capacity is elevated by the force of our hearts. Imagine chomping at the bit to do acts of kindness that are permeated with love and caring we feel for another. Viewing this through the lens of chesed means acting in the spirit of generosity to recognize the needs of other people with whom we are in relationship and making efforts to help satisfy or alleviate their needs.[295] Practicing loving-kindness (chesed) as defined by our Mussar sages means that we are rebalancing from being takers to being givers. (A quick note: Meeting the needs of

The nature of our kindness

Jewish wisdom is useful in learning how to function as good citizens and thrive as members in our new communities. The prophet Micah taught that God's will for our lives is that we "do justice, love kindness and walk humbly with God" (Micah 6:8). And we read that "the world stands on three things: on the Torah, on the service of God, and upon acts of kindness."[294] Because these ideas are central to Jewish thought and values, and they are very nuanced, it's important to clarify and distinguish what is meant by acts of kindness, lovingkindness and loving-kindness. I want to expand your thinking to consider loving-kindness as the meaning of the middah we call *chesed*. I think of kindness, lovingkindness and loving-kindness as being on a ladder that reaches toward heaven—to the sphere of holiness. All are admirable qualities. By practicing any of the three, we make this world a better place. Through acts of chesed, which we reach on the highest rung, we can bring heaven to earth for ourselves and others. Let's unpack these ideas.

Being kind, on the first rung, refers to an intentional action that reflects viewing another as important in some way. We all know people who are kind; they are friendly and extend themselves to be supportive of others. We might say to a host or nurse who served our needs "thank you for your kindness," referring to their actions on our behalf. Or, as an act of kindness, we might bake cookies for a new neighbor. In general, I'll describe kindness as being nice—it's largely an outside job, meaning that there is little about it that is deeply heartfelt.

Moving up a rung on our ladder, we step into lovingkindness; here our acts of kindness are imbued with feelings of love and deep concern for another. Acts of lovingkindness reflect the tender feelings we have toward others, with a desire to meet their needs. I submit that, at minimum, the idea of lovingkindness was behind the wisdom of our tradition cited above.

In the context of the Program, a fellow describes lovingkindness to me as the heartfelt inner drive to be of service and support those who are suffering. We have entered the heart domain. Program literature captures this, saying we love fellows in a very special way. "I cannot explain it but an energy flows through me and we both are buoyed" says a Program friend.

being ridiculous, telling me that my raisin bagel is not a real bagel. I got sucked in straightaway and needed to convince him that my bagel was legit (i.e., I am legit) and his thinking is idiotic. Do you see the stinking thinking here? (Hint: it's egotistical and inane.) The good news is that this happens less and less frequently as we mature in recovery. Nonetheless, when it does, I know in my gut almost immediately that it's on me and I must make an apology to relieve the feeling of agita that sits in my gut. It can't wait—it's just easier and better to be free of it. Oftentimes, we laugh together over our mutual missteps.

Such episodes of wrongdoing are vehicles to our learning and continued growth. I have had increasingly frequent success at averting them. Vigilance—to avoid problems as much as possible, and humility—to accept ourselves and remedy wrongs—are spiritual muscles to keep growing. Living one day at a time and failing is a chance for liberation, a new start and a cause for rejoicing. Be not afraid of growing slowly; be afraid only of standing still (Chinese proverb).

Loving-kindness (*Chesed*): A Mussar perspective on Step 10

> *The material needs of my neighbor are my spiritual need.*
> —*Rabbi Yisrael Salanter*

Integrating into new lives in Serenity Place, one goal is to form loving connections with the people around you. Becoming caring, respected members of our new communities requires work to nurture relationships. In addition to addressing our missteps, building new lives requires that we learn how to engage on a more intimate level so that we can join and be joined with others in the care and support of community.

An important aspect of our Program work is building relationships that form our new world. It's easy to focus on others, but the scope also includes us. With increased self-awareness, wrongdoings have the power of eating away at us and can weaken or even derail our recovery absent a strong Program. If they are allowed to, errors can quickly accumulate into a new mountain of wreckage and get in the way of our progress. "Getting stuck in regrets is like driving a car that only moves in reverse."[293] Perfectionism is one thing that can get us stuck, serving as a thick barrier to admitting our wrongs. Insofar as no one is perfect, holding ourselves to this standard is a form of self-abuse. While we do need to be accountable, we also need to be as kind, forgiving, and compassionate to ourselves as we would be to others we love.

We can reframe missteps and engage with them as stimuli for continued growth and feeding of our relationships. The state of our humility is a key factor. Only when we rightsize ourselves can we detour past our natural tendency to lean into JADE—Justifying, Arguing, Defending, Explaining. Staying current in our new world by cleaning out the cobwebs helps us preserve what's important and conveys to others our commitment to trying to do the right thing, albeit imperfectly. In a sense, it gives others permission to be imperfect, too, and that is a gift.

It is my experience that promptness in admitting I was wrong is not altruism, it's a form of self-care. Taking corrective measures to eliminate the *yuck* that comes with knowing I have hurt someone helps me feel better about myself and the situation. I hear the same thing from others in the Rooms with me who also feel that this is a critical goal of recovery: staying current so we can enjoy being lovingly connected to our best selves, others, and the God of our understanding. Although most of us hate the gym, we try to go regularly, knowing that staying fit has vast rewards. A Program friend reminds me that making timely amends lets you sleep with a clear conscience and start tomorrow with a clean slate. They describe it this way:

> One person in my family is my most frequent triggerer. Why is he the best at pushing my buttons? Because he installed them! Seriously, I see my pattern of reacting. On a recent occasion, he needed to be called out for

The nature of this inventory?

With regard to our inventory, our nature as addicts leads us to see the word *continue* in Step 10 as subject to interpretation. Often, the questions we pose in this area are merely manipulative—stinking thinking, seeking an easier, less uncomfortable way. As a backdrop to your approach, think about what best serves you where you are in your Program. One of the choices is whether to be intermittent in your efforts, meaning starting and stopping, or to be continuous, meaning never-ending. Think of it this way—is it better for you to clean your house constantly, every day or at some increment, like once a week. If you are messy, a lot can build up over the course of a week. Early in my recovery, staying on top of things served me best—actually, it still does.

Step 10 could be interpreted as instructing us to continue the inventory we started at Step 4. Thus, some fellows conduct an inventory with their sponsor, reviewing progress since they last met. Others do checks during the day. Alternatively, an end-of-day inventory aligns with the mental frame of doing/living the Program one day at a time, a common call to action in the Rooms. A scheduled nightly look in the mirror and clean-up avoids carrying a sack of emotional trash into tomorrow.

Whatever pattern you choose, the inventory can be viewed as a balance sheet, a simple summary of assets and debits—what was done well and what fell short. Honesty is required to avoid slipping back into old patterns. Note that regrets are meaningless and attempts to do the right thing count as successes, even if the outcome was less than our ideal. Annual or semiannual housekeeping may also be informative because sustained change can best be seen over longer arcs of time. Ultimately, the strategy is between you and your sponsor or spiritual advisor. Permit me to suggest that more is better.

Making it personal: Mama said that being prompt is being kind

Let's shine our light on the aspect of promptness in our apologies. Step 10 always triggers a memory of my mom saying that being late is selfish—it communicates to the other that you value yourself more than them and their time. I carry that voice inside me knowing that my failure to be prompt in this work compounds any hurt I caused. Golly, thanks Mom!

and, if need be, find our way home. That is provided by practicing Step 10. It provides a space in time for self-monitoring, self-modulation and personal repair, using the tools of inventory and apology to be the best people we can be.

The "S" factor: spiritual signals

We hear in the Rooms that *our recovery is a function of our spiritual condition*. Working the Steps has shown us that the inventory-apology-amends cycle is key to getting spiritually fit. As instructed in Step 10, continuing to take a personal inventory to stay or get back to a healthy balanced place seems like a no-brainer. Because the need is not always comfortable or obvious and the work can be arduous, we are reminded in Step 10 to remain vigilant in our efforts.

One goal in embracing the Program to stay spiritually fit is to recognize the signals of a wrongdoing or mistake. I am referring to being acerbic, stingy, irresponsible or foolish. Or, perhaps just judgmental, reactive and controlling. Can you relate? You may find comfort in reminding yourself that this is a learning cycle and admitting we are wrong makes us wiser than we were yesterday.

Part of our growth is becoming increasingly sensitive to the inner signals that indicate a wrongdoing/mistake. The ideal is that they register before we go awry. I am guessing that at this point in your recovery you can feel it on some level. I can say that the longer I am in the Program, the louder that bell clangs. Cleaning up after myself is the fastest way to feel better about myself. I caution you to take the time to be thoughtful and not overly reactive and not to let the opportunity pass. Action clears away debris that can stink up the rest of the day—for both us and the person we harmed. Doing what's in our power to preserve relationships that can be harmed by avoidance is the action of Step 10. Your task is to tune into your body and heart to grow that sense of disturbed serenity for yourself so you can intercede on your own behalf. As time passes, this seems to get easier for most. Perhaps the Program raises the volume of those internal signals; or maybe we get better at sensing them.

recovery we'll never progress beyond being human. Step 10 gives us a path back when we fall short of being our best selves. An essential part of this is doing an inventory on a continuing basis. Bill W. recognized that a great many of us have never really acquired the habit of accurate self-appraisal and, he cautioned, "...no one can make much of his life until self-searching becomes a regular habit, until he is able to admit and accept what he finds, and until he patiently and persistently tries to correct what is wrong."[290]

The most important aspect of this Step, I believe, is revealed in the word *promptly*, which tells us that we cannot take our foot off the pedal. Keeping in mind that we come into Step 10 having just completed a thorough housecleaning, I have heard fellows aptly say that Step 10 is about staying current with the world. Like paying our bills on time, staying current is necessary to keep our accounts in good standing (our relationships with ourselves, our HP, and with others). Teaching us how to keep our houses clean is key to maintaining the relationships that are so important to our happiness, continued growth, and recovery.

The *Big Book* says that when we have reached this point "We have entered the world of the spirit."[291] I take that to mean that we are transitioning to a way of life focused on others, which includes a power greater than ourselves. This aspect of recovery sees us shifting away from being a resident of the town called Active Addiction which was on Isolation Island and settling down to become a full-fledged part of a bustling new community called Serenity Place on the mainland. Everyone there uses a moral compass to get around and they commit to a code of staying personally fit, living with humility and embracing loving-kindness among neighbors.

Relocating to Serenity Place does not change our human nature or our unique personal traits, be they helpful or hurtful. Step 10 invites us to "…keep a finger on my [our] spiritual pulse so I [we] can cooperate with God in my [our] spiritual growth and healing."[292] We take Step 10 because we want to be the best we can be. The changes we are making in our lives and ourselves can be both exciting and challenging; life keeps happening and we have the potential to get lost, thrown off course or even swept away. Insofar as we bring our whole imperfect and perhaps fragile selves and Programs with us, we need a mechanism to intercede on our own behalf

maintaining our recovery requires that we remain vigilant and humble. Think about it a minute. Living in recovery, we reconnect with ourselves, with a power greater than ourselves, and with community. In essence, we are building a new world. Our Program work includes sustaining loving relationships; they bolster us and, through them, we can live, enjoy life, and heal.[286] As we all know from hard-learned lessons, it takes years to build a relationship but it can be destroyed in an instant. Step 10 reminds us that we are accountable to perform preventative maintenance as well as repair the occasional malfunctions that are simply part of life.

From our earlier Step work, we know the booby traps we set for ourselves and the triggers that can set us off. "This Step continues the process we began with Step Four—being aware of the things we do, and taking corrective measures without delay..."[287] In Step 4 we took a moral inventory; here we monitor our recovery. The inventory and action become seamlessly woven together here in Step 10. When put to good use, self-awareness via our inventories allows us to deploy self-restraint and, hopefully, avoid the need for apologies/amends. It doesn't always go that way, but the practice of Step 10 promotes dynamic improvement; we make our amends in real time, as soon as is feasible, when a situation arises.

The idea of continuing to practice what we began to learn in Steps 4-9 brings to mind being in the car with my father after receiving my driver's license. My father said, "Now you'll learn to drive." And so it is with the Program. At Step 10, "we are no longer learning how to work the Program. We are learning how to make the Program a way of life."[288] Because life on life's terms is ever-changing and we continue to learn new things about ourselves, this is relevant for old-timers as well as newbies. Step 10 opens the door to a new stage of our lives.

Entering and exiting the world of self

Although seemingly simple, Step 10 holds many important messages. Let's decode it together. The focus on apologies recognizes that we can't expect to do everything perfectly. A daily reading on Step 10 reminds us that we should expect to be human. "God made me a perfect human being, not a perfect God."[289] It continues by saying that no matter how long we are in

Chapter 14

Step 10: Loving-kindness

Step 10. [We] Continued to take personal inventory, and when we were wrong, promptly admitted it.

Too Little			Too Much
Disconnected	Kind	Extend ourselves	Self-Harming
Isolated	Concerned	to benefit others	Burdened
Uncaring	Obligated	Alacrity	

Let it begin with me.
—*12 Step fellowship wisdom*

Loving-kindness: A recovery perspective

Step 10 is the first in the final triad, often called maintenance steps. Collectively, Steps 10, 11 and 12 are focused on our connections—they support keeping all our accounts current (with God and people), being of service, and contributing to our community. Buoyed by the relief of completing Steps 4-9, it might seem that we can coast on the momentum we have generated. That is certainly not the case. We have some more growth and work ahead, one day at a time.

You should feel pride (not prideful) in your accomplishments; it's wise to harness that positive energy for the work ahead. Sobriety and all that flows from it is fragile, especially in early recovery. Need I remind you that we have a lifetime Program for our disease? We must invest energy to stay healthy. Woven together as they are, the ideas in Step 10 communicate that

- Restore the relationship with God and foster positive judgment.

The Work We are Doing:
- Corrective action: Live by our values.
- Do good (mitzvot). Rebalance past wrongdoing with acts of goodness.
- Return to God's ways.
- Atonement: includes apologizing, making amends, doing *teshuvah* and asking for God's forgiveness.

The Player and Their Roles:
- Prerequisite is that the offender is cleaning/has cleaned the street.
- Offender atones and God receives & decides.
- Does not include forgiveness or ensure an ongoing relationship.

Forgiveness/*Mechila*

Intent:
- Having punishment waived; lets the offender off the hook.

The Work We are Doing:
- Let go of anger/resentment.

The Player and Their Roles:
- Victim's choice. Some link this to an offender's apology, but it's independent.

- Does not include forgiveness of the victim or ensure an ongoing relationship.
- God is an observer.

Compassion/*Rachamim*

Intent:
- Validate another; remove what separates us.

The Work We are Doing:
- Stand in their pain; act to mitigate future recurrence.
- This is how to make amends—considering the other.

The Player and Their Roles:
- Offender engages humility and open-heartedness in requesting and receiving from victim; uses the shared pain to support the victim.
- God uses compassion to support us.

Repentance/*Teshuvah*

Intent:
- Stop hurting people.
- Get clean before God.
- End benefit is to remove the veils covering our inner light

The Work We are Doing:
- Multifaceted work. To stop doing harm. Seek out victims and ask what they experienced. Own our past "sins," feel remorse, do restitution, apologize. Make different future choices.

The Player and Their Roles:
- Offender gives; victim receives (and may give).
- Supervisor (God) observes/judges.
- Our inner work is to use feelings of remorse to drive change & return to Godly ways.

Atonement/*Kaparah*

Intent:
- Mitigate the harm we have done to others and to God.

IMPORTANT AMENDS-INTERRELATED IDEAS

Apology/*Hitnazlut*

Intent:
- Express our feeling of regret about what we have done.
- Convey to our victim, "I see you and what I did."

The Work We are Doing:
- Confess and take ownership of our role.

The Player and Their Roles:
- Offender gives apology.
- Victim chooses whether to accept.

Amends

Intent:
- Clean our wreckage from our side of the street so we can get on with life.
- Start to do the right thing.
- Set things right with others.

The Work We are Doing:
- To Amend: Effectively, to make ourselves better.
- Start to live our values.
- Ask what the other experienced; listen, offer restitution & an apology. Own our part. Explain changes we have made or will make so it will not happen again.

The Players and Their Roles:
- The offender (us) is a street cleaner—the maker of amends.
- The victim chooses whether to accept, being approached, the effort or the amend.

- Like a skater visualizing their routine before taking to the ice, create a visual image of what the other is describing they experienced. Draw the image into your heart.
- Meet in person with a good friend, tell them how much you appreciate them, and ask if you can give them a hug to convey and share those feelings.
- Attend Shabbat services and recite the Mi Sheberach and/or Mourner's Kaddish.
- Wear a rubber band and snap it gently till it smarts when you see a situation that touches you. Make a donation in honor of it.

Prompts for journaling or study with your *chevruta*/sponsor
- Where do you see yourself in the quote, "If I am not for myself, who will be for me? If I am not for others, what am I?"
- What impedes you from standing in someone else's truth?
- What stops you from making amends?
- How do you distinguish between codependence and compassion in relation to making amends?
- What does the slogan *Let go and let God* mean to you in relation to compassion for others?

Playlist
- "Sorry Seems to be The Hardest Word"—Elton John
- "Hello"—Adele
- "Hard to Say I'm Sorry"—Chicago
- "Please Forgive Me"—Bryan Adams
- "What Hurts The Most"—Rascal Flatts

There is no room for rationalization or defensiveness. Healthy self-esteem is essential so we can listen with generosity of the heart (*nedivut ha'lev*)—owning our part without any expected return. Those are the terms of engagement in making amends with compassion. With gratitude (*hakarat hatov*) for the strength and support we have surrounding us, we can lean into Mussar practices and create a different future.

Daily reminders to help you work Step 9

Following are some phrases that you might use as your daily reminders. Feel free to choose one or create your own.

- One mouth, two ears: Divine Design
- Cleaning up my side of the street
- Start to do the right thing
- Setting things right with others and God
- Co-Passion—Feel what the other does

Kabbalot to cultivate compassion (*rachamim*) as you take Step 9

If you lean toward too much compassion when making amends you might try:

- Discern your role in the events of note and work with your sponsor or spiritual advisor to show compassion to yourself. Not everyone you ever knew is deserving of amends.
- Create a daily accounting of your mind space and heart space and check it for balance. Adjust as needed.
- Diffuse the pain of seeing another continue to suffer; visualize handing the other person over to their Higher Power.
- Diffuse the pain of seeing another continue to suffer. Ask for help via a note that you put in your God Box.

If you lean toward too little compassion when making amends you might try:

- Put yourself on the list for amends.

So, you ask, what hardens our hearts? I posit that middot that are out of balance obstruct compassion. For example, shame and perfectionism that underly fear calcify the heart. What's on your spiritual curriculum? Only by identifying and addressing your distorted thinking can you break through the barriers that keep you from completing Step 9. Thinking of yourself as too small or too big would be a barrier to connection with others. What about emotional stinginess, anger, impatience and judgmentalism? Whatever the answer for you, engage with it, pierce it, open yourself up and reveal your beautiful light. Shine bright!

Secondary middot

Silence (*shtikah*) is an important middah. At first blush it is obvious that we should guard our tongues from doing harm. Creating a space for contemplation is another dimension of silence that's important. Alan Morinis referred to silence as pregnant; it is this aspect of the middah that intersects with rachamim and teshuvah.[285]

In the course of doing teshuvah, offering silence by listening is an act of compassion, honoring the other and creating space for them to share their personal experience with us. Additionally, the space is filled with potential for healing and spiritual growth. Thus, Morinis writes, "silence is a pregnant state out of which can emerge worlds of possibility we have no hope of knowing so long as our lives are overfilled with words and noise."

Each party who has stood with another emerges changed—with new vitality—cleansed of burdens of the past. Talmud says that compassion is a building block of creation; and I posit that it is a building block of our re-creation when powered by silence.

Faith (*emunah*), trust (*bitachon*), humility (*anavah*), generosity (*nedivut*) and resolve (*zerizut*) are also all in in play in our Step 9 work. Overcoming our fear to expose ourselves and giving space for another in teshuvah, knowing that we may be judged harshly, is a dimension of our work as we try to bear the burden with the other. We must shrink our egos to leave room for others to tell us their stories. It's interesting to note that in kabbalistic teachings, *tzimtzum* represents the concept that the Divine contracted or withdrew to create a space for humanity, including our pleas for help. We mirror tzimtzum.

domain (e.g., physical, financial, sexual or emotional well-being), making amends through the lens of compassion and focus on the areas of others' needs is an accessible way of meeting Salanter's goal and fulfilling our Divine purpose of loving others. Related to this, Rabbi Dessler noted that we are drawn closer to others by the act of giving to them.[283] When fellows talk about taking Step 9, I hear frequently that giving others the dignity of their experience by openhearted listening fulfills our Divine purpose of seeing their light and, paradoxically, it warms us. While I cannot attest to cause and effect, I can say that amends made with compassion did open relationships that I thought were lost forever. I'm not going to sugarcoat it; it's work in progress, but I am filled with hope and gratitude.

A dimension of our *turning* as we complete Step 9 is the transition into the next phase of our Program, focusing on helping others. In Steps 1, 2 and 3 we learned to trust a power greater than ourselves; in Steps 4-9 we've gotten to know ourselves better and, as they say, cleaned house. Stripping away the barriers that kept us isolated and beginning to build loving connections with others has opened the door to a different future. Going forward, our work includes maintaining the house (Steps 10 and 11) and sharing our experience, strength, and hope with others who are also seeking…working on their recovery.

For us in recovery, the next phase of our work includes learning to live on life's terms. That phase of the Program requires that we learn how to stay in balance; I imagine riding a surfboard through the ups and downs of life. The experience is like flying atop water. The ride is exciting and rewarding. Let's go catch the waves!

What obstructs *rachamim*

"Aloofness—with its sense of being remote and distant—is inimical to compassion" observed Alan Morinis.[284] The isolation of our disease easily explains our withdrawing from others. And Moses' reference to a thickening about our hearts (Deuteronomy 10:16) is especially powerful in contemplating what holds us back from making amends and doing so with compassion.

past but I am committed to being a safe, supportive place for you. It's my personal goal to do everything I can to be loving and supportive.

Cultivating compassion

Along the lines of acting our way into right thinking and not thinking our way into right action, our Sages wrote that "our heart is drawn after our actions."[280] Similarly, Jewish wisdom teaches that external movement stimulates internal movement[281] [of the soul], and doing so repeatedly cultivates our middot.[282] In other words, acting with compassion to meet the needs of others is a path to cultivate this middah. If you want to be more compassionate, practice being compassionate. Torah spells it out with the commandments to clothe the naked, feed the poor, and visit the sick.

Even when done with a sense of detached obligation, rather than out of love, it's my experience that these actions pierce my heart and open me to stand with others in their pain. Drawing up into our hearts the personal version of the experience described by the other person creates internal connectedness, aka *rachamim*.

Prior to making amends, my sponsor challenged me to imagine the interactions in my mind's eye. This is consistent with Mussar practice of visualization. Unlike some meditation practices, when our goal is to let the mental chatter float by, I have learned that experiencing the images can stimulate inner learning and help me refine how I express this middah.

The value of *teshuvah*/making amends with compassion

It was my experience, albeit unexpected, that undertaking amends pierced my heart and loosened my tight fist around those listed as deserving amends but I had categorized as "no way." There was a self-reinforcing element of doing this work. Completing the first ones with compassion for myself propelled my willingness to approach those further down my list.

As it relates to others, Rabbi Salanter is said to have taught that meeting the material needs of others is our spiritual responsibility. I interpret this teaching in terms of my personal and moral responsibility for what is important to the dignity of others. Insofar as our actions harm another, in any

Scenario 3.

Self = In Al-Anon recovery making amends to someone in the family system we hurt

Self: I've come to realize how I fell short not being there for you as you were growing up. I was so focused on controlling the chaos in our house that I neglected loving you. I was not the parent I wish I had been, and I know I hurt you. Please tell me how my actions/choices affected you.

Other: I was embarrassed to bring friends over because you were as crazy and unpredictable as Dad. I tried to do well in school so my teacher would never have to meet you. I gave up trying to get your attention.

Self: How did that feel?

Other: I was alone, kind of abandoned. I hid in my bed where it was warm and safe because you never came into my room. And I tried to protect my brother. I lost my self-confidence; nothing I did was good enough. I was happy when you got divorced. Why didn't you see it?

Self: Is there anything else you want me to know?

Action of Compassion

Self: I am so sorry I hurt you. What you described reminds me of how I felt when we came home from the lake and I finally saw the truth of our lives. It was a cold, scary, dark place.

I was too busy being a wallet and not a mom. I never want to make you feel that way ever again. You are an amazing human being—a loving and supportive Dad and brother. I was unhealthy then but I'm getting better. I have just begun working on myself and I know I can't fix what's

Scenario 2.

Self = In Al-Anon recovery making amends to my qualifier (other is an active alcoholic)

Self: I learned how disrespectful it was for me to try and control you and control your drinking. I am so sorry that I robbed you of your own experiences and the dignity to make your own choices. Please tell me how my actions/choices affected you.

Other: I drank more to drown out your whining. You stole my dignity.

Self: How did that feel?

Other: You made me angry and ashamed by treating me like a child. I felt smothered, like I could not breathe.

Self: Where in your body did you feel it? Can you describe it?

Other: I wanted an explosive burst of courage so I could just tell you to go away. I hate that you only see me as a drunk loser.

Action of Compassion

Self: I am sorry I made you feel that way. What you described reminds me when my Mom was hovering and smothering me. I have been in Al-Anon for 7 months and know I have to let you make your own decisions and stop trying to control you. I love you and will pray for you. If I lapse back into my old ways, I hope you can understand that it's out of concern for you. Just remind me to let go.

Scenario 1.

Self = Drug addict in recovery making amends to loved one I hurt

Self: I've learned that I am powerless against XYZ and I caused harm when it became my life. Please tell me how my actions/choices affected you.
Other: You made me scared, angry, anxious. I felt like I was sucked into a typhoon, unsafe, you ruined my credit.
Self: How did that feel?
Other: I felt like my head would explode, I wanted to knock some sense into you, afraid to go to sleep (always waiting for the shoe to drop), felt like I could not trust anyone.
Self: Where in your body did you feel it? Can you describe it?
Other: I got a rash, I could not sleep or eat, I lost 15 lbs., I could not concentrate and lost my job. I hate you for that. Like acid in my gut.

Action of Compassion

Self: I am so sorry for what I put you through. I have been sober for 7 months and am going to A.A. I am working again. I want to earn your trust back. What can I do? At least, I'd like to give you some money to help make up for your lost income. Here's $$ and I'll send it monthly until you are working again.

making excuses and cleaning up the consequences of addictive behaviors for another is showing compassion. Twelve Step and Mussar teachings help dispel this misperception. Paradoxically, the compassionate action in such circumstances is to allow the natural consequences of the other's choices to unfold.

Making it personal

The idea of sharing the pain (or joy) of another is at the core of impactful amends. Alan Morinis described the work of practicing *rachamim* as lowering or transcending the boundaries of self, drawing closer, so that we feel within us the truth of what is the other person's experience.[278] He goes on to describe the closeness as enabling us to "see more deeply to perceive the untainted soul that is the kernel of that being…"[279] Among fellows I have heard intimacy described as *into me you see*. Compassion is intimacy in action and requires great respect and sensitivity among the parties.

Another act of compassion is avoiding causing more harm to those we have hurt. Thus, this Step provides for exceptions to thoughtfully consider. I've worked with sponsees who are victims of abuse and others whose loved ones died from overdoses. That the wounds are too deep to withstand being revisited to support someone's efforts to make amends must be respected. It's not our job to fix the wounded or change their minds. In such instances, being willing to make amends and being respectful of the wishes of others can be sufficient. Dignity must be preserved.

Even when our efforts at amends are snubbed, it is incumbent on us to avoid reacting with judgment or, for example, with a new resentment. Looking for the Divine spark in another while we respect their boundary for self-care is an act of compassion within our power. Insofar as the traditional Jewish concept of *teshuvah* encourages repeated attempts, that is something you should discuss with your sponsor or a spiritual advisor.

Here are some examples of bringing *rachamim* to amends. Think about how these resonate for you.

action related to caring for the individual. We find a clear example of appropriate compassion in Jewish traditions around death. We are commanded to visit the bereaved. We assure those in mourning that they are not alone and the action of physically showing up shows we care. Being present in a house of mourning evokes feelings related to our own losses, allowing us to share the pain of the other.

We need not say a word but being truly present, extending ourselves to spend time in proximity and trying to comfort a mourner, conveys that we feel and join the other in their experience. It is in this way that compassion is defined as feeling what the other does.

It is my unexpected experience that in such a heart-to-heart connection both parties can enjoy some healing. Our action does not fix those we hurt or undo the past; neither is humanly possible. Yet, it is the action which begins with truly seeing those we hurt in their humanity and the shared emotion that turns our experience into compassion and fuels our recovery. As is the case with mourners joined by shared experience, the essence of *rachamim* is present in Program fellows with whom we are joined by the common experiences of our adventures and the challenge of changing the course of our lives. Based on this, I use co-passion as the focus phrase for my practice of compassion.

The relationship between compassion and codependence

Our goal in the practice of *teshuvah* is to stand with others, sharing their pain (or joy) and taking a caring action to express how we feel about them. Mussar teaches us to express compassion rather than just feel it.[276] This oneness with shared pain is necessary for emotional contact with another. An important nuance is that "we bear the burden with, not for" the other.[277] I imagine lending a shoulder as when two oxen work in a shared yoke. It is important to digress a moment with a word of caution that is relevant to being in relationship with an addict. Care must be taken to avoid enabling and codependency in the name of compassion. Enabling is doing for others what they should be able to do for themselves; codependence is an unhealthy attachment where one individual surrenders their power to another. Many are confused when they enter the Rooms thinking that

the people we harmed, may enjoy healing in the course of interacting with us; but that is not in our control, nor is it our responsibility. Nonetheless, Step 9 does lead us to be concerned about their well-being. Whether it's one attempt or many, the nature of the amends conversation is critical. From a Mussar perspective, humility is key and it needs to be elevated by compassion. "You don't apologize at a person. You apologize to them. A true and compassionate apology is trying to see the human being in front of you, to connect with them and communicate with them, to make it abundantly clear that you recognize the significance of your wrongs… and that their feeling better matters to you."[274]

Authentic amends is about listening to the truth of others—standing in their reality.[275] This idea of standing so close to another that we sense their reality with such depth that it is felt within us is the essence of the middah we call *rachamim*, compassion. *Rachamim* bridges what separates us; it brings us together, connected by a shared experience. With a Mussar lens, compassion takes on meaning that is beyond our ordinary ideas about this trait. *Teshuvah*/amends done with compassion is profoundly deep and impactful, joining the giver and the receiver in a loving connection of shared emotion.

The other's experience is at the core of *rachamim* in Mussar thought. Conventionally, we talk about compassion from our own frame of reference. It would be common to say *I have compassion for you*—meaning we feel bad that you are struggling. Still, that leaves things largely about our experience. Not to split hairs, but I believe that this is actually closer to empathy—understanding the feelings of someone else. Knowing (understanding) is a head-based experience. In Mussar practice, *rachamim* (compassion) extends beyond empathy.

Compassion in a Mussar frame of reference starts with our feelings being stirred in response to the other. Moving from the head to the heart, we are emotionally touched by someone else. Going beyond that, compassion includes a heart-to-heart experience—theirs touching ours. This starts when we feel what the emotion they name feels like. Literally, we go back in our memories to a situation that evoked that emotion for us and we revisit those feelings. Finally, compassion through a Mussar lens also encompasses

The relationship between *teshuvah*/amends and atonement

To put Step 9 in the Jewish context in which we most frequently talk about these ideas requires that we look past the boundaries of Step 9 briefly. I want to acknowledge that the interrelationships among the three parties involved here might make this a bit confusing and it's for that reason that I want to parse it out, albeit only in a cursory way. We have ourselves (the addict/offenders), our victims, and God. In the context of the Program, the God of our understanding is a resource or partner in our journey toward recovery and our best selves. Through a Jewish lens, God is both a partner and judge.

We make amends and *teshuvah* with people; we (people) atone before God. Theologically, God is the ultimate decision maker in the ongoing process of repair and self-refinement as Jews. Our goal is to earn forgiveness by God for our wrongdoings. In Jewish ritual, the effort of cleaning things up with people (*teshuvah*) is a prerequisite for getting straight with God. And, I'll note that getting straight with ourselves is key to healthy relationships with others. Atonement includes doing *teshuvah* (making amends) but extends beyond it by encompassing confession of our wrongdoings to God, culminating in our request for forgiveness by God.

Step 9 directs our focus to those we have harmed. They are instruments of our work; we are not, however, responsible for their work. Owning our wrongs with those we have hurt clears our path forward. It may not have the same effect for them. Although the idea of a happy ending with them has great allure, healing the relationship or being forgiven by the individuals to whom we make amends are not the goals of amends or *teshuvah* and should not be an expected outcome of your twelve-step work.[272] Some spiritual advisors hold that after listening to those we hurt during our amends, asking for forgiveness is the ultimate act of humility and powerlessness.[273] Again, this is a matter between you and your sponsor. It is my view that asking for forgiveness shifts the burden to the other, which is to be avoided.

The nature of *teshuvah*/amends: the need for compassion

We heal by doing this work. I have seen it over and over all around me in the Rooms and this has been my personal experience as well. Our victims,

Rabbi Danya Ruttenberg described Step work as the contemporary framework of repentance (*teshuvah*).²⁶⁶ In Step 9 we pivot away from past wrongs. *Teshuvah* is also a process of turning—changing our ways from a past pattern of wrongdoing. Like Program amends, we do *teshuvah* with people we have hurt, by confessing, owning and seeking to understand the harm we caused. So, in many ways, these are parallel projects.²⁶⁷

Both amends and *teshuvah* require heartfelt engagement characterized by humility (*anavah*). It needs to be "...with our lips, moving to say these things out loud that we have resolved in our heart."²⁶⁸ Teshuvah requires that we suspend fear of what others think of us and trust the process because we trust God and believe in our inherent worthiness. The same can be said of making amends. One difference of note is that Jewish tradition specifies the need for three repeated efforts at making our amends to individuals we have hurt. This reflects the diligence involved; application of this to your Program amends is between you and your sponsor.

Writing about 500 years after Maimonides, Rabbi Luzzatto described the idea of cleaning our side of the street as purity. He was focused on how to combat the yetzer hara, that inner drive that romances our addiction. "Purity entails corrective measures aimed at the refinement of our heart and thoughts. ...The purpose of this virtue is that a person should prevent the evil inclination from influencing his actions."²⁶⁹ Paquda also explored this idea, noting that it is clear that man fails to live up to his obligations requiring that we correct our errors and make up our loss in service [to the Divine] by repenting and returning to righteousness (living in alignment with what is good and true).²⁷⁰ Depending on your personal theology, perhaps it is more palatable to think of God as described in the Rooms as Good Orderly Direction from which we deviated. The wisdom of these Sages is that we can engage with our imperfections and, through *teshuvah*/repentance, return to the way of righteousness, trying to live by doing what's right. "Repentance makes an individual a new creature. Previously a person may be dead through sin, now he is fashioned fresh."²⁷¹ To my thinking, being able to start over with a clean slate is a great enticement to do this work.

obligations requires discernment. "…We cannot buy our peace of mind at the expense of others."²⁶⁵

Compassion (*Rachamim*): A Mussar perspective on Step 9

Bear the Burden with the Other.
—With Heart in Mind

There are several words and concepts that we toss about from our Jewish lexicon that touch on the ideas of amends and recovery. To help follow this discussion, you might want to refer to the section at the end of this chapter where we summarize these ideas and their interrelationships. It's important to tease them apart to know what our work is and is not, and where we are in the process.

The relationship between teshuvah and recovery: Judaism's answer to amends

A core idea in Step 9 seems simple enough: Do the next right thing, making amends by cleaning your side of the street as an action of righteousness. The effort is a step toward acting your way to right thinking. For us addicts, taking this action is a leap forward in turning our lives around. You may recall the earlier reference to *teshuvah*, the Jewish process for turning our thoughts and lives in a more positive direction (See Step 5, Chapter 9). We generally talk about doing *teshuvah*/repentance during the Days of Awe; repentance is on the path of returning to God in the hopes of ultimately being forgiven for falling short of righteous living. Here in Step 9, we complete our part of the process that Maimonides outlined in his teachings on *teshuvah*. To refresh your memory, Maimonides' steps for spiritual renewal were: stopping the offending behavior; feeling regret for hurting others; verbalizing our regret to the God of our understanding and whomever we have hurt; and making a plan so we don't repeat the offending choices. It's important that the process provides space for us to forgive ourselves.

theless, "the readiness to take the full consequences of our past acts, and to take responsibility for the well-being of others at the same time, is the very spirit of Step Nine."[264] The sad truth is that people may refuse to look at you in a new light, only seeing you for what you were, only seeing you for the mistakes you've made. They may be unable or unwilling to realize that you are not your mistakes or your past you. It's easy to want to ignore them—we mustn't. If you really want the relationship, it may take more time and effort. Our sponsors and others can help us navigate these challenges. Not all the outcomes are happy. Just do the work.

One aspect of amends that merits consideration here is the harm we have done to ourselves. I am referring both to the poor choices we made in our disease and the ongoing guilt and over-responsibility that gnaws away at us. Did you put yourself on the list in Step 8? There are varying opinions about this. Mine is that treating yourself with the same compassion that you extend to others is an important aspect of recovery. Fellows in the Rooms say *we will love you until you love yourself*. While we cannot control whether others are willing to accept our amends, we are in control of how we treat ourselves. Our self-examination and efforts at change are amends for the harm we may have done to ourselves and do, in my view, justify forgiving ourselves, creating an opening to moving forward. I encourage you to forgive yourself and move on.

The exceptions

We addicts will naturally be tempted to skip the more humiliating and dreaded amends meetings. The provision for exceptions within Step 9 is not intended to foster manufactured excuses or avoid consequences to ourselves. This aspect of the Step is about compassion—not hurting others to serve our wants. This risk of unintentional harm can be avoided by reviewing your plans and motives for making amends with your sponsor, a Program friend, or other spiritual advisor. Making the other person feel unsafe, opening old wounds, or revealing something about another person that puts them in jeopardy (such as bringing up an affair, bankruptcy, or other legal matter that their spouse or employer may not know about) are examples of things to be avoided. Suffice it to say that this aspect of our

In many instances, living amends is the best available mechanism for clearing away the debris and showing that we are trustworthy in our commitment to change. Manifesting the promised lifestyle or behavior changes over the course of time is what some need to see to believe that we will honor the values we claim to embrace. Permit me to share a personal example. I was an absent, emotionally unavailable parent because I was so caught up in trying to control the addict in my household. I can never give that time or attention back to my children who are now grown. In addition to making direct amends, I can go out of my way to help them with their children and be a loving listener and supporter as they walk their journeys. In the damaged relationships with my addicts, living amends has been the primary source of rebuilding trust between us and forging a new relationship. Please do keep in mind that this is not a straight line. I need to pray for guidance and strength when I approach each task and interaction. Sometimes I fall short and revert to old patterns, which for me means lies. Knowing that none of us can do this perfectly, it helps to do this work with humility and loving-kindness for ourselves and others.

The relationship between amends and forgiveness

Hidden from view as we approach making amends is the risk of an unspoken expectation that we will be forgiven. That is a potential trap for both the giver and the receiver; the obligation here is on us only. Indeed, being forgiven is not the goal of Step 9. Our dependence on forgiveness from the recipient can indicate that we have not forgiven ourselves. (Ironically, making amends may allow us to forgive ourselves.) Our work in Step 9 must be totally independent of what the injured party does. We must be careful to avoid putting that person in a position of caretaking us, having to protect us or make us feel better. We are not entitled to receive understanding or forgiveness from those we hurt.

It's important to acknowledge another difficult truth about the work of making amends. This work can be very thorny; the consequences may expose us to the risk of jail time or damage to our reputation and/or social standing. Think of these symbolically as well as literally. Family members may cut us off and friends may judge us. Employers may fire us. None-

feelings that come with revisiting painful memories or a relationship that included humiliation, anger and resentments. Were it not for Program obligations, I likely would not want to walk this path. Keep in mind that we in the Program have the luxury of our circle of fellows to encourage and buoy us; those to whom we are making amends may not have such a support system.

Another reason someone might refuse our attempted amends is that they may not hold us responsible. Or, they may have let the past go and forgiven us as part of their own healing. Ironically, it is also possible that some don't want us to change. Our being the bad guy allows them to avoid looking in the mirror at their own choices. The A.A. *Twelve & Twelve* teaches that the other person may reject our apology. "…such reactions will not deflect us from our steady and even purpose."[263] We can only control our own actions and our effort is what's important. We are not in charge of outcomes; a genuine effort is sufficient. In itself, this is enough for us to forgive ourselves and move forward.

The amends itself is intended to make restitution. Think about the various forms that your damage took. The monetary and physical damage to assets is easily quantifiable versus injury to someone's psychological well-being or social reputation. Sometimes the nature of the harm is not finite and the damage cannot be remedied with a discrete action such as repaying a specific amount of money or doing hours of service. We must not shrink from the obligation and where necessary must look for creative ways to clear our debts.

Making it personal

Direct amends are not always possible; that does not mitigate the need to do this work. If people are unwilling or unable to work with us, we can, with the guidance of our sponsor, develop a strategy for indirect amends. Depending on the circumstances, we may write and send a letter reflecting our amends. When the person has died, we may write and read a letter to them graveside. Alternatively, or in addition, donating a relevant sum of money or time to a cause that was important to the injured party can be an effective form of amends.

Here is an example of an amends from an Al-Anon member:

> I have been afraid that you will go to jail or die and I have come to realize how disrespectful I've been, meddling in your recovery program. I should not check up on your meetings and I was way out of line in calling your sponsor. It's none of my business and I'm going to let you figure this out for yourself. By the way, I deleted their number from my phone.

All of the principles we have been thinking about are put into practice in the process of our making amends—responsibility, humility, faith, trust, courage, shame, and truth all apply. And powerlessness plays out as well. We have no control over how our words will be received. Our years of active addiction created justifiable skepticism and distrust. There is truth in the adage *actions speak louder than words*. Our behavior will likely be more convincing than our words.

The response we get when making amends can influence how we feel. Initial successes may make subsequent effort easier and rejection can make it harder; we cannot allow ourselves to be deflected or to become overconfident. To renew trust, we must earn it. The dream of reconnecting with life is within our reach.

Direct amends

Step 9 refers to direct amends, meaning a face-to-face interaction with the individuals we wronged. In my experience a direct interaction is most effective for mutual understanding and mending a relationship when making amends. Being present to sweep off our side of the street makes us personally invested; the action of the other is beyond our control.

There are a variety of possible scenarios when we go to make amends. Some approaches are welcomed; in other instances, the injured party may refuse a meeting. My experience is that most will listen and a few will be willing or able to meet us at least part of the way across the street… although they proceed cautiously. We cannot know their motives and it helps to be mindful that they may simply need to avoid the uncomfortable

for you, tried to control you, etc. We addicts are quite accustomed to apologizing. It's often hollow. And worse, it's just another form of selfishness. Saying *I feel bad about that...* is often a means to have the recipient help us feel better. The fact that the expressed regret is not associated with anything being different going forward creates frustration and distrust. Another approach to accountability is that we might say *I am sorry for...* This is also misplaced; it presumes that we know what is bothering someone else. Filling the space with our voices misses the mark for building a connection; our Step 9 work must include listening in order to understand what the other person feels. Maybe this is why we have one mouth and two ears!

In contrast to simply expressing regret, making amends requires a change in our attitude and our behavior. The Program teaches that when making amends, we must take steps to right the wrong we did. Think for a moment about the meaning of amend—for example, amending the Constitution. In that realm, an amendment is an alteration made for the purpose of changing how the country will be governed. Working a Twelve Step program is a means of personally amending our constitution, to change how we govern our lives. "Apologies are basically words while amends are actions that demonstrate a new way of life in recovery. When you make amends, you align your values and your actions by admitting wrongdoing, and then living by your principles."[262]

The nature of amends

To make amends we state our errors from our viewpoint and share how we have or will correct our behavior in the future. The amends needs to reflect our regret and/or what we have learned about ourselves but goes a step further to include a future view of what can be expected of us. That we are committing to change so that the pattern is not repeated is a source of hope for many broken relationships. An alcoholic/addict making an amends might say this:

> I am sorry that I stole money from you and violated your trust. I did that while I was drinking/drugging and want to earn your trust back. I have been clean and sober for X months and I want to repay you; here is my first payment.

walking into a den of tigers, you are not unique or alone. I am reminded of our human capacity for cognitive dissonance; we can be in faith and fear at the same time. Which messages do we listen to? Recall the Step triad: trust God, clean house, help others. Since Step 4 we have been cleaning house. The relationship with a HP that has grown out of Steps 1-3 helps many people undertake the work of Step 9. Given these headwinds associated with Step 9, it is suggested that you pause and gather your resources and confirm (with a sponsor or fellow) that your Program and recovery are robust enough for you to take this leg of your journey now.

It's important to note that Step 9 is not about punishment; it is about breaking free of the shackles of the past and creating the possibility of an unfettered future for all parties involved. My truth was that I had over two dozen names on my list: spouse, children, employers, colleagues, friends. Some people had died. There was one person who would be harmed in the process; with the guidance of a spiritual advisor, that one was removed from the list. Others who I reached had no recollection of what I was talking about. Some people told me they could never trust me again; most acknowledged that I was a real jerk, yet they appreciated my asking to see them and I've reconnected with a few. "Every conversation was valuable. Each one felt like cleaning up a layer of grease on the outside of my soul."[261]

Approaching others for the purpose of making amends is not done to expose ourselves to retribution, nor is it an invitation to beat ourselves up for our mistakes. A Program friend told me that "To get straight with the world, we have to get straight with those we hurt." The experience of showing compassion for others as we make amends fuels our growth. Think of it as molting—outgrowing and shedding what no longer fits, taking on a fresh new healthy wholeness. You are about to become a beautiful bird, ready to fly anew.

The relationship between apologies and amends

Cultural norms suggest that, at the very least, we owe the people we have hurt an apology. Why then does Step 9 refer to making amends and not an apology? There are important differences between them. With an apology we might casually say *I am sorry that I was late, lied to you, let you down, lied*

Chapter 13

Step 9: Compassion

Step 9. [We] Made direct amends to such people wherever possible except when to do so would injure them or others.

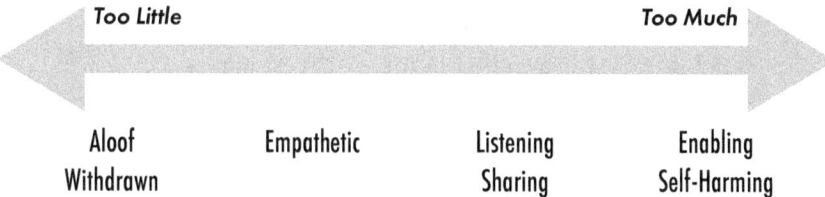

Too Little			Too Much
Aloof Withdrawn	Empathetic	Listening Sharing	Enabling Self-Harming

Do the next right thing.
—*12 Step fellowship wisdom*

Compassion: A recovery perspective

We are going to focus on the what, why, and how of amends to understand Step 9. Understanding the pain we caused others in the past is integral to [re]building/restoring connectivity in the future; this is an important dimension of recovery in the context of our real-world lives. Step 9 is not about meeting the needs of anyone but ourselves, but it does bring our focus to others. In that regard, Step 9 represents a departure from our past self-centeredness and isolation.

Those we hurt likely have memories of the harm we caused them. We know that these individuals are entitled to some recompense. While we acknowledge the need to be accountable, the unknown of their resentments, anger and reactions to us tests our faith and resolve. If stepping outside the cocoon of the Rooms and fellowship to complete this Step feels like

Prompts for journaling or study with your *chevruta*/sponsor
- What is my willingness to make a list, to name names? What's blocking me?
- What blocks my willingness to make amends?
- How am I harming myself? Where do I fall on the list of people I've hurt?
- Is the harm I've caused from things I've done or not done?
- Which motivates me more strongly—thinking of the *other* or what comes *after*?

Playlist
- "Man in the Mirror"—Michael Jackson
- "A Little Bit Me a Little Bit You"—The Monkees
- "Running Dry"—Neil Young
- "Down by the Riverside"—Louis Armstrong
- "We Can Work It Out"—The Beatles

- The first step in overcoming mistakes is to admit them.
- You're not required to like it; you're only required to do it.
- Do not desist from the work.
- Let go and let God.
- If I am not for myself, who will be for me? If I am only for myself, what am I? If not now, when?

Kabbalot to help cultivate responsibility (*acharayut*) as you take Step 8

If you lean toward too much responsibility you might try:
- Wear a rubber band on your wrist to track yourself apologizing over the course of a day. Move it from one wrist to another each time you find yourself apologizing. Is each apology truly justified or is it just to keep the peace?
- Practice pausing before intervening by using the stopwatch on your phone (or doing a silent count to 10/20/30).
- Give others the dignity of making their own mistakes/choices.
- Take a picture/make a drawing of both you and an amends target together and look for where you begin and the target ends.
- Write a note about "the other" you have harmed and practice letting go and letting God by putting it into your God box.

If you lean toward sagging responsibility you might try:
- Consider the relationship between humility and responsibility. Are you confusing them?
- Look in the mirror and ask out loud, "What's your part in hurting others?"
- Revisit your Step 4 Inventory and your part in the resentments you hold.
- Do something unexpected for a friend without being asked.
- Make a to-do list and add one thing a day that you don't want to do but must.

(so it reflects rigorous truth of what we have done). Another interpretation stems from the teaching in Pirkei Avot: "Who is strong? One who conquers his evil inclination."[259] I suppose that in a way these are connected; strong boundaries might keep us from giving in to temptations—think chocolate, carbs, cocaine, and cheating.

I am focusing here on strength that is directed inward—to moral high ground. A related but slightly different translation of *gevurah* is discipline, mental strength. We need both to complete Step 8. *Gevurah* also intersects in a very personal way with the middah of *yirah*—awe and reverence of the Divine. *Yirah* draws out the desire to make choices that avert falling short from the highest moral standards of living. I believe that is the calling of our heritage; embracing an idea such as this helps us resist the pull of the yetzer hara which lures us away from what's right and holy toward what's self-serving and comfortable. The middah of laziness (*atzlut*) that impedes the work of Step 8 reflects falling short of this inner strength to which I am referring. In Program terms, *gevurah* that we harness this way is associated with the ability to do the next right thing, practicing the middah of order (*seder*). Think about the self-restraint necessary to remain silent when someone you love is self-harming because you are honoring their right to make their own choices. It is my experience that I need every ounce of *gevurah* to honor (*kavod*) and avoid trying to control others I care about. The voice of *gevurah* says, *Don't do it*. In the case of taking accountability, the voice says, *You can do this. This medicine tastes bad but it will help you get better. Just take it—one day at a time.*

Looking at the root of the word *gevurah* (GVR/*gimel-vet-resh*) as we did to understand *acharayut* takes us to one final thought here about our qualities. Through this lens, the inner strength to stay the course is viewed as a kind of heroism.[260] The task of recovery does take heroic effort. So, as we turn to Step 9 together, let me say that *you are my hero* (*gibor*).

Daily reminders to help you work Step 8

Following are some phrases that you might use as your daily reminders. Feel free to choose one or create your own.

- All Israel is a guarantor, one for the other.

of recovery and personal growth together, we are fulfilling the Jewish ideal of becoming a holy vessel in pursuit of healing the world.[255]

It is useful for me to remember the presence of *other* (*akher*) in *acharayut*. Having actually caused harm to others, Step 8 is preparation to do *tikkun* (repair) within our personal world. Although we cannot fix wrongs and harm that we ourselves did to others, we can take responsibility for them and fix ourselves (at least repair our moral compass). This obligation is informed by Rabbi Hillel, who taught in Pirkei Avot 1:14, "If I am not for myself, who will be for me? If I am only for myself, what am I? And if not now, when?" In other words, we are responsible for repairing the world, beginning with ourselves—and sooner rather than later. Teachings attributed to Mussar master Rabbi Salanter are so apropos: "first a person should put his house together, then his town, then the world."[256]

It is important to remember the closing of Hillel's teaching. *If not now* closes with an admonition against delay. The time is now! Do not tarry. "When the power of responsibility is perfected the impossible becomes reality."[257] The work of each of us and the perfection of our individual path has the power to affect the fate of our world. What seemed impossible only seven Steps ago is now within reach.

If you are tired, perhaps it will help you to keep in mind that "when a person chooses a path and takes action, however minor, to affirm his commitment to that path, he is defined by the direction he has chosen, even if he has not yet transformed himself completely to the standards of the new path. Man is defined not solely by what he has done until now; the path that he chooses is the essential indicator of who he is."[258] Please persist; let's continue to journey together and begin restoring relationships with other people. This is the path to breaking our isolation and healing our world.

Secondary middot

There are many middot that can help us with Step 8. Based on what we have covered already I'm guessing that thoughts about courage (*ometz lev*), humility (*anavah*), and alacrity (*zerizut*) might have popped up for you. Regarding the list, the completeness of the list involves a balance between setting limits (so it's not punishingly big) and maintaining firm boundaries

in a modern context; nonetheless, this teaches that our choices at this *bechira* point affect us and others in the here-and-now and *after* in relation to the power outside of ourselves. Concerning the lazy one, in the Book of Proverbs, King Solomon says: "I went by the field of the slothful and by the vineyard of the man void of understanding; and lo, it was all grown over with thistles, the face thereof was covered with nettles and the stone wall thereof was broken down."[250] Thinking of the harm I had done as if it became prickly and stinging like nettles and thistles is strong imagery; it explained how I repelled others. Although the task is thorny, we do need to clean up our gardens.

In a closer examination of the attribute of laziness, the Sages wrote about the path to righteousness, referring back to the Book of Proverbs. They go on to teach that "…even if he were to busy himself with his field until the products grew, owing to his laziness he would lose the produce, because the stone fence is in ruin and he is too lazy to repair it, so that cattle and thieves enter and take everything."[251] Taking responsibility for the impact of our actions helps us rebuild our foundational sense of self that becomes a basis for healthy boundaries. It is my experience that this work is necessary and productive, especially in the spiritual and emotional aspects of healing. I interpret Pirkei Avot to teach that while we are not in control of what others do, we cannot desist from our obligations.[252]

How to cultivate responsibility

The prophet Micah taught that taking responsibility for our lives means that we will "do justice, love kindness and walk humbly with God."[253] For many of us, the command to do justice is fulfilled by efforts to repair the world, which is captured in the Hebrew term *tikkun olam*. We often think of *tikkun olam* as social action, such as charitable giving and acts of kindness within our communities. Often, our social justice work is a personal effort at making amends on behalf of society in general because of what we see that seems unfair and harmful to those of lesser resources or power. Taken very broadly in the context of Micah's teaching, *tikkun olam* is human responsibility for fixing what is wrong with the world.[254] Walking this journey

Making it personal

Let's be honest: the work of Step 8 is difficult. For many of us, we are dredging up unpleasant memories; naturally, most of us begin to anticipate equally uncomfortable interactions in the foreseeable future. Hearing fellows tell me to keep my head where my feet are was important. Nonetheless, there was some heavy lifting here. Our new community (the fellowship) and our key supporters (sponsor and power greater than ourselves) can help to bolster our resolve. But even the strongest among us is at risk of being diverted by our old friend, our yetzer hara, to a place of ease and comfort. It's so easy to tell ourselves we don't have the emotional or spiritual energy for this.

Twelve Step wisdom is that we don't have to like this; the challenge and opportunity is to do the next right thing. Mussar texts vividly and forcefully relate laziness to ruin. I did know that I had made too much progress to quit but, honestly, I needed some sort of inspiration to wholeheartedly engage. I leaned on an aspect of the Hanukkah story that was highlighted in a meditation led by Rabbi Angela Buchdahl.[247] Rabbi Buchdahl focused on the courage of the Maccabees to use the small amount of oil they had recovered, knowing that it was not enough for the task ahead. I was not sure I had enough resolve to face those on my list. Slogans that I had grown to think of as prayers, such as *Let go and let God*, echoed in my mind. The sense of safety in the fellowship and my trust in the Program energized me enough to take the step of completing a rigorous list without being diverted to lie, control, manipulate, and try to manage others and avoid my responsibility. I was humble and knew my place was simply to complete the task. Staying present with the work, strengthened by a leap of faith that drew on our heritage, allowed me to take this step.

What obstructs responsibility?

It is important to remember our Sages' wisdom that "through laziness the ceiling collapses and with idleness of the hands the house leaks."[248] *The Ways of the Tzaddikim* teaches that laziness is an evil quality; anyone in whom this trait is strong will find his affairs spoiled in this world and in the world to come.[249] To categorize laziness as evil does seem a bit extreme

Which approach is appropriate for you? The answer rests, in part, on your motives for asking. Avoiding the discomfort of accountability is not a good reason for a short list. Nor is laziness. In working my spiritual curriculum, my Mussar teacher told me that some discomfort is healthy, but suffering is not the goal. Growth comes from walking through what's difficult. Rabbi Danya Ruttenberg says it this way:

> ...facing the harm I caused is an act of profound optimism. It is a choice to grow, to learn, to become someone who is more open and empathetic... Accountability... has integrity and allows us to move forward. It moves us out of avoidance, blame and denial, and into the reality of what we have done—we finally face it bravely and begin to learn and grow from the experience. It's not always easy or comfortable, but it's critically important—for us, for those we've hurt and for anyone we meet in the future...[245]

Regarding our responsibility to others, Alan Morinis teaches that "we must always see that the other person has a valid point of view."[246] From my personal experience, bringing this attitude of honoring others was integral to my willingness. My attitude is a good indicator of working this step and my spiritual curriculum successfully. This all combines to help me show up as my best self.

As we work toward recovery, the expression of *other* and *after* are dynamic. Like all of our middot, they are not discrete and discontinuous. They develop differently and interdependently for each of us. It has been my experience that my honesty and accountability grew over time. This helped me expand my thinking so I could better anticipate and appreciate the consequences of my actions on myself, my Program, and on others. With openness of mind and heart, the tools and resources of both Mussar and Twelve Step programs enable us to take responsibility to do the next right thing and avoid creating more chaos. Thank goodness!

No matter how much time we have under our [Program] belt, we keep going to meetings to be reminded of what it was like and what comes after a relapse. Rabbi Salanter says that our deterrent must be palpable: we cannot simply believe that a poor choice is a bad idea, we have to feel it. That is an essential part of the experience of Steps 8 and 9. The physical act of revisiting the regrettable aftereffects of our actions is incredibly uncomfortable, as is the idea of making amends to the affected individuals. At Twelve Step meetings when we hear others tell their stories, we revisit through our own memories all the feelings we struggled with as the consequences of our addiction. The remembering is a painful yet productive reminder that we do not want to go back there. Having been given the gift of physical and mental sobriety, we must own our responsibility and take the actions necessary to sustain our clarity of thinking and purpose, lest we unleash the predictable aftermath of harm. In the Rooms, we learn the acronym PAUSE: **p**ostpone **a**ction **u**ntil **s**anity/**s**erenity **e**merges. Deployment of tools such as this gives us the power and responsibility to protect our *after*.

One important aspect of *after* relates to the power that comes from our willingness to take this step. Rabbi Walkin taught that our sense of responsibility and determination in Torah study, prayer, and character improvement affords us Divine aid so we can fulfill these obligations and rise even higher on the ladder which originates on earth and reaches to heaven.[242] I interpret this as meaning that taking responsibility for our own recovery elevates us spiritually. We are moving up the ladder toward holiness. Those around me in fellowship echo and confirm this. We go on to realize that although the task is difficult, we will enjoy the benefit of Divine aid after we make our list and become willing to undertake the uncomfortable task of making amends. In other words, you can do this!

Aspects of *other*

This aspect of *acharayut* has many dimensions. One relates to the idea that we have a responsibility to care for those in our circle. How big a circle shall we draw in listing "all persons we had harmed"?[243] Self-awareness reveals that everything is a form of relationship; we are all connected. This view would likely lead to a large circle and a long list. Rabbi Dessler brings a different focus to the work by defining the circle as those directly harmed.[244]

considered to be essential for fulfilling our divine purpose.[236] These ideas are consistent with Jewish wisdom which teaches that as long as we possess free will, we are always responsible for the consequences of our words and actions, whether deliberate or not.[237] Righting a wrong that we have done is consistent with our personal obligation to be our brother's keeper—to be kind and loving. The soul trait of responsibility, translated as *acharayut*, serves our need to be accountable for the effects of our actions toward others. There are often clues about the meaning of Hebrew words that are revealed by looking at the root of the word. Let's explore how this aspect of *acharayut* informs Mussar thinking about responsibility and the work of Step 8.

The root of *acharayut* is ACHR (*aleph-chet-resh*) which can be interpreted to mean *after* (*achar*) or *other* (*acher*).[238] These are lenses we can use in making and cross-checking our list to assure it is thorough. Responsibility through the lens of *after* relates to what comes after—the consequences of our actions. This is certainly within the realm of our Step 8 work. Alternatively, we can look at responsibility through the lens of *other*. This relates to our responsibility for the well-being of others, encompassing anyone who suffers harm because of choices we have made in the course of our disease. This aspect of our work in Step 8 falls along the lines of the talmudic teaching that "all Israel is a guarantor, one for the other."[239] We get an additional perspective on this middah and Step 8 when we think about the *other* version of ourselves—the change that we are working to create in our twelve-step journey toward a life of recovery. Because much of the harm that we caused is to ourselves and we may need to put ourselves on the list for amends, this dimension of responsibility is important. Let's look at these two aspects of this middah.

Aspects of *after*

By virtue of our intelligence, humans are unique in their capacity to understand the relationship between before and after. This aptitude carries with it responsibility. Related to the idea of responsibility and preventable harm, the Mishnah teaches that humans are always responsible for their actions[240] and that whoever has the ability to prevent harm from occurring but does not do so is held accountable for the harm that occurs.[241]

the place. In Steps 1-6 we came clean with ourselves and the God of our understanding; in Steps 7-9 we are cleaning up things with others and with life. With a goal of taking responsibility for our lives, our work in Steps 7-9 is focused on turning outward and cleaning up our relationships. Maimonides' Laws of Repentance, an oft cited source of wisdom, tells us to begin with naming and owning the harm we have caused.[234] Step 8 aligns with that ideal completely.

Traditional Jewish observance embraces this type of housecleaning; at a minimum we are to examine and address issues in the circle of our personal relationships during the Days of Awe. This period between the Jewish New Year (Rosh Hashanah) and the Day of Atonement (Yom Kippur) is devoted to repentance and renewal. We are to take an inventory of the year passed, identify instances where we missed the mark as defined by our Jewish moral compass, and work wholeheartedly to make amends so we can move on to the next parts of our lives. Why, you may wonder? Alan Lew describes the loose ends of unresolved issues as "tearing us away from the present-tense reality of our experience, from the present moment, the only place where we can really have our lives."[235] The preparatory work for the Days of Awe is especially important because the stakes are high—obtaining God's blessing and being renewed in the book of life for another year. (See Step 9 for more discussion of amends, repentance and atonement and how they relate to our work.)

Personally, I think of the reference to life here in spiritual terms. I see being alive as the gift of being free to live fully—connected to others and the universe, being able to experience joy and love. That contrasts with spiritual death—being imprisoned by secrets and shame, where it is cold, dark, and lonely and there is no room for God (or any another power greater than ourselves). The pre-work for Judgment Day includes making things right with those humans we harmed (in addition to making things right with God). The work of Step 8 parallels this Jewish practice. In both, we are responsible to discern who we have harmed and to become willing to make amends. These traditions of Jewish thought and practice provide a strong foundation for the work of Step 8.

Owning up to our past choices is necessary to move past them. This step lays the groundwork for personal accountability, which is an attribute

Willingness

We have talked about willingness before. As was the case in Step 5, willingness here in Step 8 is a process—we have some space to become willing. Ask yourself what's blocking you. Courage? Trust? Who can help? You can lean on Program wisdom or reach out to your Higher Power. There's an acronym for encouraging willingness: WILLING (**W**hen **I** **L**ive **L**ife, **I** **N**eed **G**od). Also, I found comfort in being reminded in the Rooms that it's not until the next step, Step 9, that we will need to develop strategies for how we will right our specific wrongs. To keep them separate, the phrase *I have to keep my head where my feet are* may help you stay focused on the work of Step 8. We do not have to make amends yet; we just have to become willing. Also, as we hear in the Rooms all the time, *You don't have to like it, you just have to do it.*

As we close this aspect of our journey together, the teachings of Rabbi Danya Ruttenberg come to mind. She said, "we can't undo the past, we can address the present with integrity and endeavor to create a future that is much more whole than anything we can imagine from here."[233] Her words encapsulate for me the power of the healing work we begin in Step 8; I hope you will venture forth with me.

Responsibility (*Acharayut*): A Mussar perspective on Step 8

Am I my brother's keeper?
Genesis 4:9

The nature of responsibility

In the Rooms of recovery, we talk about Step 8 as part of our housecleaning. In the context of our Twelve Step work, to this point, we have inspected our house and grown to see our past more clearly. We discovered that our foundation had some longstanding cracks; we uncovered some "decorating" issues in the form of denial and the patterns that played out in "crazy" reactions and poor choices. Truly, our free will had the run of

defect made me do it." Also, you need to do this work to improve yourself regardless of whether the other individual harmed you. Whatever the approach, beyond the "who," Step 8 challenges us to contemplate how we harmed the other, our relationship with them and whether we are willing… to make amends to repair what we can. The required honesty makes this Step frightening for many. Al-Anon's *12 & 12* encourages us to embrace the fear and do it anyway. This seeds the growth of courage and positive feelings about ourselves, both of which are self-reinforcing.

This [blasted] opportunity to know ourselves on a deeper level can take multiple forms. My sponsor told me that because of the games I play in my head, I needed to write it out. The most basic approach is a simple list. Insofar as we commit to go to any lengths for our recovery, I suggest a more rigorous, five-column format:

1. Name of the person we harmed
2. The individual's relationship to us
3. How we harmed them: harming actions (e.g., lying, cheating, demeaning)
4. The reason for amends: what we are trying to rectify (build trust, show respect)
5. Our degree of willingness to make amends

Note that this does not include why we did what we did. In general, the question why triggers defensiveness. Staying away from *why* here avoids the diversion of the JADE pattern described earlier. In fact, to stay focused, it may be helpful to put a limit on the amount of commentary for each answer—stick to two or three lines. Regarding willingness to make amends, it's okay to qualify your willingness using terms like *quickly, harder, very difficult, never*. Talking with others about this work confirmed that for them, too, looking at how we caused harm is the hardest part for many. And, I need to confess that I was not willing to make all the needed amends on Day 1. Step 8 says I *became* willing. I became more willing over time; as I made amends to some, making amends to others became easier to contemplate.

tionship with an active addict is challenged to be generous and forgiving, often beyond the limits of their comfort. Acquiescing in these diverse circumstances is almost always out of love. Paradoxically, we can love them to [their] death because we prevent them from hitting bottom. And, the stress and anxiety that we carry when facing these choices can affect our physical, emotional and spiritual health. Both parties are harmed despite the best of intentions. This too falls within the scope of consideration of Step 8.

The unintended consequence of addiction produces a ripple effect that extends far. Recall that we speak of addiction as a family disease. An entire family system can be destroyed as an unintended consequence of one person's disease. A recent case grabbing national headlines saw a socially prominent attorney steal millions from his clients and his law firm to hide an opioid addiction. The lies he told himself and his family ended in his being convicted of murdering his wife and one son, leaving a surviving son whose life as he knew it was destroyed.

Children are especially vulnerable to the chaos in a home with the disease present. Often both parents are emotionally unavailable. The well-being of children can also be threatened in a more insidious way when they are neglected while a so-called sober parent obsesses over an alcoholic spouse or other loved one. Knowing that I harmed my children with the choices I made related to addiction in our home is the hardest truth to stomach. While this is an ugly reality, by continuing to work the Program it does not have to be the reality that defines our future.

The list

You can start a fresh list in Step 8, or it can be a continuation of the work you started in Steps 4 & 5. In either case, we look at our memories through a lens of harm, focusing on our role in the conflicts. It's entirely normal if you have difficulty with this step. The *A.A. 12 & 12* makes clear that fear and pride can conspire to divert us from making the list of those we harmed. Examining the details is essential to the work. Being rigorous means you are accurate and exhaustive. A key to this work is looking through the eyes of those you have made uncomfortable. I caution you to resist the temptation of justifying your actions by claiming "my character

someone in the throes of addiction, we can obsess over them and ignore our well-being entirely. We might not sleep or eat properly. I personally depleted retirement savings to fund multiple stints at rehab clinics, pay bail bond and cover my loved one's debts and legal fees. Crazy, I now know. Other examples of self-harm include: saying yes when we wanted to say no; liver and brain damage from excess alcohol consumption; constant anxiety over the uncontrollable; suppressing our feelings so we would not trigger our addicts; holding onto resentments and allowing other people to run our lives by manipulating or controlling us. Believe it or not, there may be some point in time when you need to consider putting yourself on the list. Do any of these describe you? You are not alone!

Harming others

Codependency can be part of our addiction to others. This is present when we do for them what they should be able to do (but do not). Consider this please. With an addict we love codependently, we may try to shield them from the consequences of their actions/choices. We may, for example, call the boss to cover their hangover-related absence from work because we are scared about our financial security should they get fired. Bailing them out of jail after being arrested for a DUI so they don't have to miss a family event is something I did. Usually, it looks like our motives are good but underneath we rescue them to make ourselves feel better. The truth is that shielding them from the consequences of their actions is a form of harm.

Are you getting in the way of your loved one's recovery to make yourself feel better? An unexpected consequence of rescuing others is that we deny them essential learning experiences. Our actions also convey our lack of confidence that they can manage their lives. Sending that message to the addict I loved disturbed me deeply once I became aware of what I was doing. I came to realize that this is one aspect of my disease in which I have to work my Program hard, including the related amends for my failure to treat the addict I love with respect.

A slightly different but common story in the Rooms is helping the addict with ordinary life responsibilities such as the rent or a car repair. Maybe it's to protect a child or grandchild. Frequently, the "sober" party in a rela-

responsibility to practice self-care and avoid harming others. Self-care here refers to doing what's needed to create and maintain physical, emotional, spiritual and financial health. It is possible to manage the symptoms and keep the physical and mental aspects of addiction in check with a lifetime program of self-care. Being an addict might be an explanation for certain of your actions and choices, but your disease does not excuse your continuing to make choices that harm yourself or others. Whether it is intentional or unintentional, direct or indirect harm, Step 8 is the point in our Twelve Step journey where we take ownership of the impact of our choices as we continue to work toward recovery.

There is a range of distortions related to responsibility for us addicts. We may confuse caretaking with responsibility and have an exaggerated sense of our obligations. Many of us start Step 8 convinced that we did not cause any harm, but instead have been harmed by others. Those of us who take too little responsibility often fall into a pattern captured in the acronym JADE (**J**ustify, **A**rgue, **D**efend, **E**vade). We perpetuate the ruse to minimize or forget our part in things. The *A.A. Twelve & Twelve* warns that our emotions easily default to defensiveness when we contemplate the state of our relationships with others. Such skewed thinking can easily lead to resentments and a sense of being the victim. Others take too much responsibility and are overly self-critical, believing that they are the "...source of most of the pain and suffering in our [their] lives and in the lives of those around us [them]."[232] Both are distortions. Another common scenario is looking back and sharing in broad strokes with a sponsor or spiritual partner: *I'm sure I've hurt people. I was wrong. I won't do it again.* That's not good enough—it's likely just an attempt at avoidance. For durable recovery/sobriety, we must feel and acknowledge the impact of what we have done. Step 8 provides an opportunity to learn the difference between what is and what is not our responsibility. A sponsor is a key partner to help us truthfully navigate the heart and head components of this work.

Self-harm

It's important to note that the harm we are exploring in regard to our Step 8 lists can be harm to ourselves as well as to others. As was noted earlier, it can be a function of something we did or did not do. Loving

efforts to fix and control them may cause them to lose self-worth; that harm also merits attention. To be clear, blame is not the focus of Step 8—honesty, humility, and accountability are. Recovering our dignity and integrity requires that we own our part of what happened to others while we were active in our disease. Steps 1-7 give us the tools to break these patterns; here in Step 8 we set the table for creating a different future.

The relationship between harm and responsibility in addiction

Personal responsibility is generally accepted as an obligation of membership in the human family. Society generally assumes that we will be trustworthy, decent citizens of our communities, accountable for our personal choices and actions. Hurting ourselves and others is unacceptable. Perpetrators of harm should be accountable for their actions and should seek help to address whatever problems prompt their harmful behavior.

A common stance is *If you do the crime, you do the time*. The topic gets thorny very quickly when underlying problematic behavior relates to a disease. Perhaps a brain tumor causes aggressive behavior, resulting in a physical assault of someone. Or, let's say that depression prevents someone from working, so they are delinquent in paying their rent. We would not hold these people responsible for their disease; we likely would hold them responsible for seeking medical care and remaining compliant with treatment protocols because those are choices within their control.

Now, please consider the question of personal responsibility for someone with addiction. Let's separate the matter into two parts. First is the compulsion to use something (alcohol, drugs, sex, love, controlling behavior, lies) that modifies how one feels but damages themselves and can cause harm to others. Second is patterns of selfishness, arrogance, submissiveness, control, lying, anger, etc. that are also part of the disease spectrum. When you take the substance out of the system you are left with an individual who still has these underlying "sick" patterns of being and whose behaviors can be harmful to themselves and others. Where does responsibility for harm from these aspects of the disease begin and end for us addicts?

It's important to be clear that we are not responsible for causing addiction. For those who suffer from the disease, accepting the diagnosis and becoming aware of the consequences is an opportunity to take on the

release us from this pain. The ultimate outcome sounds appealing; but speaking for myself, I can admit that I was petrified when I envisioned the task ahead. Please trust me and push through concerns that might hold you back. For the purpose of Step 8, the focus is simply on making the list of those we have harmed and cultivating the willingness to make amends; I will caution you not to jump ahead. The steps are in order on purpose; stay with me on making your list, thinking and praying only about being willing to be willing at this point.

Let's start by acknowledging that we all cause harm on occasion. That's not the focus of this list. Here, we are talking about longstanding patterns of behavior that damage people and relationships—directly and indirectly. Addicts can cause financial, emotional, social, religious, physical and sexual harm because we are blinded to the truth. Victims can suffer an infinite range of damage—ruined reputations, credit and joint tax problems, STDs, social isolation, anxiety, etc. Responsibility for such harm is clearcut. Perhaps less so, but no less important, is the damage we cause with our tongues. As addiction runs its course, we likely will have been judgmental, impatient, and maybe even vindictive because of our frustration and fear. We cannot take back hurtful words we have spoken. Our being triggered and justifiably frustrated or angry may explain the harm we cause but that does not excuse it.

Less obvious are instances where we misled others or ourselves for our own gain or benefit. Both the addict and the Al-Anon can do this to the other. The consequences are insidious, such as the loss of self-confidence, self-respect or the ability to trust others. This also falls within the work of this step. A person to whom we lie to hide something clearly belongs on our list. Overtly lying to a spouse to hide a job loss or DUI are obvious. Failing to be rigorously honest or truthful with someone also entitles that individual to be on our lists to receive amends. For example, hiding a relapse by attending meetings although still drinking/drugging/controlling may cause someone to doubt their mental competence. Although we did not tell a lie, not telling or owning our truth (because we are manipulating the other) falls within the scope of the list we are to build in this step. Let's also look at the other side of the street. If you are supporting an addict, your

Chapter 12

Step 8: Responsibility

Step 8. [We] Made a list of all people we had harmed and became willing to make amends to them all.

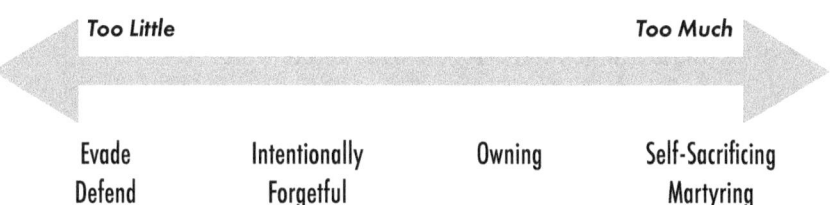

Too Little			Too Much
Evade Defend	Intentionally Forgetful	Owning	Self-Sacrificing Martyring

What's my part?
—*12 Step fellowship wisdom*

Responsibility: A recovery perspective

Addiction is a disease of isolation. The isolation may be insidious or overt. It may be self-imposed to protect our secrets about the disease in ourselves or those we love; or it can be the consequence of being cut off because of the harm we have done to ourselves, families, friends, colleagues, neighbors, and perhaps even our communities. This step is said to be the beginning of the end of isolation from our fellows and from God. Taking Step 8 begins the process of building a new foundation for future relationships with ourselves and others.

The nature of harm

The core idea behind Step 8 is that the instances when we have caused harm created negative residue that we continue to carry as shame, guilt, anger, and resentments. Like secrets that keep us sick, this emotional debris blocks us from loving relationships. Owning up to our responsibility will

- Eat matzah at every meal as a reminder to be less puffed up.
- Put a slip of paper in your pocket that says *I am but dust and ashes*.
- List 3 examples of unjustified arrogance: things for which you took credit that belonged to someone else, such as plagiarism of someone's words, taking credit for a colleague's success.

Prompts for journaling or study with your *chevruta*/sponsor
- In what situations do I shrink and in what situations do I take up too much space? What helps me rightsize?
- What obstacles keep me from working Step 7? Do I compare my insides and others' outsides?
- How are anger and arrogance related to humility?
- What does it mean to say that the "I" in humility is silent?
- Do all virtues and duties depend on humility?
- What defects am I ready to have removed? How do I humbly ask God?

Playlist
- "Nothing from Nothing"—Billy Preston
- "This is Me"—from *The Greatest Showman*
- "Within You Without You"—The Beatles
- "With a Little Help From My Friends"—Joe Cocker
- "My Way"—Frank Sinatra
- "I Gotta be Me"—Sammy Davis, Jr.
- "God is God"—Steve Earle

Imperfection for you to chew on as you do your work to cultivate your own practice of honor and humility:

> A man went to Wahab Imri and said:
> "Teach me humility."
> Wahab answered: "I cannot do that, because humility is a teacher of itself. It is learnt by means of its practice. If you cannot practice it, you cannot learn it." [231]

Daily reminders to help work Step 7

Following are some phrases that you might use as your daily reminders. Feel free to choose one or create your own.
- Allow time and space for others.
- Claim my seat.
- I am dust and ashes *and* the world was created for my sake.
- I am made in the image of holiness.
- I came from but a putrid drop.
- Honor myself as I do others.

Kabbalot to cultivate humility (*anavah*) to take Step 7

If you lean toward excessive humility, you might try:
- Plant some flowers and celebrate your power to unleash a piece of creation.
- Find a bench and enjoy taking your space.
- Pray for a bit more audacity. Enjoy a puff pastry to feel being puffed up.
- Wear bold colors.
- Put a slip of paper in your pocket that says *The world was made for me*.
- List 3 things every day in which you have pride.

If you lean toward sagging humility, you might try:
- Look at the night sky and think about your place in the universe.
- Find a bench and rightsize your space to leave room for others.
- Wear muted colors.

when we can no longer hide from the insanity of our lives that we fall at last into the arms of humility."[221] The key to taking Step 7 is speaking from the strength of your limitations. Alan Morinis says that "being humble doesn't mean being nobody; it just means being no more of a somebody than you ought to be."[222] To this I would add: being no more than anyone else. Our tradition teaches that "authentic humility inspires joy, courage and inner dignity."[223] I'm all in. What about you?

Secondary middot

We talk here of middot that we can lean on when feeling challenged or wanting to strengthen the practice of humility. Closely related to the idea that we are all children of God is the teaching that we are "each and every one, holy soul."[224] This is a daily reminder for the middah of honor (*kavod*); however, humility also challenges us to respect everyone simply because we are all the handiwork of God.[225] I believe that honor is a perfect fit here.

As with humility, honor is based on accepting others as they are. Rabbi Jonathan Sacks taught that this "means honoring others and regarding them as important, no less important than you are. . . .It does not mean holding yourself low; it means holding other people high."[226] That does not mean we are to demean ourselves relative to others. To be humble is not about comparisons[227] and neither is honoring others. Jewish wisdom teaches "Who is honored? One who honors others."[228] Thus, we are to let the honor of a friend be as dear to us as our own.[229]

The opposite of humility is arrogance. Adjectives that come to mind when thinking of arrogance include egotistical, boastful and overbearing. Jewish wisdom is filled with warnings that arrogance is the consequence of falling short of humility. Rabbi Salanter teaches that arrogance is pursuing honor and, in fact, as you just read, I posit that one way to avoid arrogance and cultivate humility is to practice honor/*kavod of others*.

Other Jewish scholars have also written on this topic. On being righteous, we find an entire chapter in *Ways of the Tzaddkim* making the point that arrogance "is the root of all evil soul traits."[230] That's an ugly thought. I don't know about you, but I prefer the idea of having my feet planted and giving root to goodness. Here is a closing parable from *The Spirituality of*

ducting ourselves humbly—in our speech, our physical presence, even the seat we select. Two things are notable about his teachings. First is that the consequences of falling short are dire: he warns about falling into "...the class of pseudo humble and evil people, whose hypocrisy is greater than any evil found in the world."[215] All that from just a little haughtiness!

His teaching that changing one's behavior brings about the desired internal change is also noteworthy.[216] In the Rooms we hear that *you can't think your way into right action, you must act your way into right thinking*. Luzzatto explained that your feelings are not under your control, but your actions are. Trying to control the uncontrollable is futile; the only sensible approach is to change that which is amenable to change. It's interesting how this aligns with the Serenity Prayer which is almost a mantra in Rooms of recovery (and beyond).

While Luzzatto seemed to focus on our smallness ("we come from a putrid drop...")[217] and our propensity to enjoy arrogance (flatterers), the earlier Mussar text, *Duties of the Heart*, draws attention to healthy pride and staying connected to the source of the gifts bestowed on us.[218] Rabbi Abraham Twerski, a contemporary expert on addiction and a spiritual guide, draws these ideas together in his commentary on *Path of the Just*.

> As a practical example of how one's ego can be obstructive, let me quote an observation of a highly accomplished professional person who recovered from severe alcoholism. "There is no way I could've recovered by my own efforts. I know that G-d did it for me. He was always trying to do it for me, but I kept getting in his way. What the recovery program accomplished is to enable me to get out of the way so that God could do his thing without my obstructing him." A humble person can recognize his achievements but he also knows where they came from.[219]

Consistent with this, Olitzky & Copans observed that it's "Not until you pick yourself up from your bottom and begin to live again that you can be humble."[220] Along these lines, Rabbi Rami Shapiro notes that "It is only

Speaking from personal experience, accepting the reality of imperfection was a big challenge for me (actually for my ego). Two aspects of imperfection threatened my sense of value. The fact that I had failed at so many things made me feel useless, which was discouraging and I needed to guard against it being self-defeating. My feelings of inadequacy were compounded by the fact that I could not actually fix everything and everyone—not even myself. My self-worth was restored by Jewish wisdom that "it is impossible for any person regardless of the level of perfection he has achieved to be without numerous faults. These may derive from his own nature, from his family and relatives, from certain things that have happened to him or from his own deeds."[212] Insofar as humans are imperfect by design and we all deviate from perfection constantly, I was comforted to know that Judaism provides space for an individual who has made bad choices (and seeks Divine will, if this is your North Star). Knowledge that there was path back by doing things differently fueled my recovery.

Another teaching that was helpful to me was that "one who offers humility to God and man shall be rewarded…"[213] I had previously understood humility to mean weakness. Clearly, this related to my humiliation as an addict and reflected my egocentric focus. This teaching about being rewarded for humility made me reconsider, especially since Program and Mussar wisdom spoke to the importance of humility. The words "offers humility to God and man" were the key to my changed thinking. I moved from selfishness to a spaciousness that I could create by being humble in my interactions with others.

The last piece of text I want mention is from Torah, which commands us to walk in God's ways.[214] The kabbalistic idea that God made and filled the world and then contracted to create space for us is the ultimate description of humility to me. I took this to mean that we must make space for others. I surely had much room for growth.

Cultivating humility

Our Sages taught that acquiring humility requires both thought and action, reflection and deeds. Rabbi Luzzatto advised that we start with cultivating an inner commitment toward humility and proceed with con-

route to our destination. In terms of our actual shortcomings, the tools of the Program and Mussar practice give us this new routing.

Step 7 also directs us to ask for help, humbly. I have an inherently poor sense of direction; stopping to ask someone for directions is an old habit. I give myself permission with ease. In a Mussar sense, I am leaving room for others, not exceeding my space by pretending to know the way. Rav Kook taught that genuine humility inspires courage and inner dignity.[210] Learning that we all have faults and weaknesses boosted my courage to ask for help and take Step 7. Offering yourself to receive help from others does, in fact, build humility that comes from a place of strength.

The last piece of Step 7 I'd like to explore here is the *Him* part (ask Him). From the Seventh Step prayer, one might assume that *Him* is God. To the extent that you embrace the idea that your personal blueprint was a Divine design, going back to the source for needed adjustments makes sense. Indeed, Talmud says wherever one finds the greatness of God there one also finds his humility.[211]

Alternatively, *Him* as written in the Step can be interpreted as anyone but me. In the context of humility, if my lens is distorted, then looking through your lens may provide me a better view. Some people think of Program fellows as God with skin on. Others look to the Program itself as their Higher Power. The message here in Step 7 is that we should look outside ourselves for guidance.

Making it personal

Regarding ego, self-esteem and humility, there are some uniquely Jewish ideas that were important in fueling my recovery; perhaps they will buoy you. The teachings that we are created in the image of the Divine by the breath of God are important starting points. By virtue of our disease, we addicts may find ourselves lacking any sense of inherent goodness, purity, capability or connection to anything outside ourselves. Facing my truths in working the Steps, it has been reassuring to be reminded that I have inherent greatness as the possessor of a Divine soul. We don't have to change to become good, we are good. The work of recovering and growing via Mussar practice is to remove the veils that cover our inner light.

and the natural suffering Reality contains."[209] Our work of recovery and Mussar practice is to return the ego to its rightful place in the psyche. While the ego can keep us sick, humility shows up in recovery as we heal. That is so important that I want to repeat it. Living in the solution of recovery means that we must refine our middah of humility. This is why the sages of Twelve Steps and Mussar teach that humility is a foundational trait.

Digging deeper into Step 7

Step 7 looks pretty straightforward; but as you've now learned, all the steps have multiple embedded ideas and we need to explore the pieces to capture the full value of each. Looking at Step 7 through the Mussar lens of humility is useful. On the one hand, *no more than my space* means that we must leave room for others to help us. On the other hand, we must also step up to do what we can to meet the goal of taking *no less than my place*. We can apply these ideas to the three concepts within Step 7. Let's explore together 1) removing our shortcomings, 2) asking for help, and 3) Him.

To start with removal of our shortcomings, permit me to revisit an earlier discussion. Through a Jewish lens, shortcomings are not defects. I take exception to the language of the Step (and the Program). God does not create defective people. How about calling them imperfections? We all know that we are imperfect. Let's think about them as potholes. Driving into a pothole is jarring and unpleasant, and often damages our vehicle. Our character traits can be like potholes—they can make us irritable and can make our fellow travelers uncomfortable. That captures it well: they are things we fall into that can hurt us and others.

Familiar strategies for dealing with potholes include complaining to the municipal authorities (blame) or making mental note of them so as to avoid them the next time we're on that street (doing our footwork). My experience in the arena of potholes and my imperfections is that new ones pop up as soon as an old one is fixed, so the need for readjustment is dynamic and never-ending. Jewish wisdom related to accepting our imperfections, combined with Mussar teachings on doing what we can, teaches that a good alternative, using available resources, might be finding a different

from a challenge or overstepping our place and taking on problems or situations that are not ours to fix. In what seems like a contradiction, addicts are often described as egomaniacs with inferiority complexes. Does that apply to you?

Ego: disease || Humility: recovery

In our disease, most of us live in ego extremes and we do not think of others. We think only of ourselves. Some of us show up to life with an inflated ego as victims or controllers. We blame others for everything that is wrong—spouses, children, bosses, banks, etc. It's all their fault. Paradoxically, for others of us, the wreckage and/or our failure to successfully control people, places and things causes us to feel totally defeated and deflated. Losing jobs, our health, marriages, friendships, cars, etc. breeds self-doubt for many. We believe we are at fault—that we are not good enough.

In the chaos of active addiction, there is little room for nuance. As we discussed in Step 1, our internal storylines reflect falsehoods that we tell ourselves to explain our situations and/or justify choices that are self-satisfying. Our inflated ego may have us try to manipulate or control an addict we love, thinking that we can get them clean. Or ego may allow us to find ways to justify our lying, stealing, and cheating to protect our [drug] habits. Feeling deflated, based on the falsehood that we are useless and worthless, touches on the other side of this middah. Neither of these perspectives allows room for anyone else. Perhaps this helps you understand the Program slogan EGO: **E**asing **G**od **O**ut.

Ego is the part of our self that drives our self-will. It is the lens through which we see everything and everybody else and, for us addicts, our ego is often distorted. "As long as there is an ego factor, one is preoccupied with oneself; wherever there is an element of self-interest, one's thought processes are invariably influenced in that direction."[207] In contrast, "humility keeps a person from haughtiness, arrogance, pride, vainglory, domination and the urge to control everything…"[208] Rabbi Rami Shapiro teaches that "…when the ego over reaches its rightful place in the psyche and imagines that it is the True Self, it, distorts its perception of reality… We need ego, but we don't need the walls ego has erected in its a mad flight from Reality

feed the pigeons? Do you jump up and give your seat away to anyone? To whom? Why or why not?

Showing up to life from a place of arrogance, entitlement, and control is associated with having little or low humility (an ego that's too big). This type of person would be loath to share the bench and likely would also devalue or disregard the contributions of others to their successes. On the other hand, an inferiority complex results when humility is too high (the ego is too small). This manifests as feelings of inferiority despite our strengths and successes. What is your tendency?

Being at either extreme is problematic; spiritually, both high and low humility veil our inner light and interfere with our connectedness with God and our ability to be of service to others. I find these ideas about the relationship between ego and humility to be confusing; when one is big the other is small, etc. To make them easier to remember here is a summary of the interrelationships we are discussing.

Big Ego / Low Humility

How we treat others: Intimidate, dominate, and manipulate.

The bench is all mine. I got here first and am not moving an inch for anyone.

Contracted Ego / Excessive Humility

How we treat others: Surrendering our voice and power to others.

The bench is open to anyone. I may need to find a new bench if someone wants to use mine.

This example of the bench assumes that we always show up at one or the other end of the continuum. That, of course, is an oversimplification. Because we each have a unique array of strengths and weaknesses and attitudes about them, there are times when we may be in either place. And the human condition is complicated. While we might feel like we lean toward high or low humility naturally, life inevitably gives us chances to step into the other attitude. The key is becoming aware whether we are running

you know people who are introverted or extroverted, naturally athletic, musical, or speak multiple languages? What are your strengths and what makes you different? Where do our capabilities and attributes come from? What controls the limits of our potential? Are we talking about gifts that we receive, or are we creators?

One school of thought posits that who and how we are is solely attributed to how we were endowed with the breath of life. Such an idea of pre-destiny is hard for many people to accept. An alternative view rests on the belief that by virtue of free will we each have the power to control our development, which is unbounded. This approach would suggest that any one of us could become Olympic athletes or iconic painters. What do you think? Each of these ideas seem somewhat extreme. We all need others to realize our potential. A question is whether we recognize and acknowledge that. Doing so is the reason that here in Step 7 we look beyond ourselves for help—and do so with humility.

Debating our role as recipient or creator is actually a question of who is in control. The question stems from the human capacity to develop a sense of self (ego). Ego plays a big role in how we see ourselves relative to others. Are we smarter, richer, better looking, etc? Our ego wants a place in the world; it wants the glory of the spotlight center stage. Left to its own devices, ego wants to run the show from a place of power. One of our human tasks is to keep our ego in check and in a healthy balance, meaning that it does not get too big or too small.

Humility/*anavah* is a soul trait important in the relationship of self (ego) to others. Humility counters ego; it is the attitude we embrace in regard to others, and it is a choice. Regarding *anavah*, a Mussar view of humility is encapsulated by the phrase "no more than my space and no less than my place."[206] A park bench is my favorite metaphor for thinking of the space we take/occupy relative to others. Imagine that you take your lunch break in the park on a beautiful spring day. You have a backpack with your personal things, plus a coat, thermos, and your lunch sack. Do you spread out your stuff on the bench and crowd out others while you immerse yourself in a book or do you leave space for them? If someone else comes to sit, do you move your stuff out of the way? What if they want space so they can sit to

others takes this idea to the next level. Being of service is not being servile. It is simply being open to what those around us might like or need. Where would they like to go for dinner, what movie do they want to see, offering to unload the dishwasher, relieve someone of burdensome responsibilities, etc.

Think for a minute about a healthy balance in your sense of self and self-importance—we are neither too small nor too big. Self-centeredness, arrogance, and selfishness leave little room for anyone else, including a spiritual connection.

I hope this helps you understand why humility is the foundational principle for all Twelve Step work and that you are sufficiently encouraged to embrace this ideal and personal practice. Over time, you will come to appreciate that humility is what makes the Program and your recovery durable.

Humility (*Anavah*): A Mussar perspective on Step 7

> *No more than my space; no less than my place.*
> —*Everyday Holiness*

Our Sages have long taught that humility (*anavah*) has a place of importance in Jewish thinking and Mussar practice. The middah of humility reflects an attitude about how we show up in our lives—how we relate to God and our fellows. Humility is frequently viewed as the first step on the ladder of self-refinement and is foundational in Mussar thinking. The idea that all virtues and duties are dependent on humility is found in *Duties of The Heart*, written almost 1,000 years ago.[205] This thinking is clearly in sync with the guidance of Twelve Step programs for becoming our best selves. Let's explore how these teachings relate.

A good starting point for thinking about *anavah* is to ponder: How do we come to be as we are? One approach to this question is captured in the nature versus nurture debate. Have you ever seen a child prodigy? Do

individuals who have a disease and, while we have made some bad choices, we are not bad people. *We are children of God and people of worth.* Dr. Edith Eger teaches that "no one can take away from you what you put in your mind."[202] It's time to replace those old recordings that come from a place of learned helplessness and regret. I encourage you to create a positive mantra that captures this shift in thinking and repeat it to yourself whenever you feel any self-doubt in your recovery.

So, for whatever reason, addiction is part of our journey. Although you may think of it as a burden that condemns you to a life of misery, I can assure you that if you continue on this path of recovery you will come to appreciate many hidden blessings. "Our painful experiences aren't a liability—they're a gift. They give us perspective and meaning and an opportunity to find our unique purpose and our strength."[203] In fact, while you may be unaware, many of your shortcomings have already been removed owing to your work. Yes, there is more to be done, but you should not think of humility as accepting defeat; quite the contrary. When you harness humility, you become your own liberator.

The second half of this maxim is *humility is thinking of yourself less.* "Without humility, you won't be able to recognize, admit, and address your shortcomings, and you will fall into the trap of being overly prideful and making excuses for your behaviors."[204] Here in Step 7, we start with intentionally taking the focus off ourselves and our ideas. After all, our best thinking hasn't worked out so well so far. Rightsizing ourselves, cultivating openness to hear and receive from others, is a critical part of growing humility. The 3 Cs remind us that we are not God: we cannot cause, control or cure addiction. Nor are we entitled to adoration or attention. As it relates to God or your Higher Power, a phrase commonly heard in the Rooms is *thy will, not mine.* As it relates to our defects, this is the start of letting them go and deferring to the ultimate authority when in doubt about what action to take.

Within the Program, sharing our experience, strength, and hope shifts the focus to being of service, sharing and helping others. Working with others in the mutual pursuit of recovery and beginning to think about being of service takes the focus off ourselves, our problems, and our choices. Outside the Rooms, thinking about how we can help meet the needs of

It was important for me to learn that letting go of old patterns created a space for new helpful traits. Nature abhors a vacuum. The transition was uncomfortable at times. Think of changing your hairstyle or wearing a clothing style or color that is very different for you. It feels awkward and uncomfortable… until it doesn't. Not only do we each have to become accustomed to the changes, so do those around us. My reality was that out of habit, I sometimes tried to take back my old, unproductive ways. Although counterproductive, it was easier to slip into old ruts than embrace new habits. Beware, that's our trickster at work.

Remember that Step 7 is written as "humbly asked Him to remove our shortcomings." The *our* in this case reflects the universality of this work for everyone working to live in recovery. We hear constantly in the Rooms that we have to live the Program one day at a time. This axiom surely applies to our work in Step 7. Although we become willing for all our defects to be removed, the change is a gradual process. The work is never complete, although with our initial efforts we will move on from Step 7. On any given day we might discover that a new or different defect has been lifted or revealed or that an old shortcoming has resurfaced. It is important to remain vigilant and continually renew our efforts.

Humility requires balance

Before leaving this discussion, I'd like to share a concept I've heard in the Rooms in relation to humility: When we think about the space we take up in the world, we should be neither too big nor too small. This is a high-level Program concept. It will mean more to you as you progress with the Steps and with each passing day that you live and love in recovery. One fellow who works a great Program reminds me often that this is the essence of recovery.

Let's explore the first half of that concept: *humility is not thinking less of yourself*. It is easy to confuse humiliation with humility. Coming into the Program, I felt *less than*; many of the people around me in my old life seemed to relish reminding me of how I repeatedly fell short. My wreckage of the past was a constant reminder of those truths.

What I know today is that you need to dismiss, right off the bat, that we addicts somehow deserve to be humiliated, reduced to a lower position in relation to anyone else. Being in recovery means that we accept ourselves as

sible. This idea is equally true for those of us who love addicts. We need the help of something bigger than ourselves—despite our best efforts, none of us can successfully recover without help. Perhaps, like me, you find yourself questioning the word *humbly* in this step. Humbly here reflects the way we ask *her/him/them/it*, as you prefer; it also describes our standing relative to the Higher Power of our understanding.

Asking humbly means that we have humility—modesty, a lack of arrogance. One common and inaccurate image of humility is "a spiritual pauper wearing sackcloth and ashes."[201] Interpreting humility as being weak or meek feeds attitudes of self-criticism and can lead us quickly to feeling stuck in a quagmire of humiliation. Rightsizing ourselves is the sweet spot of a life in recovery. When we are humble, we are in balance. We let go of the notion that we are big and in control. In working Step 7, I finally came to understand the oft heard phrase *we are children of God and people of worth*. Perhaps you can envision humility as a continuum where harboring false pride and meekness are at the two extremes of too little and too much, respectively. Humility is a midrange, grounded in the idea that we are not in control but that we are individuals with the power to act independently and to make our own free choices—which includes actively seeking and accepting help.

The key to my willingness to take Step 7 was learning that reaching out for help was an act of strength; confidence in this knowledge to the level of belief (confidence in my personal sufficiency and worthiness) helped me act with courage and open myself to what might happen.

Out with the old

So, letting go and letting God becomes the call to action in Step 7. While I previously had a list of reasons for not letting go, working the Program propelled me past willingness to a place of wanting to overcome my shortcomings. Appreciating the power of creation and the potential for re-creation that I saw and felt all around me among Program fellows and the larger world made me believe that change and healing were possible. I admit that I was comforted by knowing that only those defects that were in the way of my being in meaningful relationships with others were the focus. My trust in fellows, in the Program itself, and a newfound sense of my potential for happiness were very motivating.

perience validated what I had heard in the Rooms, that *a changed attitude can aid our recovery.*

The irony is that although we see our part in problems, we may resist letting go of these parts of ourselves. Fear of the unknown is often the root cause of our resistance. Speaking from personal experience, I had three unknowns in play:

1. What would be left of me if these traits/habits were removed? Would I like myself, and how would this new me fit into the world?
2. Fear of God stopped me from even getting started. Would that power of the universe help little ol' me? How do I ask?
3. Fear of asking for help. Would others see me as weak?

Does any of this resonate with you?

I learned in the Rooms that all three of these were excuses; they reflect an ego-based desire to feel like we are in control. Taking Step 7 challenges us to step out of our egos and into relationship with our HP, whose help we need. The power of the Program, our sponsor and/or the creative force of the universe was revealed in our work on Steps 1, 2 and 3. In Step 5 we connected to a power greater than ourselves when admitting our wrongs. We were challenged to acknowledge and reveal our truths. This was, generally, a one-way, outgoing monologue. It's not that I am keeping tabs, but I did not think I could get more humble than I was when surrendering in Step 1 or admitting all my wrongs in Step 5, or submitting myself to accept whatever this power-greater-than-me has in store in Step 6. Let there be no doubt; Step 7 is also an action step. We open ourselves to ask that God, as we understand it/him, work on us. We are strengthened by recognizing that we are more than our mistakes and actively partnering in the work of this step. We take Step 7 from a position of balance and strength; therein lies an important aspect of humility that informs our efforts.

Living in humility

A.A.'s *Twelve & Twelve* explains that achieving greater humility is foundational for all of the Twelve Steps and without it, staying sober is not pos-

Let's move on to explore Step 7 together so you too can enjoy being where it's warm.

Letting go

Congratulations on your personal reflections and discoveries thus far. As we leave Step 6 and approach Step 7, it's important to take a moment to acknowledge the many strengths that you uncovered, in addition to thinking about your defects of character. The positives are often overshadowed by the negative consequences of our addiction but they are not to be dismissed. Embrace them as a source of healthy self-esteem and personal value on which to build. Having discovered that your addiction could not be relieved by any human power, and that your Higher Power could and would help if you asked, Step 7 creates the opportunity to ask for help to release those things that no longer serve you well. Please don't rush past this opportunity; take a moment to let the ideas migrate from your mind to your heart. It might go something like this….

> HP or God of my understanding, I am now willing and pray/ask that you will remove from me any aspect of my character that interferes with my usefulness to you and my fellows. Take all that you deem necessary, whether good or bad, and grant me courage to venture out and do as you direct.

Working the earlier steps "…put us in a position to relinquish self-will and experience the will of a power greater than your own."[199] This reflects a huge step forward in your recovery. I don't know about you; for me, this requires heavy lifting! Contemplating the removal of any part of ourselves is bold and requires trust. The ask here is all or nothing. "Half measures availed us nothing," says the *A.A. Big Book*.[200] Asking for help is hard enough; asking for God's help takes it to another level of difficulty altogether. Learning in the Rooms that reaching out for help was an act of strength changed my perspective and was essential to my ability to take Step 7. Transforming my perspective this way changed my view of myself, and helped me feel courageous and open to what might happen. This ex-

Chapter 11

Step 7: Humility

Step 7. [We] Humbly asked Him to remove our shortcomings.

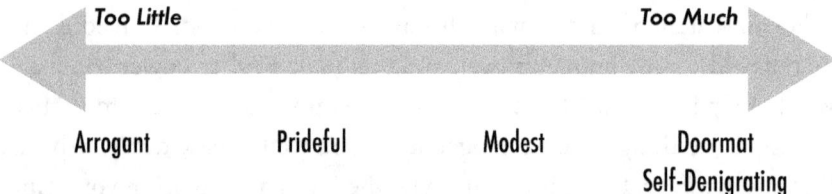

Too Little			Too Much
Arrogant	Prideful	Modest	Doormat
Self-Denigrating

Let Go and Let God.
—12 Step fellowship wisdom

Humility: A recovery perspective

Up to now, our program focus has largely been on understanding and engaging with the reality of our disease. Beginning in Step 7, we turn toward the work of recovery! One Program friend described her experience this way:

> Honestly, in Steps 1 through 6, I was continuing to slide downward. My descent was diminished a bit by getting sober, but I was still disconnected from reality and others; I was stuck in a dark, cold hole. And despite my best efforts, I could not climb out. Standing up at the edge, fellows told me it was beautiful outside. It was not until Step 7 that I was willing to accept the truth that I needed help and was willing to ask for a ladder so I could go where it was warm and beautiful.

- What blocks me from readiness and willingness? Obstacles?
- Bring perseverance to our inner energies through your meditation practice.
- Describe the difference between procrastination and patience (*savlanut*).
- *Hineni*=I am ready. Use me. Discuss.

Playlist
- "Do It Now"—Ingrid Michaelson
- "Keep the Fire Burning"—REO Speedwagon
- "If Not Now, Tell Me When"—Carrie Newcomer
- "Fight Song"—Rachael Platten
- "Unstoppable"—Rascal Flatts
- "I Will Survive"—Gloria Gaynor
- "I Am Ready for Change"—Carrie Newcomer
- "I Am Changing"—Jennifer Hudson
- "One Small Step"—Peri Smilow

- Run to do good.
- Each moment, choose good.
- Arise and engage.
- Progress, not perfection.
- Feed the fire.

Kabbalot to cultivate alacrity (*zerizut*) as you take Step 6

If you lean toward excessive alacrity you might try:
- Before taking an action, talk with someone about your motives.
- Before you take an action, grab piece of gum and "chew" on the situation for at least 5 minutes before you decide what to do.
- Prepare a hot beverage to symbolize your energy and wait until it cools to take an action.
- Before you take an action, take a walk or a bike ride as a reminder to stay on your side of the street.
- Choose a situation where you have too much enthusiasm and ask yourself which part of this situation is yours?

If you lean toward sagging alacrity you might try:
- Go to the hardware store and buy a pack of springs—put some in your pocket, on your desk, etc., as a reminder to "spring" into action.
- Choose a situation where are you are lacking enthusiasm—writing a will, giving to charity, working on a relationship with someone from whom you've been estranged, visiting someone who is sick, making a shiva call. Visualize it, feel what comes up, and say out loud, "What is blocking me? Please give me insight." Listen for the answer.
- Repeat out loud *"Hineni"*—I am ready, use me!
- Visualize adding wood to the fire of your energy center.
- When you feel the impulse to answer a request with no, say yes.

Prompts for journaling or study with your *chevruta*/sponsor
- What would my life would be like if I did not exhibit *zerizut*?
- What can I be grateful for that would inspire me to have *zerizut*?

Do you remember the idea that a key aspect of Mussar is making our hearts feel what our minds know? When we bring alacrity to the performance of a mitzvah (such as cleaning things up), being speedy to take action will arouse our inner zeal even further. Thus, acting with alacrity cultivates the soul trait of alacrity, and living in recovery grows as an inside job. Writing 700 years ago, Rabbi Luzzatto recognized that vigilance is the key to alacrity.[196] "True zeal consists of one's heart being alert, his mind being wakeful, and his limbs being light for the performance of his labor…"[197] Jewish wisdom permeates Steps 1 through 6 of the Program and conveys how we can be entirely ready.

Secondary middot

You have already been introduced to gratitude (*hakarat hatov*) as one middah that relates to *zerizut*. Another is *charitzut v'bechira*, called decisive choice making.[198] In the context of Step 6, this middah accounts for the "entirely" aspect of our readiness. Specifically, I am referring to being at the *bechira* point and making the choice to surrender to truth and work toward recovering our best selves. We talk in the Program about aligning our will to God's will for us—committing your energy to hold yourself open and not to limit the answers you are willing to accept.

Silence (*shtikah*) and patience (*savlanut*) also intersect with *zerizut*. Silence will allow you to envision your destination and begin to separate your voice from the Divine. The middah of patience comes into play while sitting with the discomfort of waiting. Were it not for patience it would be very easy to succumb to our willfulness and jump into problems. We must work the Program, not the problem. This can be challenging when we (or someone we love) are in pain or danger. As I am sure you have experienced, there are times when the decision to do nothing, to harness *zerizut*, is the next right thing—and the hardest choice to make.

Daily reminders to help work Step 6

Following are some phrases that you might use as your daily reminders. Feel free to choose one or create your own.

- Whose will?

ercise discretion and strengthen our practice of this middah. Please do be aware that *zerizut* may be needed in some areas of your life and not others. For example, personal finances may be a mess but the house may be very clean. Please do not dismiss the value of cultivating *zerizut* because your problem is confined. Your yetzer may be trying to confuse you to dull your energy. That's even more reason to turbocharge.

Cultivating alacrity

What can we do to intensify our enthusiasm? A good starting point is awareness of the stories you tell yourself. Ideally, you clarified these in your inventory work. Addressing the obstructions with your sponsor, therapist, or fellows will go a long way in getting you started.

In addition to pushing through what holds us back, we can lean into *middot* that draw us forward. Many teachers agree that an attitude of gratitude can fuel the fire of enthusiasm. The Hebrew for gratitude is *hakarat hatov*, translated as "recognize the good." Reading this carefully, gratitude is not passive; it's an action. The good is always there; we need to look for it, savor it and convert it into propulsive energy. Just as we eat over the course of the day to sustain ourselves, we can replenish alacrity by connecting with the power of the universe that envelops us. It only takes a moment of mindfulness—marvel at the many shades of green you can see, feel the sun's warmth on your skin, do a random act of kindness, study Torah, light Shabbat candles, pray or meditate.

Even in the depths of our addiction, we can find something deserving of gratitude: finding the Program; benefiting from its wisdom; the love and support of a sponsor; a crisis that brings our disease into the light and opens the possibility of treatment—all are reasons to be grateful. The Hebrew says *Wake up! Give thanks!* Thus, even before getting out of bed we are to recite a prayer of thanks (*Modeh Ani*), being actively grateful for the gift of a new day. We can observe with gratitude, but the act of engaging elevates us further. Starting my day with an expression of gratitude implants a message that repeats itself throughout the day: you have been given the gift of life; use it wisely and make it good for yourself and others.

in Step 5 as a metaphor for cleaning our spiritual houses. Alan Lew notes that turning, related to our High Holiday preparation, is "the conscious decision to change, letting go, letting the walls of identity crumble and turning toward that which remains."[191]

It's good news that every moment contains the opportunity for us to make such choices. Alan Morinis describes them as "invitations from God"[192] and our Sages' teaching reinforces the concept that we must not let an opportunity to do good go stale.[193] *Zerizut* is the middah that we can call upon to help us push through the internal barriers, to engage with the challenge, so that we do not let a chance for turning slip away.

The mindset of seeking recovery as a mitzvah is a perfect launching pad for putting all our defects on the table as the ultimate measure of our engagement. Living a life of alacrity means engagement even when we might rather avoid it.[194] We might prefer that the removal of our defects be partial or gradual but we are challenged to commit to the whole nine yards. Entirely ready means that we shift from willfulness (our will) to willingness (of God's will). *Zerizut* carries us the full distance to whatever God has in store.

What obstructs alacrity

Much has been written by Sages across the generations about what undermines alacrity. Willfulness, laziness, rationalization, a closed heart, fear and anxiety have been identified as obstructing enthusiasm. The inverse is also true. We are not to be overly hasty. "One who runs too quickly is very apt to stumble, and one who runs too quickly falls….things cannot be done correctly in haste, but only in patience…" Thus, we are advised, "be patient in judgment." As if speaking to us addicts, we are told "one must not… pursue his lust, exert himself for his pleasures, and pursue evil deeds."[195]

Sit quietly and pick your poison. Many of these traits that hold us back are second nature for us. I think it's fair to say that we addicts have experience with how each of these can distort our reality. The cunning and baffling nature of our disease makes it a mighty foe. The death we see around us among our fellows is a stark reminder of the high stakes in our choices. This calls on us to heighten our awareness and work our programs to ex-

that Torah wisdom provides an important message related to willingness and our practice of *zerizut*. God said to the Israelites, "….I have put before you life and death, blessing and curse—therefore choose life!"[186] Was he talking to us? I think, yes, absolutely. Since nothing we have tried has worked, this crossing seems to be the only solution to choosing life. Letting the opportunity pass would be a failure to exercise the gift of our power to choose life. Openness gives us a chance at change for the better.

To sign up for this "swim," we must be willing to fight the undertow, sharks, and jellyfish (the defects that are our jailers and constitute our yetzer hara) that have the potential to weaken us and draw us back into our willfulness (and our addiction). *Zerizut* is the force that combines with our openness and willingness to make us ready. It powers our plunge into the water and our full-throttle swim. Alacrity is like potential energy—it lets us tap into the physical and emotional resources we need to go the distance. Consistent with our effort to redirect our will to do good, our Sages teach that "zeal [a synonym for *zerizut*] promotes Torah and *mitzvos*…"[187] Quoting *Ethics of Our Fathers*, they wrote that *zerizut* enables us to "be bold as a leopard, light as an eagle, swift as a deer, and strong as a lion, to carry out the will of your Father in Heaven."[188] It is a "trait of the righteous" reflecting our goal of aligning our will with God's will, moving from willfulness to service.

Entirely ready

Abraham Twerski, a modern psychiatrist who also happened to be a rabbi, wrote that by doing everything in our power to rid ourselves of our shortcomings, we become entirely ready.[189] I see something deep at play here that can hold us back. Fear! Losing the self I know and you know is a challenge to the ego. Rami Shapiro puts this in the frame of death; not the death of body, but the death of "I."[190] The proposition of being in the world in a new way is hard to imagine. He said "I will be a different me" and explains that Step 6 is possible when we abandon the need to know the future and simply take up the challenge of the present. "I surrender. I am ready."

We can also look at this through the of lens of Tisha B'Av. This is the holiday that commemorates the destruction of the Temple; it came up

Nachshon made the commitment to enter the water. He did not wade in; the text apparently says that he jumped into the sea, the water rising to his nose.[184] Would you have been the first one in? Neither raging water nor fear deterred him. Facing death due to drowning or at the hands of an army in chase, he chose to lean toward change for the good of the people. I assume that he relied on faith in the Divine to make the crossing possible. This story demonstrates the essence of *zerizut*—acting with full-throttle, deliberate enthusiasm for the greater good.

Zerizut and Step 6

Let's explore how alacrity applies to the work of Step 6: "We were entirely ready for God to remove all our defects of character." Our deliberation in Steps 4 & 5 revealed that our moral compass had been hijacked by our defects of character. We found that we had lost our capacity to make well-reasoned choices and create lives centering on the Divine will. We were willful, focused on meeting our needs and wants at any cost. Although skepticism is natural, uncovering the blockages that connect us to a power greater than ourselves, revealing our light, recovering our beauty, and restoring our connectedness to others are worthy motives to take this next step forward.

Beginning with nonjudgmental curiosity (*hitlamdut*), we become mindful and envision the choice (*bechira*) before us. We know that our efforts alone are not enough. Here we are standing at the shoreline with two choices—going back and accepting the dismal state of our affairs, or considering the opportunity to do something about the patterns which continue to derail us and through which we hurt ourselves and others. The removal of these shortcomings requires that we enter and cross our own Sea of Fear to swim for freedom. What exactly do we fear? What do we need in order to be ready? To actualize our goal, we must first be open to the necessity of the swim. Rabbi Mendel taught that at such moments we must harness alacrity to assure that the opportune moment does not pass.[185]

What attitude will we bring to the task? We can carry the extra weight of heaviness from resentment, anger and fear or we can be buoyed by gratitude, hope and trust to take a path that leads where we want to go. I believe

- Be Deliberative. (Review, Consider and Decide). Reminds us to reason things out (e.g., talk to your sponsor) and stay focused on good, orderly direction, bringing non-judgmental curiosity (*hitlamdut*) to our choice or decision point (*bechira*). There is a nuance here that I want to emphasize. Applying *zerizut* to poorly conceived choices is a misuse of the middah. Strictly speaking, the decision or choice itself stands just outside the boundary of *zerizut*. We decide on an action to which we apply *zerizut*; part of our Mussar work is discerning whether the action is appropriate.

In the storied past of the Jewish people, we can easily find ancestors who model alacrity. Think about Abraham (Genesis 22:1-3). He rose early in response to God's command that he should take his son, Isaac, to Mount Moriah where he would sacrifice him to God as an offering. The willingness (enthusiasm) Abraham showed to undertake this mitzvah, grounded in belief and trust in the Divine, exemplifies *zerizut*. You might take issue with whether his compliance was discerning; I will say that it's hard to argue with "the boss" and I will ask you to think about this in terms of making God's will your will.

Unimaginable is the word that comes to mind for Abraham. A contemporary take on this reveals that his willingness is not as unthinkable as you may imagine. If nothing else, Step 1 teaches us that we are not in control and ultimately must submit to a power greater than ourselves. Imagine, for example, parenting a child who identifies as other than their gender at birth. Isabel Rose has lived this story.[183] Like Abraham, she described it as giving a son up to God, aligning her will to the Divine. I'm guessing that if you look, you will find similar situations in your life circle. Bringing *zerizut* to our lives can have very personal meaning; that's the power and beauty of these teachings.

Nachshon also personified alacrity. I admire him so very much. Do you remember the story? According to the Talmud, as the Israelites fled Egypt they found themselves trapped with the Egyptian army behind and the Red Sea ahead. Freedom was almost in reach, across the sea, but no one wanted to be first into the water. They were trapped at the water's edge with Moses praying for Divine guidance. Intent on escaping the Egyptians,

Related to the idea that we practice the principles of the Program in all our affairs, our Jewish Sages taught that this *middah* is the foundation of all the traits.[180] Fifteenth-century Mussar teachers recognized that zeal is an ornament to all the other traits and that it perfects all of them. By way of example, Alan Morinis said if you are going to be generous, how much better to give with enthusiasm and to be zealous in defense of the honor of your friend.[181]

Permit me to insert a cautionary note here that is important in light of our tendencies as addicts/alcoholics and Al-Anons. As we move into action, we must be sure that our motives are clean. As we try to do the right thing, we need to know we're doing it for the right reasons. This is not about attempting to control what's good for us, such as taking action to get what we want. Alacrity supposes that we are aligning our will with God's will, not the other way around. It's important that we not justify recklessness or impulsiveness by naming it as the practice of *zerizut*. These behaviors reflect an imbalance in alacrity, leaning toward the side of excess along our continuum.

Alan Morinis described this middah as "proper, positive, balanced enthusiasm, done with a full throttle, once review, consideration and decision have set you on the right course."[182] The antidote to our reactivity is deliberation, albeit it seamless and perhaps almost imperceptible. In many ways, integrating the practice of *zerizut* into our Twelve Step programs can be transformational for us addicts. Guided by this definition, let's look at how these attributes of alacrity help us be our best selves:

- Be Proper. Reminds us to consult our moral compass as a guide for our decisions and actions, which should include bringing the Divine into our choices.
- Be Positive. Reminds us not to hurt ourselves or others.
- Be Balanced. Reminds us to look at our motives, not to be impulsive or manipulative, and to stay on our side of the street.
- Go Full-throttle. This is a double-edged sword. Some must throttle down overzealous action; others need to open the throttle and exert themselves to step out of isolation and shame because their voice and their light in the world matter.

amby-pamby for you, perhaps the reason to keep going through the Steps is as simple as the fact that your sponsor, who is trustworthy, has told you that you are harming yourself and others. If neither of these compel you, perhaps a better question for you is *why not*. Work with your sponsor to mine your inventory for insights that help break through this barrier. You can do this!

Alacrity (*Zerizut*): A Mussar perspective on Step 6

> *Be bold as a leopard, light as an eagle,*
> *swift as a deer and strong as a lion*
> *to do the will of our father in heaven.*
> —Pirkei Avot 5:20

Step 6 is the point in our Step work where we pivot and focus on change. Up to this point, we have concentrated on what we can learn from what was—the ways we have been. In Step 6, we begin to imagine the way things can be and we take action to start making it so. The middah we will focus on is *zerizut* (alacrity). The Hebrew *zerizut* is difficult to translate because it is multidimensional, encompassing both the attitude and energetic qualities of our actions. Cheerful readiness is a good starting point. Alternative explanations are that the idea starts with enthusiasm or energetic responsiveness and it refers to springing forward without hesitation or obstacle.[177] Alacrity is playing to win, not playing not to lose. It drives the intentionality and commitment we bring to face life.

According to Alan Morinis, the basis for this middah is found in Torah instruction on how to eat the sacrificial lamb at Passover. "They shall eat the flesh the same night…"[178] Morinis interprets this as teaching that we shall do what is spiritually beneficial with no delay.[179] We must not let opportunities to do mitzvot slip by. Our recovery is spiritually beneficial, we should proceed with due haste—alacrity.

ture faith, trust and courage is also essential; many add prayer to the mix. The idea that you are what you think is a powerful stimulus. We are also told to imagine who we will be when our defects are replaced by healthy choices. This envisioning has been very effective for me when I let it be.

Going to any lengths is a related Program concept that challenges us to be accountable to being open and willing—entirely ready. "If you're interested, you will do what is convenient; if you're committed, you'll do whatever it takes."[173] I knew that my disease was killing me—physically, emotionally and spiritually. I was committed to recovering myself and my family. The decision to risk being open, bearing the discomfort of fear and pride, seemed like an acceptable price to pay for freedom from the toll of addiction on me and my family.

A well-known teaching in the Rooms of recovery is this: *willingness without action is fantasy*. Daily questioning of your willingness will increase your ability to be increasingly willing.[174] A *yes* mindset as it relates to working a program is a great starting point for creating change; following through by doing what you say you are willing to do is what ultimately cultivates willingness.[175] I was taught to fill the holes with the inverse of what was removed. If it's dishonesty, do something honest; if it's an attitude of arrogance, do some anonymous service. Our outer actions inspire inner zeal. Overall, we must practice living life on life's terms with an attitude of gratitude and humility. As Joan Didion said, "the willingness to accept responsibility for one's own life is the source from which self-respect springs."[176]

Please keep in mind that recovery is a lifetime job which we do one day at a time. Step 6 asks us to aim high; my sponsor and fellows help me take comfort in knowing that none of us can do this to perfection day in and day out. That's to be expected in our humanness. We are told to keep coming back and keep working at the change we desire. It's helpful to keep the long game in mind. If you harbor doubt about whether you want to keep going, the Program provides compelling reasons to stay the course. First is teaching that removing our defects removes that which stands in the way of our being useful to God/HP and our fellows. In other words, taking Step 6 is the preparation for becoming useful human beings. It's hard to find fault with the idea of becoming useful to others or God. If that's too

logue of self-encouragement and self-motivation, or we can choose one of self-defeat and self-pity."[172] Willingness is a make-or-break component of readiness and it is clearly a challenging part.

Step 6 requires us to be entirely ready—not just ready, but *entirely* ready. Keep in mind that the scope of change that we are asked to commit to in Step 6 is the possible removal of all our shortcomings. Entirely ready means enduring the discomfort of abandoning willfulness (aka control) as the solution to our problems. It means being all-in—invested in success, welcoming the shift to offering no resistance, no negotiation, no holding back. Willingness is a decision point, a choice. In terms of having our defects removed, we can, for example, be arrogant, stubborn and resentful or we can choose to be grateful, willing and compliant. Which attitude brings you closer to God and your loved ones? We clearly don't like it, but we know the answer. No one said we had to like it; we just have to do it!

This attitudinal part of Step 6 is especially challenging because the Program often requires us to do things that we do not want to do. In my workday example above, doing the right thing is inconvenient and means having to fight traffic, deal with crowds in the stores and maybe lose some leisure time. All that, in addition to eating humble pie. Willingness becomes harder (and resentment bigger) when what we are giving up has a high emotional toll. We may need to leave old friends and stop eating at our favorite neighborhood tavern or stop attending family holiday gatherings, typical triggers of our addictive thinking and old, harmful patterns of reacting. While these were things we enjoyed, we might easily be resentful that *we* are the ones who have to change. But tough choices are often necessary to protect our recovery.

Think for a moment... what would need to be true for you to be entirely ready—to surrender and open yourself up to change? My musts included accepting that I could not fix "it" myself and that I needed to know I could trust whatever I was leaning on. In the case of my defects, both are surely true. There is no arguing that I have seen the Program work for others and that I don't have a solution of my own. Leaning on the ideas of Steps 1, 2 and 3—*I can't, He can, Let Him* also supports my willingness and readiness. I repeat this as a mantra as well as *let go and let God*. Taking the time to nur-

atic, they are the devil we know. Our defects feel safe and, on some level, they do something for us that feels good.

> We must admit that ...we exult in some of our defects. We really love them. Who, for example, doesn't like to feel just a little superior to the next fellow, or even quite a lot superior? Isn't it true that we like to let greed masquerade as ambition?... Self-righteous anger can be very enjoyable.... procrastination, which is really sloth in five syllables.[169]

Without realizing it, these defective solutions keep us stuck. Eventually they stop working, becoming troublemakers themselves. There's a saying in the Rooms about being sick and tired of being sick and tired—that's when we say enough is enough, and open ourselves to change. The awareness that we developed in Step 5—that we are harming ourselves and others—cracks open the door to willingness. When we are burned out, the lucky ones among us experience the combination of openness and willingness and we become entirely ready.[170]

What will be left after they're gone?

While we surely want to be freed from the burdens of our present lives, the idea of removing them can be worrisome. Swiss cheese is OK with holes, but will we be OK when parts of what defines us are removed? Many people express worry about what will be left when these aspects of our character are removed. There is a fear that we will become invisible, that we'll be normal or boring.[171] Will we like ourselves? These questions reflect a battle between wanting help and wanting to be in control. Honestly, for the longest time, this held me back from saying here I am, I am ready. Willingness is the key to continued growth and progress in our recovery. So let's look at how we can cultivate this attitude.

How to cultivate willingness?

It's been said that attitude is everything. "It governs how we perceive the world and how the world perceives us. We can choose an inner dia-

chance to clean out the cobwebs so we are more effective, etc. The bottom line is that if we were in a corporate office, we'd have to do our errands after hours. Now substitute or add in having a beer along the way—in addition to the time, we may not be fully present upon our return. It's a slippery slope. Rigorous Program honesty requires that we admit that it is stealing (time), and that it's a willful, dishonest, harmful choice. Step 6 asks us to be ready (open and willing) for God to remove the willfulness that allows us to justify such a pattern of thinking and action.

Our relationship with our character defects

Shortcomings related to our sense of self are intensely personal and hard to lose. But they are especially important issues for us addicts because we are our largest problem. Some of us have a deflated and some an inflated sense of self-worth and self-confidence; some suffer with both at the same time. These spell trouble when, out of false pride and judgmentalism, they turn into tearing others down to elevate ourselves or tearing ourselves down to make excuses for our addicts. Blaming ourselves for causing someone to drink or use, or for being deficient because we can't get them to stop are other patterns of sick thinking—and they have no good purpose in serving God, others, or ourselves. Character defects are sneaky and, as we all know, our habitual patterns are hard to change. Why? Mohandas Gandhi explained how habits become so deeply engrained and powerful. He taught that "your beliefs become your thoughts, your thoughts become your words, your words become your actions, your actions become your habits, your habits become your values and your values become your destiny."[168] In other words, we are what we think. The distorted thinking that characterizes our disease is our personal saboteur. We need to battle Shame D. on that darn committee in our head who is screaming at us to try and save his job as well as everyone in the chorus of family, friends, employers, lawyers and more to forge a new life path. It's dizzying and, when we are in despair, it is very easy to close down under the weight of fear and confusion.

All that said, our defects are old friends. They are comfortable. Although our patterns may have stopped working for us, or worse, may be problem-

absurd. For me, the answer required that I fully understand the nature of character defects and our relationship with them.

The nature of character defects

In addition to the actions we take, character defects include our thought patterns and attitudes when making choices (which are reflected in our actions). To be clear, I'm talking about such things as selfishness, rationalization, anger, judgmentalism, false pride, greed, blaming, and perfectionism. You know them well—they are the tactics we all adopt and adapt to get our wants and needs met. These traits are instruments of willfulness that we deploy to fix, manage, and control other people and situations.

Without us noticing—because we are consumed by the progression of our disease and we isolate from others—we lose our sensitivity to balanced judgment. Our traits morph into patterns of stinking thinking that poison our ability to reason in line with our values. For example, we become habitual liars. I once heard someone in the Rooms describe himself as a pathological liar. After he got sober (in his case, stopped using drugs) and became self-aware, he lied even when he had no reason to—because lying was all he knew to do. In our disease, we lie to ourselves and others. With self-centered willfulness, we feel entirely okay asking others to lie for us to cover our tracks and get people off our backs. "If you love me, you'll do this" is a common refrain as we take others emotionally hostage. It's a no-win for everyone, which is often then compounded by compelling those we pressure to tell their own lies to hide their shame about our addiction. In this case it's easy to see the destructiveness. Why tell a painful truth when a little lie will do?

Willingness includes a decision, a shift from willfulness. In reference to our actions, that means making it a priority to do the right thing (remember your moral compass?) rather than satisfying our impulsive, selfish desires. Consider someone with a hybrid work schedule who has the habit of running errands during the workday. Clearly, it's more convenient to do them midday, and it seems there's no harm. We all can easily justify such a choice—our work always gets done, it's only a half hour or so that we may be gone, everyone has to take breaks now and then, the break gives us a

of thought and action that contributed to our problems. Removing the causative shortcomings sounds like a decent idea. Although it feels rotten to say that I am my problem, despite my best efforts I had not been able to fix myself, so at the very least I needed help to find a solution.

We can move toward a solution in Step 6. We hear in the Rooms that *change is God's job; our job is to get out of the way.* So, looking to God to remove our defects of character seems like an attractive option; however, I was not sure that I wanted to hand over control. Step 6 only asks that we get ready, not that we do it or even just agree to give anything away. For me, it seemed a low risk to proceed. I was left more aware that I might want to cultivate faith and trust in HP. Are you with me?

My fellows in the Program were proof positive that this removal is somehow possible and they buoyed my faith and trust. Those who were further along in the Steps were surely in a better place than I was and they assured me that the solution was simply doing what the Program said. I learned in the Rooms that starting Step 6 required that, at a minimum, I needed to be open to the possibilities. Since I had nothing good to lose (losing these defects would seem to be a win), I was becoming willing to be pleasantly surprised and that brought me closer to being entirely ready.

The committee in my head was chewing on the following facts: 1) you have a hard time trusting anything outside yourself; 2) you don't have the answer; 3) you need an answer; and 4) it needs to be more powerful than you are alone.

What's so hard here? My trust in God as my caretaker varies (wildly) from day to day although I have high confidence in my Program pals (who I view as God's messengers) and 100% confidence (faith) that some power keeps the universe moving in a **G**ood **O**rderly **D**irection (is that God?). There is little harm in allowing room for that power to do for me what my Program friends told me is possible and, in fact, I didn't want to risk being wrong…so, I decided to hold my doubt in one hand and extend the other to the possibility that the God of the universe could lend me a needed hand.

This is how we inch closer to being entirely ready and it brings us face-to-face with the very real question of whether we are willing to have our defects removed. My honest answer was, "It depends." I know that seems

open to the prospect that our HP can or will remove our character defects, allowing us to recover our best selves and create lives of joy and serenity. Being willing and open means we are not restricting something. To help you feel more comfortable, I will admit that I was open to the idea of my shortcomings being removed; at the same time I was not entirely willing because of fear about the consequences. We will discuss this aspect in a bit.

I believe Step 6 encourages us to aspire for total willingness, an attitude that reflects a level of energy and enthusiasm for welcoming what follows. Insofar as we are stuck and are looking to improve our lives, I interpret being ready in Step 6 as embracing the prospect of change, opening our minds and hearts to whatever God has in store. It's a tall order indeed. Change is scary but in the case of our disease, being stuck is scarier. Taking Step 6 reflects our making a decision and committing to do what it takes.

As we dig further into Step 6, it's useful to keep in mind our learnings from earlier steps. Step 6 stands on the shoulders of concepts such as faith, trust, courage, acceptance, surrender, and decisiveness. My decision to take Step 6 triggered a number of questions for me. Clearly, you will see my disease of control rearing its head.

- Do I believe that God/HP could remove character defects in general?
- Was HP doing this for me… or to me?
- Would doing this be a good thing?
- Do I want to ask God to do this and why not, if that applies?
- How would I become entirely ready, i.e., open and willing?

While we can consider these questions separately, they interact and are integral to the practice of the Program. Taking the time to tease them apart is essential here at Step 6 and in your recovery overall. Be patient and gentle with yourself. Remember, it's a journey.

To start, please remember the triad of Steps 1, 2, and 3: *I can't, He can, Let Him.* In other words, yes, God has the power or capability to do this for me. Step 6 is about *Letting Go and Letting God*—releasing your pride, fear, and ego, surrendering to a Higher Power, and being willing to accept the help of God (whatever that may look like). After Steps 4 and 5, most of us could see that we were a mess, our lives were a mess, and we had patterns

Chapter 10

Step 6: Alacrity

Step 6. [We] Were entirely ready for God to
remove all these defects of character.

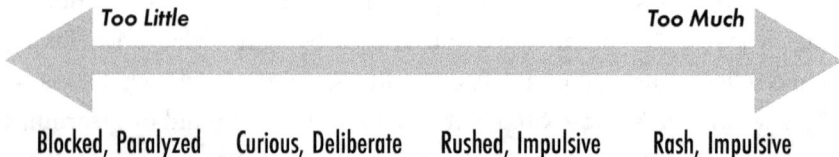

Too Little			Too Much
Blocked, Paralyzed	Curious, Deliberate	Rushed, Impulsive	Rash, Impulsive

Half measures availed us nothing.
—*A. A. Big Book*

Alacrity: A recovery perspective

Step 6 is a vital part of our recovery work. Hang in there. The language of this Step has the potential to be a bit confusing, so let's start by trying to understand what it means to be ready...for God to remove our defects of character. To be ready is to be prepared mentally or physically for some experience or action. Insofar as this Step relates to our shortcomings as seen in patterns of negative or destructive thought and action, I would suggest that we want to prepare ourselves with an eye to right thinking and right action. Thus, being ready for us addicts would mean that we have shifted our thinking and action from willful and self-serving to well-reasoned and guided by a moral compass.

Even more than readiness, it is willingness that takes center stage in Step 6. Willingness means that we are open to something. Here it's willing to be

- When do you take on the destructive attributes of shame? How might you do it differently now? How does that relate to accepting help? What about the positive aspects?
- Humility is telling the truth about yourself. Humiliation is when someone shames you for being you. What does that mean to you? How does acceptance release you from guilt and shame?
- What does your sponsor have that you want?
- What does it mean to you to have a hardened heart? How does it apply to you?
- Mussar teaches that lack of sensitivity reflects a heart that is blocked by the residue of inner qualities that are out of balance. Do you think any part of your heart is blocked or hardened?

Playlist
- "Hello"—Adele
- "This is me trying"—Taylor Swift
- "Secrets"—Mary Lambert
- "I'm Moving On"—Rascal Flatts
- "I Forgot to Remember to Forget"—Elvis Presley

- The world was created for me; I am but dust and ashes.
- From foolishness to discretion.
- Bring these hidden aspects of our nature into the light.
- What's my part in it?
- I will not regret the past nor run away from it.

Kabbalot to cultivate shame (*bushah*) as you take Step 5

If you lean toward excessive (destructive) shame you might try:
- Practice building inner awareness with 5-10 minutes of daily meditation. Imagine a beam of light penetrating your body, starting at the crown of your head. Watch it move through your brain into your spinal cord, moving through your arms and out your fingertips, down through your torso, legs, and out your toes. Release any shame that creates a restriction.
- Make a list of self-recriminations that you would like to release on a piece of toilet tissue. Flush it away. Write about the experience.
- Make notes for your pockets—the world was made for me; I am but dust and ashes.
- Tell your sponsor one secret that is making you sick.
- Share at a meeting.

If you lean toward sagging (building) shame you might try:
- Ask your sponsor to help you discern your role in a situation that is troubling you.
- Make notes for your pockets—the world was made for me; I am but dust and ashes.
- Soften your reactions to one problem each day and practice pausing until you have considered what the blessing might be.
- List inner qualities that are out of balance and obstructing your heart.

Prompts for journaling or study with you *chevruta*/sponsor
- "The shamefaced go to heaven/the world to come." What does that mean to you?

es. Humility is also key to the space we hold to forgive and love ourselves or others, and to allow others to help us see our way, which may include correcting distorted thinking.

One of my favorite insights from our tradition relates to this challenge. It says that everyone must carry two slips of paper, one in each pocket. One slip says "the world was created for me" and the other says "I am but dust and ashes." Depending on the situation, we can review the one that is appropriate. When we feel low (ashamed), being reminded that the world was created for us will raise our spirits; when we feel (overly) proud (no shame), we can be reminded that we are but dust and ashes. What a great tool to find balance in humility and *bushah,* as well.

The middah of *zehirut,* translated as illuminated awareness, is also fundamental to Step 5 and supports repair of our middot (*tikkun middot*) and work toward recovery. In Step 4 we took the first step toward tikkun middot by practicing *hitlamdut,* nonjudgmental awareness. This practice allowed us to recollect our stories. The next step toward tikkun middot practice is the *bechira* point, having choice and a range of options. Here in Step 5, we take the next steps toward recovery, examining our actions and becoming intentional in our choices about whether to sustain our historic patterns or seek change. In an essay on this topic, Alan Morinis interpreted this middah as "introspective self-knowledge of right from wrong," he connected that view to Maimonides' idea of illumination by naming it illuminated self-knowledge.[167] As we are instructed in Step 5, we illuminate our awareness by inspecting our actions to determine whether they are right and desirable. Morinis is referring to the attitude of thinking that we bring to our decision-making. His reference to light is significant and relevant to our blindness to truth and choices that come with being trapped in denial and stinking thinking when our disease is active. Awareness allows us to choose our response with intention rather than reflex.

Daily reminders to help work Step 5

Following are some phrases that you might use as your daily reminders. Feel free to choose one or create your own.

- One who possesses *bushah* will not easily sin (Nedarim 20a).

that we are not God. This is an idea that aligns with the teaching in *The Ways of the Tzakkidim* that the trait of shame results in humility.[164]

Eliyahu Dessler wrote that learning Mussar enables us to feel shame.[165] Humility, which is said to be a foundational soul trait, has a pivotal, paradoxical role in our cultivating bushah. Lack of humility is a barrier to feeling shame; too much humility engenders false shame. Some adjustment on the humility scale is necessary in order to open the heart and allow shame to penetrate and also to prevent it from depleting our spirit. Working with a sponsor, hearing other people's stories, and getting feedback on our self-perception are critically important to opening our eyes to the truth and using it help us make better choices. Guarding against extremes such as recklessness and paralyzing fear need to be priorities in our work.

Rabbi Luzzatto wrote about vigilance as a pathway for embracing bushah with the benefit of preventing us from individual wrongdoing. Acquiring Torah and living in accordance with it was his prescription for success in this arena. About this he says, "Align the course of your feet and [thereby] all your ways will be corrected."[166] Surveying future and past deeds for what was good or bad is what Luzzatto proposed to embrace the middah. The moral compass about which we spoke earlier is a useful tool for checking that we are headed in the direction that is in line with our values and our sense of personal purpose. When it sounds a warning of danger ahead, the internal voice of Shame B. (aka bushah) can be useful and direct us back to the intended path.

A last thought. It is useful to consider the extremes of the middah of bushah on your continuum. I see recklessness/impulsivity on the end for too little of the middah and paralysis and fear on the opposite end. As is often that case, too much or too little shame results in soul sickness.

Secondary Middot

Several middot share connections with the work of Step 5. Two come to mind as central. One is humility. The basis of this connection was explained in the preceding section. Cultivating humility (*anavah*) is important to being at peace with bushah. In the context of recovery, balanced humility is necessary for us to hold ourselves appropriately accountable for our choic-

It is important to acknowledge that we have a choice regarding the unsettled feelings about ourselves. We can become hard and closed or pliable and open, willing to change and learn from our mistakes so we can nurture meaningful lives and relationships. Our challenge is finding a healthy balance. That can only be possible if we set proper boundaries. Getting beaten up by brutal truths is no healthier than sugarcoating the facts of our past or ignoring them. Letting Shame D. hijack us is another form of imprisonment. Growing in recovery does not mean we need to succumb to that.

Talking about our experiences, revealing our secrets, and asking for help as directed in Step 5 is not easy for anyone—but it is necessary to get others' perspectives for us to see where our own might be distorted. Pirkei Avot teaches that "the shy person does not learn."[163] Going to meetings, getting a sponsor, praying and studying literature and sacred texts are pathways to the learning we seek. Shame B., from our committee, may show up for us as our *chevruta* partner, our sponsor, or another fellow in our recovery programs. In addition to helping us recalibrate our own [distorted] judgment of ourselves, alliances with others can give us the strength to consider the views of Shame D. from our committee, without ceding control and losing our balance.

Wrestling: a learning attitude

Learning from what we get wrong becomes productive, as our tradition encourages, when we feel regret for the hurt we cause without indulging in self-loathing. The story of Jacob exemplifies this. Jacob lied to his father, colluded with his mother, and stole from his brother. I did all those things, too, in my disease. I lied, cheated and stole others' dignity by manipulating them to get my way. It was all symptomatic of denial, driven by the desire to be in charge, to control and manipulate.

With time Jacob wrestled with life, learned from his mistakes, embraced his shame and regret, and refined his character to change himself. You may recall that Jacob's transformation was associated with a name change: he came to be called Israel, which is often translated as God wrestler. In our journey to recovery and righteousness, most of us struggle with the idea

furnace than to embarrass another person in public." I'm not sure if that fiery imagery would have stopped me from any of my antics when I was active in my addiction, but now that I am sober (trying to live as my best self), it is a potent reminder to stay on the right track. Even stronger warnings are found elsewhere in Talmud (Bava Metzia 59a): one who whitens his friend's face (i.e., shames him in public) has no share in the world to come. It even describes shaming another as a form of murder—the red blood leaving and the white pallor following.

A related and personally real aspect of this topic is what to do with the feelings of regret that we deservedly hold from having hurt others in the course of active addiction. Mussar teaches that we must engage with it. I draw on teachings of Rabbi Marc Margolius and the sacred use of memory for mindful forgetting to deal with this painfully important issue.[161] Mussar master Rabbi Paquda is also supportive. In teachings on reflection, he notes that forgetting is an essential element of a healthy, wise life.[162] Were it not for the ability to forget, he says, a man would never be free from melancholy. Provided that we reflect on the past with honesty and without judgment, and that we consider our impact through the eyes of others who we might affect, we can learn from our missteps and grow from them. In this way shame is productive.

How to cultivate shame

It is instructive to consider cultivating the middah of bushah—the healthy aspect of shame, that is. Denial blinds us; it keeps us locked in the prison of our distorted thinking. We may tell ourselves stories that we have not caused any damage. Or, we may be swayed by Shame D., from the committee in our head, that we are irredeemably bad. In either case, denial blocks us from truth that can nurture learning and growth. Although it may well trigger our dis-ease, the perspective of Shame D. might actually have some merit and should not simply be dismissed. Even if there is no merit to be found, looking for it has worthiness in itself. The consideration is the essence of honesty, openness and willingness about which we have spoken already, and these are the keys to this prison cell.

Both Twelve Steps and Mussar give us a choice—a *bechira*. The attitude we bring to situations is the mediating factor. The middah of bushah is lauded by Mussar masters. Let's see what our Sages had to say and consider how that supports recovery.

Shame (*Bushah*) is a blessing

Orchos Tzaddikim (The Ways of the Tzaddikim) looks directly at middot that need to be refined as we walk the path to righteousness. Shame is among the 28 traits described as a gate (meaning spiritual passage) in this cherished 15th-century Mussar text. Writing on the Gate of Shame, our Sages teach that "intellect is shame and shame is intellect."[158] Say what? In other words, shame is a kind of intelligence. We are smart to embrace shame because it keeps us out of trouble. The chapter underscores the positive value of shame, advising that shame and trustworthiness are interconnected: one who has shame keeps his faith with all men; one who does not keep his faith has no shame.

We can think about a properly developed sense of bushah as a mechanism to prevent us from individual wrongdoing. The middah may be likened to "a great fence and an iron barrier against all transgressions."[159] These ideas bring to mind the teaching of Pirkei Avot about putting a fence around Torah study; they both evoke an image for me of a wall to lean on when contemplating an action in my newly sober life. Regarding shame and teshuvah, our Sages taught that "all who commit a transgression and are ashamed of it are forgiven for all their sins… and the shame-faced one—to *Gan Eden* (heaven/Garden of Eden."[160] These teachings align with the idea that feeling shame about something we have done reflects a healthy regret, and that redeems us. I like that idea!

So how might the middah help you look to the future? Twelve Step programs and Mussar are blueprints for living, applicable in all our affairs. Although using a middah as a deterrent is generally not productive, I have found that imagery associated with causing shame is a useful red flag that does motivate me to stay the course in pursuing a life of integrity and recovery. I reframe shame as a reminder to live with intentionality and purpose. Talmud (*Sugya* 59a) states, "It is better for one to throw himself into a fiery

It so happens that there are two members of the committee with the same first name. Interestingly, they almost always have opposing views although they both say they have my interest at heart. Permit me to introduce these members of my committee to you. First is Shame D. I'd describe Shame D. as loud, critical, and always bringing up my past failures and deficiencies, fearful that I will repeat them. It seems like Shame D. expects me to be perfect. Truth be told, I have created a mountain of wreckage with my fingerprints on it so there is likely some validity in what Shame D. says. When I hear Shame D. talk about me, I feel fear, self-doubt, and self-loathing. I suppose that is better than rejecting the comments out of hand and remaining reckless. Shame D. is a destroyer. Shame D. is concerned about job security so an element of what's said is self-serving and I need to be on the lookout for the motives behind the messages.

Shame B. shares nothing in common with Shame D. Shame B. is soft-spoken, nurturing, and hopeful. I am struck by the way Shame B. motivates others and promotes openness to guidance, assistance and personal growth; Shame B. leaves room for me to grow, in part learning to lean on others—including the power greater than ourselves. As much as Shame D. focuses on yesterday with regret and on the future with anxiety and fear, Shame B. believes that we can learn and grow from our mistakes and focuses on being present in the here and now, confident that we have what we need to live life on life's terms. Shame B. is a builder, using lessons learned as a springboard, and wants me to avoid being traumatized by D.

Now, let's go back to the question. Is bushah a negative soul trait? I have come to see that all middot must be considered in context. No trait is simply positive or negative. For example, envy sounds like it's negative, yes? My envy of my teachers' knowledge of Mussar motivated me to continue learning. And my stubbornness (usually viewed as a negative) helped me overcome a *D* grade in high school biology and ultimately earn a PhD in a biomedical science. On the flip side, humility sounds like a positive. And it is unless you have too much of it and you shrink from responsibilities. Middot are not simply good or bad—and believe it or not, that is especially true of bushah/shame. Clearly, it can be negative but it can also be positive. Viewing shame with a learning attitude opens a door to growth.

rassment and humiliation, as we confront our own truths and fears about being judged for doing things that were dishonorable, immoral, or illegal. The middah of shame (*bushah*) is commonly highlighted as lingering and is an important aspect of what many discover in their work. With regard to our spiritual curriculum, Alan Morinis states that "the real quarry is traits that appear as sources of suffering, confusion, conflict, or any other negative outcome."[156] Shame feels like it hits the mark for Step 5. I am taking the liberty of focusing here on shame/bushah. Although the Mussar view on this middah is unconventional, it has great importance and power in helping us live with our disease by engaging with it and growing spiritually as we move forward.

The nature of shame

Shame is the first emotion mentioned in the Torah,[157] and the rabbis of the Talmud viewed shame and embarrassment as a positive moral quality. But shame has a negative connotation in our modern culture. So is shame a negative or positive middah? The question is not easy to answer but it's important, so let's look at it together.

I want to digress and talk briefly about committees; we all know they can be helpful in assuring that we have diversity of input when making decisions. Working with committees also has some well-known risks, including that the loudest member can take control of the conversation and the committee can get trapped in groupthink if members do not feel safe to voice their views. Managers can avoid making choices, deferring to the committee for tough decisions rather than considering the input and formulating a solution for the problem at hand.

I bring this up here because I have a committee in my head. It has its own meeting schedule and rules of order. I am an ex officio member because they use my conference room (my brain) but I do not have any power over the members and their chatter. Recently, my boss (the God of my understanding) has encouraged me to sit in and observe the meetings so I can better understand the dynamics and the output. I'm grateful for the chance to see what's going on; it has helped me know how to use the report-outs.

(confession) is essential to both *teshuvah* and recovery."[153] Lest there be any confusion, permit me to restate this as I hear it—for us addicts, seeing our part in and taking responsibility for how we harm ourselves and others is a step toward sober living. An attitude of accepting mistakes, being self-aware, confessing, and correcting ourselves is an important aspect of how Jewish practices enrich the work of recovery, including Step 5.

Making it personal: The relationship between Mussar practice and Step 5—admitting our wrongs

In taking Step 5 we admit the nature of our nature—how our patterns of thought pulled us off center and led us astray. Bringing our focus to creating better selves and healing our world, we embrace our responsibility to practice teshuvah. Our Mussar practices to repair those soul traits that are out of balance is at the heart of our Step 5 work.

Speaking as an addict whose story includes an array of unwise choices, I find it comforting that Judaism provides pathways for us to learn and return from our blunders and to reconnect with a God *of our understanding* and our community. Our tradition provides us with the opportunity to learn and grow from our mistakes. Jacob, who colluded with his mother to deceive his father and steal his father's blessing from his own brother, traveled a path to healing and wholeness with appropriate reflection and self-correction.[154] This is not to say that we will be free from consequences. Moses, for example, was denied the honor of leading the Jewish people into the Promised Land when he disobeyed God's command.[155]

Our mistakes can teach us what not to do in the future. They can also shed light on character traits that we need to improve in the here and now. It's worthwhile to note that Jewish wisdom teaches us to focus on this work one day at a time, as does Program literature. Knowing that our Sages did not intend for mistakes to shackle us in self-loathing or perpetual punishment helped me face the fear of doing Step 5. In fact, this aspect of our tradition allowed me to engage with my fear and be willing to look—and keep looking—at my past as an opportunity for learning and growth.

Often, integrity is identified as the principle underlying Step 5. For a variety of reasons, Step 5 begets lots of negative feelings, including embar-

undertake in Steps 4 and 5, can help us discover what is in our spiritual curriculum. It is important to look at the harm we cause ourselves as well as others. The less admirable parts of our stories include patterns and cycles of deception, manipulation, enabling, denial, blame, anger, and shame; and frustrating, hurting, and embarrassing others. These are important sources of understanding—they unlock fertile territory for the work of recovering our best selves through a life of balance in our middot.

I caution that the self-knowledge of Step 5 alone is not sufficient to achieve and sustain recovery or teshuvah. It's necessary to do the work of the subsequent steps to experience substantive relief and healing, to find a zone of recovery in which you can experience stability. That said, we must know ourselves to be able to confront what may be ugly, painful, or shameful within us. This knowledge of who or what we are changing from is the necessary starting point and the key learning in Step 5.

Finding meaning in the words

In our work to heal the world (*tikkun olam*) and ourselves (*tikkun middot*) as Jews and as addicts taking Step 5, we reflect and begin to see the harm and pain that we have caused others, as well as our transgressions against God. This is the prelude to cleaning up the problems, which is the work of Steps 6-9. Step 5 uses "admitting" as a primary tool for doing the housework.

Our Jewish Sages and our modern prayer language refer to the action of admitting, calling it confession. The act of confessing is intended to be part of our daily personal prayer practices, and it takes on heightened significance during the Days of Awe as the starting point for turning back to our best selves and a life that follows a path guided by spiritual principles, In reciting the *Vidui*, our core prayer of confession on Rosh Hashanah and Yom Kippur, we itemize how we have fallen short of the mark over the past year, and we acknowledge our failings and our character defects. Rabbi Joseph B. Soloveitchik concluded that "confession is the concretization of repentance" and a key component of teshuvah.[152] He taught that "speech, the verbalizing of confession, endows the thought of repentance with reality." Writing about Step 5, Rabbi Dr. Abraham Twerski shared that *"vidui*

how we must clean away what blinds us to the reality of the harm and hurt we are creating.

I posit that Tisha B'Av is also symbolically important to our efforts at spiritual understanding and renewal. Tisha B'Av, which occurs seven weeks before Rosh Hashanah, commemorates the destruction of the First and Second Temples (586 BCE and 70 CE). Why do I mention this here? As if describing the work of Step 5, Lew describes Tisha B'Av as "the moment when we turn away from denial and begin to face our estrangement from God in our alienation from ourselves and from others."[150] Lew's description evokes an image of choosing to turn away from the denial and isolation associated with our disease. Lew goes on to say that Tisha B'Av represents the time when we seek to understand and reconstruct ourselves, bringing focus to the difficult truth that "…catastrophes will keep recurring in our lives until we get things right, until we learn what we need to learn from them." Tisha B'Av represents hope that we can build a new future. Collectively, these traditions help us see how our nature has influenced our choices and prevented us from living healthy and rewarding lives. The many links to the work of this Step and the Program helped me surrender to my Step work.

Turning toward a solution

Torah teaches that committing any wrong toward a fellow human is breaking faith with God and requires that we confess and address the wrong that we have done as soon as we realize our error.[151] *Teshuvah* (turning or return) is how Judaism refers to the work of correcting transgressions. Maimonides described a step-by-step process for practicing teshuvah with the goals of taking responsibility, correction, forgiveness, and growth. His prescription for spiritual renewal includes stopping the offending behavior, feeling regret for hurting others, verbalizing our regret to God and whomever we have hurt and making a plan so we don't repeat the offending choices. According to Maimonides, the measure of our success is actually breaking the pattern by not reacting as we did in the past when confronted with a similar trigger.

Our Step work clearly parallels this Jewish process for spiritual renewal. In Mussar terms, the examination of where we have faltered, which we

iors. Rabbi Marc Margolius defines *bechira* as "opening our eyes and growing in our capacity to see that which was hidden."[145] Thinking about how blind we are to our truths, to our part in our disease and actions, perhaps these ideas will resonate and help you embrace Step 5 as the path to change.

I would like to offer a word of caution about reflection grounded in Jewish thinking. Taken to an extreme, self-accounting can be harmful. The contemporary philosopher Martin Buber wrote that one who had done ill and dwells in it cannot turn from it. Buber noted that "his spirit will grow coarse and his heart stubborn, and he may be overcome by gloom."[146] Mussar similarly encourages caution about dwelling on our past wrongs as an important aspect of engaging with our middot and self-accounting. Sharing what we uncover as part of Step 5 is a potent means to engage with our truths and merits tenderness and honor for our sensitivity and frailties.

Connecting Step 5 and Jewish practices of spiritual renewal

Beyond reconstructing our memories of specific events, Step 5 helps us spot our part in the recurring disasters of our lives. Because imperfection is simply a fact of life, we have many Jewish traditions that relate to the damage we do by missing the mark of "walking in God's ways."[147] The period of the Hebrew month of Elul and the Days of Awe (from Rosh Hashanah through Yom Kippur) call for heightened personal efforts to understand and confront ourselves as part of an annual cycle of self-accounting and renewal. Rabbi Alan Lew asks us to think about "the unresolved events and feelings that keep bringing us back to the same moment over and over again."[148] In the context of our addiction and pursuit of recovery, this idea—like Step 5—makes me mindful of resentments, destructive thinking, intergenerational trauma, fears and more that fill my inventory.

Regarding self-accounting, we read in *Duties of the Heart* that the yetzer hara weaves a curtain over our hearts, blocking the light of understanding; and that the longer it persists, the thicker it gets, until the sunlight cannot reach our house.[149] The traditions of Elul which help us clean house so that our lease will be renewed for another year serves much of the same purpose as Steps 4 and 5. To my thinking, this is another way of describing

The work in Step 5 to understand the exact nature of our wrongs has a strong foundation in Jewish practices and ideas. Undertaking the Step with quiet reflection (*hitbodedut*) and nonjudgmental curiosity (*hitlamdut*) allows us to bring a spirit of discovery into the work of developing awareness of our harmful and hurtful patterns, which is key to our healing.

Mussar teachers across the centuries identified self-accounting as the path to fulfilling our obligations and to protecting and purifying our soul.[142] Take a moment to reflect on the Talmudic quote at the start of this section; its meaning is not obvious. The shamefaced go to heaven? The teaching that those who are humble and self-aware are headed to heaven reflects the redemptive value of the work we are doing.

Mussar wisdom describes the consequence of impulsive, unexamined behavior as becoming lost in darkness and unable to discern good and bad.[143] Some invoke the *yetzer*, a concept of Jewish mystical thought, to help explain the choices we humans make. It suggests that the dominance of our *yetzer hara* (the inclination to be evil—i.e., selfish and self-serving) over our *yetzer hatov* (the inclination to be good) is one hidden aspect of our nature that contributes to our poor choices (refer back to Chapter 5 to refresh yourself on this *yetzer* concept). Indeed, the (im)balance of these inclinations might be an aspect of our nature that comes up in our accounting to explain lives of addicts like us that are inundated by wrongdoings and stinking thinking. Remembering my blindness—my denial—in the darkness of my active addiction, it is noteworthy that ibn Paquda promised that as a result of rigorous accounting, "the evil inclination will have no way of reaching you and misleading you."[144] Of course, the Program and Mussar are tools that guide us into the sunshine of recovery. Understanding our nature holds the key to altering our reactions.

Turning

While I do not believe that we can control the disease itself, I do believe that we can exercise choice in how we live with it. With this as a frame of reference, we can begin to envision a choice point where free will is at play and where we can break the cycle of reacting to the habitual thoughts and emotions which have distorted our thinking and fed our addictive behav-

of humiliation and pain that could have deterred him from being a repeat offender. Be patient. Over time, the brain fog and murkiness will recede.

In the Rooms, I learned that I was not unique in these feelings, and that there was no way around them. I had to engage with them and walk through them. The *Big Book* and other A.A. and Al-Anon Program literature do not deny our guilt, nor do they dwell on it. My sponsor promised me that as long as I didn't pick up my drug of choice, working Steps 6 through 11 would keep the toxic shame and humiliation in the past, where they belong. With the grace of Divine support, we can learn to let go of the toxicity, and we can begin recreating ourselves by harnessing our inner energy for good.

When we abandon the self-destructive manner of living, we grow in our sensitivity to the protective signal that we are about to do something wrong. I call that my conscience—it is usually a gentle voice that asks me if I am making a choice that aligns with my value system or moral compass. Shame feels bad and resonates like a loud bell. Perhaps its value is as a louder voice, a backup to guilt, giving us a stronger signal that we may be crossing a boundary, ignoring our values, and possibly hurting someone, ourselves included.

Proceeding with humility and gratitude along with appropriate guilt can serve us well. In my addiction, I had silenced these signal systems and was clearly lost in a forest of lies, deceit, rage, manipulation, blame, etc. Step 5 finds us looking deep into our forests. In my Step 5 work, I held onto an image created by C.S. Lewis, who described "shafts of delicious sunlight" or "Godlight in a wood." One of the recovery slogans is "go where it is warm." C.S. Lewis's imagery helps me keep walking through the woods looking for the warmth of recovery. I hope you will keep walking with me.

Shame (*Bushah*): A Mussar perspective on Step 5

> *The arrogant are headed to hell and the shamefaced to heaven.*
> —*Pirkei Avot 5:20*

I encourage you to resist holding anything back. With the benefit of time, I can say that my sponsor's most important questions were, "What did you leave out and what aren't you telling me?" That last lie, incomplete truth, or intentional omission has the power to negate the value of Step 5 work. Step into your full, true, beautiful, humanly imperfect self. The *Twelve and Twelve* of Alcoholics Anonymous explains that by beginning to tear down the wall of isolation, we set about becoming who God would have us be. I expected to feel empty and ashamed after completing Step 5, but instead I was able to accept my imperfect self. I felt empowered and wanted to take on the task of living. My confidence was bolstered by knowing that I could remain connected to the Program and my sponsor, who I began to trust, feeling loved in a very special way. Shedding the weight of regret opened space to love and be loved.

Guilt and shame

For many, Steps 4 and 5 open the gates to a flood of feelings related to the mistakes we've made, the people we have hurt, and all the things we wish were not so. My sponsor helped me understand this to be guilt and shame. The guilt—regret for doing something bad—may be deserved, but the shame we feel after the fact—feeling I am a bad person because of my actions—is toxic and unproductive. Transforming shame into something positive is a skill to be learned. In the meantime, *we must not confuse making bad choices with being bad people.* If we continue to ignore the warning bells and do something we know or believe to be wrong, that's a poor choice; guilt would be an appropriate response. The self-indictment of shame is not appropriate, though.

Being stuck in guilt and shame becomes a vicious cycle until we stop running and face ourselves. I supersized guilt into shame by internalizing it with a message I had crafted—that all the bad things I did made me irredeemable and worthless. Recovery opens us to awareness of choices that we had not been able to see. It's important to note that in this process, many of us become aware of the handicap of our brain fog. One fellow explained that the murkiness prevented him from drawing up and using memories

nerable than I had ever been with another soul. Digging into motives and how I thought through choices revealed a lot about my inner nature. I saw my part in things and began to see where I could make different choices going forward.

My sponsor pointed out my positive attributes and accomplishments in addition to discussing the patterns I had identified, where they came from and how they played out in things I had done in my disease. There was no second guessing, mockery, indictment, or judgment of what I shared, and no advice. In fact, there was some laughter and a lot of affirmation that I was not unique in some of what I had done. In sharing what I felt made me different, I discovered how alike we really are. The insights gave me hope that—with work on myself—I could break the cycles of my past and create a different future. My sponsor was vulnerable, too. She shared parts of her story with me which also helped me feel safe.

Insofar as I view my Program fellows as "God with skin on," being rigorously honest and vulnerable with someone else as we are called to be in Step 5 is an expression of trust in God as well as ourselves. Walking through the fear to complete Step 5 gave me a sense of safety and pride that I had not felt in a long, long time. The work helped me recover some essential part of myself, and I recalled microseconds of feeling good about myself, notwithstanding the damage I had done and needed to repair. Feeling unconditional love from my sponsor and my HP was an unexpected gift of this work. It was overwhelming, intoxicating, and frightening all at once. I felt so fragile, and I felt the weight of wanting to learn how to live with integrity and feel more connected. I faced a mountain of wreckage, but the work of this Step gave me a sense of confidence that I need not be alone and that I had the capacity to recover.

Feeling seen, loved, and relieved are important aspects of Step 5, and it goes both ways. The teller feels seen in a safe and affirming way. The listener is given the less obvious but no less important gift of being seen as a trustworthy and trusted recovery partner. They have grown from being perceived as an unscrupulous, pathological liar who was too unreliable to go to the store alone and who is now entrusted with someone's deepest, darkest secrets. Transformations like that are miracles of this work.

that make us wonder what happened to those good times. In this part of Step 5, we can do a deep cleaning by identifying and understanding what is no longer useful and triggered us to behave hurtfully.

A note of caution as we move on to this next part of Step 5. Just as it does not help to focus on getting older, shorter, and fatter, it is important not to get bogged down in guilt, judgment, and self-destructive shame. Quite often, it was these degrading messages that kept us drinking, raging or using. They hold us in the past. Instead, this is a time to get rid of the outdated items in our inventory and the secrets we've locked away for fear that they make us unlovable. Rather, we can keep it simple and pinpoint the areas that we want help with, focusing on what that will look like with the changes we must make.

You're as sick as your secrets. That is what we are told when we first come into a recovery program. Bringing the secrets into the light has many benefits. By working this Step, we begin the process of taking back the power which we had ceded to destructive obsessions. I saw many places in my life where I repeatedly acted like a child, hiding from responsibility and lying about my feelings. I was also able to see the things that I needed or wanted to change. Although I was scared, my trust in the Program and a power greater than myself pulled me forward and gave me the courage to keep moving toward change and healing.

Admit to another human being

Finally, (after I had moved through admission to God and to myself) came the challenge of sharing my inventory and perspective with another human being. I will not lie to you: I was terrified—heart pounding, palms sweaty. I hated my truth and was sure they would hate me, too. It is important to choose this confidant carefully. Look for someone who you feel will listen with an open heart, love, and curiosity—and then let go and practice trust. The fear that your listener will think less of you after hearing all that you have done is natural. It helps to keep in mind that they have their own stories and path to recovery.

I reviewed my inventory with my sponsor at the kitchen table. She did not skip a word I had written. I considered my story to be horrendous and embarrassing but I found the wherewithal to be more transparent and vul-

I encourage you to unburden yourself in whatever way feels right for you. The ease of working this Step will definitely depend on the nature of your relationship with the Divine. The belief in a loving God allows many people to easily draw the courage or companionship they may need to complete this work. You might reach out to a priest, rabbi, imam, or other spiritual advisor, or you might go to a place where you feel the presence of God and recite it out loud. Remember that being an agnostic or atheist is not a barrier to completing any of the Steps, including this part of Step 5. Think about who or what your personal HP is. Is it the Program, Mother Nature, the memory of a loved one? Connect to that source in whatever way is comfortable for you and share your inventory—out loud, of course. I have heard people describe reading their inventory out loud on a sun-drenched hillside or by the sea, accompanied by the soothing sounds of the incoming tide. The benefit is the same—you are setting the stage for becoming consciously honest with yourself and your world.

However you choose to do it, physical action is key. Release your ego. Feel the words. Look around and absorb the fact that you are not alone—you are embraced by unconditional love. I'm not sure how it works, but my experience was that the willingness and action taken in this first part of Step 5 softened the fear of becoming honest with myself in the next part of the Step. I know it sounds strange, but it's almost as if our ego gets to eavesdrop on the news, and the foretelling somehow softens the harshness in our truths.

Admit to ourselves

Having completed the admission to God, you are now at another point of choice, a *nekudat bechirah*—are you willing to look honestly at and own the behaviors identified from your past? You may have heard that in Steps 1-3 of the Program we learn to trust God. I hope that makes sense to you now. Trusting God gives us a wall to lean on as we continue moving through the Steps. Step 5 lives within a group of Steps referred to as "cleaning house" which spans Steps 4-9. Step 5 is our first opportunity to confront the facts of our past and learn from them. Like cleaning out a closet, some of what we find in our inventories will be patterns that are worn or out of style or no longer fit us. Other items might prompt us to recall wonderful memories

The inventory of Step 4 is taken in the solitude of our minds, and isolation creates the risk of self-deception. In our disease, most of us detach from our actions to spare ourselves feeling self-degradation, judgment, guilt, and perhaps even shame or sinfulness. Step 5 has us bring these discoveries into the light of reality by sharing the findings with someone else. The Program is gradual, but this hardly feels gentle. The verbal dimension of confronting damage we have done—like having to verbally apologize for some misdeed—solidifies our offenses so that they are tangible. For me, hearing and feeling my words fall off my tongue created a whole-body sensation. The tingle that comes with our admission in taking Step 5 is the movement of self-knowledge from the head to the heart, where it can energize us to recreate ourselves into the spiritual beings we were designed to be.

Admit to God

Much has been written about the order of disclosure described in Step 5—God, ourselves, and another human being. I was told that this sequence reflects the priority we should give to relationships as we work through recovery. In practice, this hierarchy lays the foundation for our becoming honest with ourselves and with our ability to feel loved and accepted.

A positive, safe relationship with some Higher Power is critical to the Program and certainly for proceeding with Step 5. This is one place in the Program where you can't fake it till you make it. Worry and distrust that we might be punished or seen as inadequate in the eyes of our HP are barriers to completing this Step. If you struggle with trusting your HP, be patient and take a step back to do more work on that with the help of your sponsor or spiritual advisor. That said, don't take your foot off the pedal. The *Twelve and Twelve of A.A.* cautions that the failure to complete this Step and break free from the past can put our recovery at risk.

If you are like me—looking for shortcuts or the easy way—you might ask why this Step is necessary at all if God knows everything already. This part of the Step is not about what God does or does not know. This is about us being willing to tell it all to our HP. There are some things that we must walk through—we cannot avoid them or walk around them—and walking through this gate is one of those things. Our admission to our HP is practice in setting aside our egos, coming clean, and showing up in our imperfection.

This is a classic example of the mismatch between someone's insides and outsides. The storyline about addiction being the cause of her problems was very real to the teller, who was trapped in misery, until the truth about the obsessive fear of personal risk was tested under the light of the facts and seen as a self-destructive pattern. Working Step 5 brings clarity to the exact nature of the wrong. We are all familiar with the addictive array of control, manipulation, resentments and lies, embarrassing moments, and words spoken in anger. Step 5 challenges us to look for the deeper motives and patterns of thought that underlie these behaviors or our reactions to them, and to harness the energy of inner pain and shame resulting from this self-awareness to power the work of seeking change.

Step 5 eases us into our truths, but there is no sugarcoating the ugliness or the importance of the work. Rami Shapiro describes the task with crystal clarity:

> We have to see the dark side of ourselves to really feel how the madness of our lives has darkened the lives of others perhaps even to the point of permanent stain. We have to be so painfully aware of our own wrongs and feelings that the very idea of repeating them makes us sicker than the sickness that drives us to do them.[141]

Admitting/entering

Let's turn to the aspect of Step 5 that asks us to admit our wrongs to God, ourselves, and another human being. I interpret the word "admit" here as allowing entrance, like entering through a gate or portal. Specifically, we are discovering newfound insights and allowing them to move into our consciousness, the understanding of our inner selves. The various circumstances that we recalled in Step 4 were windows into these insights which had been shuttered as secrets protected by denial. My Step 5 work revealed many places in my life where my pattern of thinking that I was not "good enough" lured me into or trapped me in unhealthy relationships or in situations where I was hurt or I hurt others. Hurt people hurt people, including our relationship with ourselves.

it. Eating carb-laden comfort food because we feel unattractive is an example. Seeing such patterns for what they are and uncovering the hidden aspects are essential to repairing them. The premise is that no defect can be corrected unless we clearly see what it is. Permit me to clarify this with a story recounted by a PhD executive who earned a six-figure salary and appeared to have it all—big job, big title, expensive vacations, kids, jewelry, house, etc.:

> I commonly said yes when I wanted to say no. I stuffed my feelings and stayed in an empty, toxic relationship for years. I almost killed myself in my efforts to people-please. For a long time, I thought this was what I was supposed to do to be a good spouse. He was a good provider, and everyone thought he was funny and such a good guy. They didn't experience his barbs or see him after 8:00 p.m., angry, hypercritical of others or passed out. And sometimes he'd go away with a "buddy" for a few days, leaving me to hold things together. Of course, he said he was just relaxing because his work is so stressful and I'm always on his back. Leaving him was not an option that even crossed my mind. He was constantly reminding me that without him, the house would fall down around me, that I'd have to live in a rented room, our kids would hate me, and I'd end up old, alone, and destitute.
>
> Working Step 5 helped me see that I was driven by destructive fears and shame. My fear of financial insecurity arose from issues my parents had, my shame was fed by personal insecurity that began in my childhood, and both were reinforced in my marriage. Although I wanted to blame the addiction in my home for everything that was wrong, my inventory revealed that the problems with my inner self long preceded my marriage. I had a bad case of stinking thinking.

Chapter 9

Step 5: Shame

Step 5. [We] Admitted to God, to ourselves, and to another human being the exact nature of our wrongs.

Too Little			Too Much
Recklessness	Remorse	Discretion	Paralyzing Fear
Impulsivity	Regret		
Selfishness	Guilt		

> *I am enough, I have enough, I do enough.*
> *12 Step fellowship wisdom*

Shame: A recovery perspective

You've already seen that the Twelve Steps are in a specific order, and that each builds on the foundation created by the Steps before it. Your Step 4 inventory will be the focus of work in Step 5. Like Step 2, Step 5 has some steps within itself that gently immerse us in the work. There is much to explore.

Buried treasure

On the surface, Step 5 seems to ask us to admit our wrongdoings. You may say, "I just did that when I wrote my inventory in Step 4!" But Step 5 is actually asking for much more. Our misdeeds, which seemed to pop up like weeds in our Step 4 work, are symptoms of underlying problems. These are self-destructive patterns in which we are stuck without knowing

- Put on a wristband in the morning and move it to the other wrist when you have left your comfort zone. If it has been moved by the end of the of the day, celebrate yourself.

Prompts for journaling or study with your *chevruta*/sponsor
- What middah is most important to your doing Step 4 safely?
- What prevents you from working Step 4?
- What positive traits can you use as a support wall in doing Step 4?
- How can you enlist the support of your Higher Power to help you in Step 4?
- How are your character defects related to your good traits?
- What have you learned about the role of secrets in your disease and recovery?
- How has Step 4 changed you?

Playlist
- "Warrior"—Demi Lovato
- "Not Afraid"—Eminem
- "This is Me"—Keala Settle and the Ensemble Cast of *The Greatest Showman*
- "Brave"—Sara Bareilles
- "Hero"—Mariah Carey
- "Roar"—Katy Perry

Daily reminders to help work Step 4

Following are some phrases that you might use as your daily reminders. Feel free to choose one or create your own.

- Yes, I can.
- I will be strong and of good courage.
- I face my fears and do it anyway.
- I can leave my comfort zone.
- Embrace a learning stance of nonjudgmental curiosity.
- Claim my seat.
- Gentle Strength.

Kabbalot to cultivate heart courage (*ometz lev*) as you take Step 4

If you lean toward excessive courage you might try:

- Zip your lip when you think someone else is wrong.
- Do not offer unsolicited advice. Instead, ask "Do you want to know what I think?"
- Try saying, "You may be right" to someone you are trying to convince of your way.
- Hold back from jumping in. Invite someone else to go ahead of you.
- Put on a wristband in the morning and move it to the other wrist when you have left your comfort zone. If it has not moved by the end of the of the day, try harder tomorrow.

If you lean toward sagging courage you might try:

- Envision being the "Little Engine That Could."
- Change your user ID or password to *ometz lev* (replace some letters with numbers, like a 0 instead of an o, for a more secure password).
- Speak out each day on truth that you would usually have hidden.
- Put a compass on your phone's home screen as a reminder of your moral compass.
- Talk about your failures without apologizing.

teaches that we can "hold a memory and enable it to serve its purpose of prodding us to grow, or to mindfully forget and release its power as a stumbling block."[140] Margolius challenges his students to "befriend their shadow and drain its toxicity," to "confront and defeat" it. He promises that we can grow in wisdom in relation to the past. That, in fact, is the promise of Step 4. Exercising these choices to recollect the past definitely takes us out of our comfort zone, and we must cultivate the middah of courage that derives from our inner spirit to do so.

Secondary middot

Recall that Step 4 demands a moral aspect of our inventory. Let's bring together the ideas of a moral inventory and courage to consider moral courage in our inventory. Risking embarrassment, exposing our vulnerabilities, and facing our fears all require courage. The willingness to do the next right thing and even do the inventory, including truth-telling of the hurt and damage we have caused, is an act of moral courage. Challenges such as this, although they may be anxiety-producing, activate *ometz lev*, courage or strength of heart. We can summon the strength we need for this middah by tapping into the faith and trust that we feel in the domain of our spirit, where all our middot reside.

Faith (*emunah*) and trust (*bitachon*) obviously interact with courage (*ometz lev*). They are essential to getting started in Step 4. I submit that without either faith or trust, it would feel impossible to consider undertaking the work of Step 4. This is a step in which just showing up is not enough. Two more middot that are also helpful at this stage are alacrity (*zerizut*) and the strength of discipline (*gevurah*). The work of Step 4 is taxing. It is best to approach it as a marathon, not a sprint. Bringing energy and the strength to go the distance is critical to completing the work with the necessary thoroughness and fearlessness. For many, confronting their truths requires the willingness to sit with the pain of what we recall and uncover. This is the embodiment of patience (*savlanut*) and requires that we cultivate self-compassion (*rachamim*). Mussar provides an array of resources to help us accomplish this important work.

stressful. I was driven by fear, naivete, and the shackles of denial. I did get fired and divorced, and my kids crashed and burned. I assumed it was all my fault, that the messages I was getting about my many shortcomings and failures were entirely true. The facts were that I was living with an active disease—my spouse's and mine—and that our kids were the victims. Oh, how it hurt to admit that.

Among other things, my inventory—which spanned over 14 typed single-spaced pages—helped me see how I had come to be in that situation. I became aware of how I had lost my way due to things that happened in my childhood and repeated themselves as a pattern to which I was blind until I looked over the arc of time. The insights also revealed that I had choices, as well as responsibilities, that I was neglecting. It was insidious, and I was so distant from who I wanted to be! With the help of my sponsor, I found compassion for myself; I also discovered the first glimmers of hope that I had the capacity to rebuild myself and my life.

Cultivating *ometz lev* (heart courage)

The inventory done in this Step inevitably engenders fear and shame for us addicts, and our discomfort is intensified because we can no longer dull it with chemicals nor divert ourselves by obsessing over someone else. Regarding the fear that holds us back, Luzzatto acknowledges the natural resistance that each of us has in thinking about our past. Rabbi Luzzatto recognized the missed opportunity in our reluctance.

One of the reasons we go to Twelve Step program meetings is that hearing others' stories reminds us of our past, including all the associated loss and pain. This helps keep us sober. Equally important, in the Rooms we hear our fellow travelers' encouragement to be strong and courageous. Does this sound familiar? When Moses was turning over leadership of the Israelites, he said to Joshua, "Be strong and of good courage."[139] Remembering these messages is critical for us addicts, for whom recovery—like the Israelites crossing the Jordan River—is a choice for a better future.

In Rooms of recovery, we often hear about "looking back without staring." Doing so is a challenge; we must find the courage to remember to forget. Rabbi Marc Margolius refers to this as "mindful forgetting." He

find what has been hidden. Remember the power of denial that we had to deal with in Steps 1 and 2? Jewish wisdom recognizes that

> ...the will is extremely effective in hiding evil from our mind. It is also very successful in leading us astray with a multitude of errors and delusions. But *Hashem* demands from us nothing less than the truth, and nowhere more than in dark places of the heart. ...God demands that we find the truth even in those parts of the mind which the will has succeeded in plastering over so they are almost inaccessible.[137]

In his essay addressing the search necessary to realign with our Higher Power, Rabbi Dessler described the effort as a "painstaking [search]...in all the nooks and crannies of the mind like searching for *chametz* [foods forbidden during Passover]." He said, "the waves of our wrongdoing are hidden deep and will reveal themselves only to the patient and determined seeker."[138] All of that sounds pretty thorough. And need I remind you that hitlamdut *demands* that we look and not judge? Jewish tradition rejects humiliation as an acceptable outcome of the search. That ideal is surely applicable when doing this work.

Making it personal

I recall one year during my annual checkup that I mentioned to my doctor that I was having periodic feelings of light-headedness and doom. At the time, I was in my mid 40s and generally healthy. The doctor asked if I was under any stress, and my answer was a definite no, nothing unusual. Another probing question or two revealed that I was worried about losing my job because of the consequence of drinking; both kids were out of control, one filled with anger and the other secretive, delinquent, and failing school; and I knew I was letting my spouse and family down because my spouse was always telling me so.

Honestly, I thought I was fine and that all young managers like me had lives like mine: chaotic, unpredictable, unfulfilling in the moment, and

was fulfilled. If the middah was not actualized there was a lesson to learn for the future. This might be considered a precursor to the column-based inventory described in the *Big Book*, although Levin's inventory lacked the thoroughness and quiet reflection of the *Big Book*. That said, many of Levin's ideas remain in use today. For more details, refer back to Chapter 4. Also, hold onto your ideas of daily review for your work on Step 10.

Subsequent to Levin, Mussar teachers appreciated that achieving change at the level of our middot (our inner lives) required an approach that penetrates deeper than the intellect. Our work is to uncover more profound insights than is possible with intellect alone. Disciples of Rabbi Salanter introduced introspective practices into yeshiva curricula beginning in the 20th century. Taking time away from intellectual activity of Talmud study to guide students in cultivating individual traits with personal Mussar practice was a major innovation.[135] In essence, the inventory chart was refined and adapted to become a practice of daily journaling, an approach to *cheshbon hanefesh* which is now commonly complemented by meditation (*hitbonenut*) and silent retreat (*hitbodedut*). Please note that all these techniques take advantage of silence, quieting diversions and chatter whether from within our own minds or from outside of us. The journaling mentioned here is the seed of the autobiographic inventory. Like the writing we do in our Step 4 work, the written accounting of our soul traits enhances the impact of our efforts.

As we wrap up the application of a Jewish wisdom to Step 4, I want to mention an aspect of mindfulness, a practice of inner learning that is critical to cultivating courage of the heart. *Hitlamdut* (the ongoing process of learning how to learn) is the first step in a practice called *tikkun middot* (healing our character traits) which we will explore further in the steps that follow. Hitlamdut requires a "stance of non-judgmental curiosity," which is the necessary condition for our self-study.[136] This concept fits perfectly with the idea of non-judgmental observation that is so important in Step 4.

To continue learning together, let's put a Mussar lens on the remaining ideas in Step 4, starting with the searching and fearless aspects of remembering what's forgotten. As we've said, the goal of our search for self is to

Clearly, Jewish teachings on the value of knowing ourselves are consistent with the concept of inventory that is captured in Step 4. The Program also teaches that remembering reveals strengths on which we can build and helps us understand what we need to bolster in order to live in recovery. Along these lines, Jewish wisdom says:

> Woe unto a person who is not aware of his defects, and who does not know what he must correct. Much worse off is the person who does not know his strengths, and who is therefore unaware of the tools he must work with to advance himself spiritually.[131]

Similarly, we learn from Jewish teachings that

> …the process of recollection opens the way to a reassessment of the past and that's also to the possibility of a different view of the future. The tendency not to remember mistakes and stumbles (except, of course, those of others) perpetuates the present path. Only a re-examination of the things that slip from memory, of the matters that one does not wish to recall, creates a new opening and allows one to choose a different path.[132]

How to do an inventory

Rabbi Levin was the first in the Jewish world to offer a method for living in constant pursuit of self-improvement. His book, *Cheshbon HaNefesh* (1808), aligns with the technique that Benjamin Franklin laid out in his autobiography (published in 1790) and called the "Plan for Attaining Moral Perfection."[133] Using a system of charts, code words, and a nightly inventory, the individual was meant to set out to live without any faults. Levin's method was time efficient and easy to follow, and it used a daily inventory to track progress.[134] Middot were studied on a rotating basis, and the nightly inventory was used to consider if the intent of the middah being studied

recovery that healing allows us to reach a point where "We will not regret the past nor wish to shut the door on it."[124]

Memories can be a source of joy and pride, but they can also be a source of discomfort. One of the most sacred periods on the Jewish calendar is the Days of Awe, from Rosh Hashanah (Jewish New Year) through Yom Kippur (Day of Atonement). During the month of Elul that precedes the Jewish New Year, we are supposed to look deeply into our hearts and practice *cheshbon hanefesh*, an accounting of the soul. We are challenged to remember what we did well and notice where we fell short in the year that has passed, with an eye toward learning where repair and growth are needed. There is a lot of heavy lifting in this contemplative work. Rabbi Alan Lew describes this work to know ourselves in preparation for the Days of Awe as setting aside time "to engage in self-examination and self-judgment and engage in a spiritual accounting."[125] I interpret this as taking an inventory of how we are showing up and moving through the world, how we are manifesting our values through our middot. Insofar as our soul traits are the heart-based expression of how we are living Torah, it seems right to examine them as part of our preparation for the Days of Awe.

Beyond such annual traditions, the idea of an inventory as a tool for self-assessment and development of positive character traits has deep roots in Mussar tradition. Self-accounting was viewed as a fundamental principle of a spiritual life as long ago as the 11th century.[126] The idea has survived hundreds of years, retaught many times over by generations of Mussar masters. More than just remembering, our tradition teaches that "we must vigilantly contemplate and survey our actions and conduct or risk the loss of our soul and walking in darkness."[127] We alcoholics and addicts know that our disease is a shroud that wraps our lives in darkness.

Ibn Paquda saw this accounting as a constant obligation to heighten our awareness of being observed continually by God.[128] A technique for performing an ongoing personal inventory was first advocated in the Mussar text *Cheshbon HaNefesh*[129] and later embraced by Rabbi Israel Salanter, the father of the modern Mussar movement. Salanter believed that character building requires that self-evaluation (and self-criticism) be performed at least weekly, preferably daily.[130]

Seeing it in black and white is an opportunity to break the cycle of hiding from the truth. This action of writing also helps us slow down so that we have the time and space to really think about what we hear ourselves saying and learning.

Once you have completed your inventory, do stop and congratulate yourself on this accomplishment, but don't stay there long. Being fearless and thorough is likely to have brought some unpleasant feelings and facts into the light of day. Harness the courage it took to complete Step 4, or borrow some if you need it, but definitely push yourself to keep going. Contact your sponsor to accompany you in taking Step 5. I know it sounds impossible to believe, but I promise that relief will come after you have shared. You are surely one step closer to the serenity and joy of recovery. These principles and practices reappear in Step 10 as part of maintaining our clean house. The repeated cycle of self-examination is something I have come to love as an integral part of my healing, growth and serenity.

Heart Courage (*Ometz Lev*): A Mussar perspective on Step 4

> *We must know from where we came to know what our legacy will be.*
> —Pirkei Avot 3:1

Step 4 is about knowing ourselves through remembering. Judaism has a lot to say about remembering. In fact, Jews are a people of memory.[123] The Torah instructs us over 150 times to remember, and remembering is a significant part of Jewish life. We are exhorted to remember the Sabbath and the generations who came before us, and we commemorate important events of the past such as the Exodus from Egypt, the destruction of the Holy Temple in Jerusalem, and the Holocaust. Jews recall and retell stories, stories that bind us together in shared history and as sources of wisdom, because it is important to learn from the past. This core idea, found in teachings that go back to our earliest sacred texts, aligns with the idea in

the risk that we might deceive ourselves. Indeed, each time I do Step 4, new things come to light.

Beyond the direction provided by the *Big Book*, rehabilitation facilities often have their own preferred process and format and many of the other Twelve Step programs have workbooks to assist with the action of taking a personal inventory.[122] By answering questions on a variety of topics related to character traits, both positive and negative, each addict comes to their own conclusion about their moral condition. The *Blueprint for Progress: Al-Anon's Fourth Step Inventory* is an excellent tool for anyone willing to undertake a rigorous inventory. There are many others readily available. For those who need structure, workbooks are a great tool.

One thing you need to guard against in Step 4 is comparing yourself. Looking at our character traits in relation to some external ideal carries the risk that we will punish ourselves needlessly for falling short of perfection. We are warned not to compare and despair. Comparing myself to others, like those on the CNN List of Heroes or *Time* magazine's Person of The Year was my pattern, and it did not serve me well. This is generally unproductive unless we can find inspiration in seeing someone else's strength and resilience. I have spoken with people whose reference standards come from their religious traditions, such as the seven deadly sins in Christianity or the 613 commandments of the Torah in Judaism. While such an approach may reinforce awareness of the need for Divine assistance, I can't get even close to perfection, so I worked with my sponsor to look for an approach that was most motivating for me. Whatever your approach, we will process the inventory in Step 5 to get a big-picture perspective on our patterns. The insights we develop will help us focus on what boundaries were missing so that we can repurpose our feelings and fortify our inner systems to consider choices going forward.

A final thought: Talking about it makes you *feel* better; working it helps you *get* better

The Step 4 inventory is a powerful tool for confronting ourselves, albeit an uncomfortable process for most. I want to recommend strongly that you write it out in whatever format you and your sponsor decide to use.

which I had internalized as my being *not good enough*. No one ever told me those things. My brain wrote the story all on its own, starting from those childhood experiences. Working with my sponsor on Step 5 helped me link this Step 4 nugget to patterns that cast a long shadow and persist in my adult life. I promise you that this work can be very powerful if you open yourself to it.

So that you realize how innocent and potent these triggers can be, I can tell you that the origin of my distorted thinking was a severe food allergy that required intense parental intervention beginning when I was a small child to assure my safety. My unconscious takeaway, however, was that I was weird and incapable of taking care of myself. Many of my addict and alcoholic friends also felt "less than"—they were either explicitly labelled so or just felt not smart enough, not funny enough, not wealthy enough, too short, too ugly, too much or not enough of something compared to everyone else. In any case, our inventories revealed that we all felt we did not fit in and we self-medicated in one way or another to relieve the distress and feel better. And thus our addictions were born.

An alternative to the autobiography is a list inventory. A.A. uses resentments and fears as focal points. The inventory starts with making a list of people, institutions, and ideas with whom they are angry. Next is capturing what caused their resentment and how it affected them—low self-esteem, financial insecurity, not meeting personal goals, failed personal and sexual relationships, etc. The final list is capturing their part in the situations. Things like selfishness, dishonesty, self-seeking, rage, manipulation and fear are common. As with many of us, my list included resentment about getting fired from my job. The *who* this resentment was directed toward were the HR representative and my boss. The event of being fired triggered shame and financial insecurity. My part was that my attendance was unreliable and I was insubordinate. Someone else I know was fired after getting caught using drugs on company property. After all these years, I do see my part and accept that I did a lot to myself. In contrast, my friend protested that "I was in *my* car when I was using, not company property!" The amount of time it took for me to see my truths reflects that such an approach carries

to be. Self-awareness helps us see our triggers or the signs of our decline, and opens a space where we have the choice whether to reach out for help rather than risk relapse. Along with fearlessness, moral courage means that we are willing to do what's right—which in this case means looking at our role in the problems we are battling.

Taking our inventory

Are you chomping at the bit to proceed or terrified to do so? Perhaps a little of both, worried about what you will find and not knowing how to proceed? There is no one right way. Most of us in the Program are likely to suggest doing what our sponsors asked us to do. My experience, having done Step 4 many times myself as well as working with sponsees, is that the key to this Step is just doing it. Permit me to tell you a secret: there is no perfect inventory. Beware that perfectionism may be a mask for fear. Whatever the cause, it will hold you back. The method you use will be fruitful because this Step is not about the method. The value is in becoming open to learn something about ourselves. The inventory is something you can and will likely get to repeat over the course of your recovery. Each time reveals a new part of the puzzle. Also, keep in mind that the effort is not useful if your focus is on labeling your characteristics as good or bad or reinforcing self-hatred, intense self-criticism, or blame. Open-mindedness, honesty, and willingness—you're golden if you bring those learning attitudes to the task.

Writing an autobiography is one approach to doing an inventory. Memories may reveal where feelings about ourselves came from and help us see what led us to make choices that made us feel better but were not healthy. Looking over the landscape of our lives may show how patterns or themes were often repeated in one way or another, fueling our spirals. By way of example, my story included memories involving food-related events. I know that it sounds silly but recalling a birthday party at age five or six and a camp experience at age 12 was revealing. In both instances I was given special food because of an allergy. Remembering, which includes feeling the discomfort of being singled out as different from so long ago, led me to an insight about an early childhood message of being different,

our intentions. In other instances where we have gone astray, our good points or assets—as given by the Divine in our personal design—may have been ignored or misused, and they need to be recalibrated or simply reloaded. Because we are human, our inventories will indeed reveal certain things we did that were morally wrong, and we will identify some people to whom we owe amends. Let all of that go for now. That is not the work of the day.

In living day to day, our moral compass guides our judgment, decisions and choices that are not necessarily fact-based, and these are reflected in our behavior. My compass kept me out of trouble until I stopped consulting it which, not coincidentally, was around the time that my addiction started to progress. I think it's fair to say that as part of our disease, our moral compass gets lost or stuck in our pockets. We lose sight of right and wrong, and we find ourselves lost in lies we tell ourselves or others. Typical moral lapses I've heard addicts admit in the Rooms are that they are cheating employers and stealing from those they love. For example, many asked spouses to lie to their boss about being late or out sick when they were in jail with a hangover and DUI—a form of stealing time from the company. Some lied to a spouse about taking a client to dinner when the truth was that they were stopping for a drink before coming home. Others lied to relatives who they solicited for money to help with the rent because their rent money had gone up their noses.

For almost all of us addicts, our choices and behavior go askew because our substance of choice (which may include sacrificing our well-being to rescue another) clouds our thinking and judgment. Systems of self-regulation that were thrown out of balance as we did battle to protect our disease trap us in the zone of unwise choices. Failing to consider our values or ignoring guidance that we do not like is evidence of emerging and progressive insanity that we dismiss but that is part of our disease.

The purpose of Step 4 is to understand how our character traits—thoughts, feelings, and actions—have failed us, or rather how we have failed at them and allowed our addictions to spiral. The inventory brings to light the gap between who we say we are and who we really are, and shows us how we can start recovering to become who we want and were created

Please don't be deterred if this prospect is frightening, even if it causes you to have second thoughts about the Program. I sat on the pity pot so long that my feet fell asleep. Rest assured that Step 4 is not meant to make you feel bad about yourself, past or present. It was helpful for me to think about it in a God's-eye view. From this perspective, our experiences are valuable sources of learning—opportunities to grow and learn to do the next right thing—and it's never too late to start. We can bring curious compassion to bear, provided we are taking steps to open the door to change and recover. Although Step 4 may fill you with fear, searching fearlessly empowers you to move forward.

The moral part

The last imperative of Step 4 is that our inventory is conducted though a moral lens. Insofar as morals relate to our values, this aspect of the step brings our focus to the standards we use to make choices. We learn some values from role models, and others seem to be inborn. Not all of us are lucky in regard to our teachers, but this alone does not cause or prevent our disease. I've heard an array of stories about people who had families with infinite resources, some who lived with active addiction, some with dry drunks, and even some with felons. As the stories vary, so do all the players in them. Some people lost their way, while others remained on a straight path. For many, the stories have surprising and happy endings. Negative circumstances can't be ignored, but they need not be life sentences. They contain lessons that can help us grow into the best version of ourselves, if we can remain open. Taken together, the set of beliefs that we form from the totality of our experiences becomes our moral compass. We rely on it to help us stay within the boundaries of what we believe is right and wrong.

The points on our moral compass could be called aspects of our character. Some of these characteristics are beneficial and some have negative value. The negative characteristics are commonly referred to as "character defects" in the Rooms of recovery. It's important to say here that having character defects does not mean we are defective! Character defects are simply traits that don't serve us well. They may be defenses that just don't work anymore, or they may be tendencies that can lead us to fall short of

whispering about me. My family talked about me as if I were not present, so I often felt like a pariah.

Learning in the Rooms that I was a child of God and a person of worth gave me a different perspective. I learned to lean into this "Godness" to stabilize myself. I was not trash because I was an addict; I was sick. And although I felt alone, I was not. The God of my understanding that was talked about in the Rooms was there for the taking. Engaging with faith and trust fed my fearlessness. I've heard it said that courage is fear that has said its prayers. Courage—fed by my faith and those all around me in the Program—helped me to take the action of undertaking Step 4.

A passage in the Al-Anon reader *One Day at a Time* is right on point. When we concentrate on today's activities, there will be no room in our mind for fretting and worrying.

> Just for today I will not be afraid of anything. If my mind is clouded with nameless dreads, I will track them down and expose their unreality. I will remind myself that God is in charge of me and mine and then I only have to *accept* his protection and guidance....If I live just this one day at a time, I will not so readily entertain fears of what *might* happen tomorrow.[121]

I don't know anyone who relishes the idea of doing Step 4. Personally, I started several times before I carried through. The scope was so overwhelming that I was paralyzed. I feared what I would find, especially knowing that Step 5 required revealing it to someone else. Ultimately, I found courage by listening to fellows and my sponsor, who assured me that Step 4 is simply about getting to know ourselves better. Being fearless in doing our inventory is the key to finding the truth about ourselves. I was shocked at what I found—specifically that although I had been wounded, which explained certain patterns of thought (and errors in my inner computer code), much of my misery and the damage around me was self-inflicted. I also saw that blaming others for our shortcomings leaves us living in victimhood. That was not a place I wanted to be.

a springboard for believing in ourselves and neutralizing the power that our weaknesses and destructive thoughts have over us. You may have heard the common saying that those who forget the past are doomed to repeat it. Learning to see the past as a learning experience opens hope for a different future. Even a tiny opening leaves room for courage to poke its head out and prod us forward. In this way, the inventory through which we reconnect with ourselves can empower us to live with ourselves in sobriety. The courage to engage with our fear and leave our comfort zone lies within our heart, the seat of our spirit, and that is where Mussar can exert its power.

Fearless

Let's pivot and look at the fearlessness aspect of Step 4. Being fearless does not mean you will have no feelings of fear. Rather, it means you will not let your fears stop you from being thorough in your inventory. Most of us are fearful when we arrive in the Rooms. The prospect of death or illness from the disease, financial insecurity, or broken homes and careers is scary. Taking an inventory is anathema to what we think we need. For the longest time, I allowed myself to believe that if I didn't look, I could pretend that there was nothing there to see. This is like blaming the dryer when my pants are too tight: As long as I don't get on the scale, I don't have to look at my eating habits and weight as the problem.

If you are like me, you might be beating yourself up with thoughts of all you've done wrong, and resist getting on the scale. My insanity included catastrophizing. In that frame of reference, I was punishing myself and driving myself to hide in fear and victimhood. But there was a paradoxical relief from the work of Step 4; I discovered that things were not as bad as I feared they could be. How surprising is that? Growing self-awareness allowed me to see that my fears about taking my inventory were tied to shame and the idea that I would be judged by others as a failure, a loser, or a malicious individual. My feelings of being less than enough keep cropping up in my history and turned out to be a root cause of my choices, many of which did not serve me well. In my past, people did not want to be with me. I was all too familiar with walking into a room and sensing that people were

with them, and find the strength to keep moving forward and accomplish difficult tasks like our inventory. Tapping into that spiritual domain via reflection, prayer, and community gives us the courage to follow through on actions that are necessary to break the cycle and would otherwise be impossible for us.

The first three steps, each of which builds on the previous steps—combined with the support of a sponsor and the fellowship—are the resources that can sustain you as you take Step 4. You can do this! Although paralyzed with fear at first, I felt motivated by finding the courage to engage in doing my inventory, and further encouraged by what I discovered. I urge you to trust the process. Let's move on together and unpack how the Step tells us to approach this work. Your future self will thank you.

Searching

I interpret the searching part of Step 4 to mean that we need to be thorough. Searching is a word that connotes something more than looking. For example, when I misplace my phone or keys, I search for them. There is a palpable intensity in my efforts to find what I am searching for. This contrasts with simply looking for beautiful flowers while on a walk. Step 4 challenges us to conduct our search with that kind of dogged energy.

Having become stone-hearted in the grip of our disease, to protect ourselves from things like judgment, guilt, and fear, Step 4 requires that we do a 360-degree search. As we begin to think about the unhappiness we've caused, we look around at relationships with family, friends, employers, etc., and we look at our relationship with the Divine. Rigor in our inventory also means that we must turn inward and delve into the corners of our heart and memories to get in touch with our full story. We cannot pick and choose the good stuff—this Step challenges us to look in the rearview mirror and acknowledge all the stuff we don't want to look at or let anyone else see. The goal is to see it, not stare at it.

I do not know one single person among us, when they are active in their disease, who wakes up in the morning happy with themselves or their history. The survey of our lives, from childhood to hitting bottom, reveals that we are more than our addiction. Rediscovering our strengths can be

this early stage in recovery to feel exposed and vulnerable, filled with fear, self-doubt, shame, and regret. Feeling those feelings is progress! Don't despair. The first 30 days in rehab is often called "feelings school," reflecting the flood of newfound emotions that go along with the fact that we are not numbing ourselves. I was so detached from myself when I first walked into the Rooms that I did not know what I felt, what foods I liked, what clothing style felt right, or how I enjoyed spending time on my own. Feelings like self-loathing and shame may pop up. I had no goals and was guided by a warped sense of right and wrong and good and bad. I was lost. I was relieved to learn that I was not inherently bad. I was sick; I simply had some bad code. The same likely holds true for you.

This isn't easy, but it's worth it

While human nature tends to draw our attention to flaws and mistakes, I assure you that the purpose of Step 4 is not to tear you down. Most people who are in the Rooms with us carry heavy cargo such as guilt and regret. It may be justified by our past behaviors, which were selfish and dishonest, but that's not our whole story. Although long ago forgotten, most of us will remember accomplishments and relationships for which we can feel pride and gratitude along with the ways we fell short. This is solid ground on which to start rebuilding. HOW? The honesty, open-mindedness, and willingness that gets us through the first three steps and to the threshold of Step 4 can fuel our courage to keep going.

Please keep in mind that, like much in life, the inner resolve we need appears intermittently, but over time we do have the resources to prevail. Here is one way I think about it: The word willingness is long and has a "g" near the center. Among the many straight letters, we find the source of the goodness that is uniquely ours and the qualities of our "Godness" such as courage that we all have within.

Now, recall that in the Step 1-2-3 triad, we cultivated faith and trust in something bigger than ourselves, and we became willing to try relying on it. These were actions of the heart, the spiritual domain where our "Godness" (courage) lives along with faith and trust. Courage of the heart helps us push through. Our Godness enables us to feel our feelings, engage

how we were molded and how we continue to hurt and damage ourselves and others. Hurt people hurt people. As if we are on an archeological dig, we search for nuggets among the mountains of dirt that we move to find what's hidden. Our inventories help us expose dormant talents, secrets that make us sick and dreams that we abandoned. We look for clues in personal tendencies and traits, in our patterns of thought and behavior, and in past relationships and memorable events. The output of Step 4 will be carried into Step 5 where we will incorporate awareness and realization to construct a powerful road map that shows us how to better navigate the future.[120]

The relationship between our inventory and our spiritual domain

The process of taking our inventory gives us some structure for finding and facing the root cause(s) and consequences of our addictions. Through remembering, we begin to see our part in the story. Over time, the patterns of thought and action that contributed to the choices we made (or avoided making) become clear. The realization that our problems are not always someone else's fault shatters the delusion that others are solely to blame. But we can't stop there if we want to get better. Beyond intergenerational influences and our genetic predispositions, we must be willing to search for and look at the hidden dynamics that drive us for the work to be effective. This is a frightening prospect. At a high level, for example, we may identify the desire for power and control, security, attention, or prestige that grew out of neglect in our childhood homes. Looking more deeply, many find that fear, anger, ingratitude, self-pity, or resentment lurk below the surface. In a variety of ways, these are barriers to accessing our spiritual domain, and breaking through these barriers is key to change.

The focus of the work ahead in Step 4 relates to the inner domain that we were endowed with as we received the breath of life. This aspect of us is a source of our unique beauty. Think of your inner makeup as the computer code that makes an app work. If the code is corrupted, the system does not work well. Now, imagine that life circumstances corrupted some of our code. Our work in Step 4 is to locate the bad code that leads us astray.

We addicts suffer from maladies of the soul that are not pretty sights, and these aspects of ourselves can be hard to accept. It is very natural at

our identities—our unique mix of strengths, weaknesses, preferences and, most importantly, a healthy sense of right and wrong.

Our inventories are focused on gathering self-knowledge. The value of this has been taught since the time of the Greeks. In fact, the maxim "know thyself" was inscribed on Apollo's temple in Delphi about 2,500 years ago. For our purposes here in Step 4, we learn that the value of the work is in understanding how our perceptions and reactions were shaped and perhaps distorted by past experiences and we become aware of how we misused our God-given instincts.

For example, growing up with parents who were active in their disease might have taught us that no one is trustworthy, that we are invisible or need to people-please, or we might internalize their being emotionally unavailable as our being unlovable. Such misinformation and scars of developmental misfortune cast a long shadow, contributing to how we relate to others today, including unhealthy patterns. Such misinformation might cause us to stay in a bad relationship or protect an active addict because we think—based on past input—that no one else will have us. In fact, it is common for the child of an alcoholic to marry an alcoholic because the chaos feels so familiar. One friend in the Program told me about a life-changing insight that had come from Step 4 work: "In my case, I had a series of memory tapes that were 'recorded' both in my childhood and in my marriage to an addict abuser. Until I saw my patterns and became willing to do the work to change, all my relationships were essentially doomed."

Because we isolate to hide our shame, those affected by addiction in themselves and those they love often describe feeling alone both emotionally and physically. Some make themselves small so they won't be noticed; some of us inflate ourselves to mask our insecurity. Recall in Step 3 how willingness fueled our progress. That continues to be the case in Step 4. Here we again harness the energy of willingness to fuel the engine of courage needed to undertake an inventory and come face-to-face with our truths. Taking Step 4 is another example of setting out without being able to see the whole staircase.

Our goal in Step 4 is getting to know ourselves again, and we begin by collecting memories. Through inspection and reflection, we learn about

Chapter 8

Step 4: Courage

Step 4. [We] Made a searching and fearless moral inventory of ourselves.

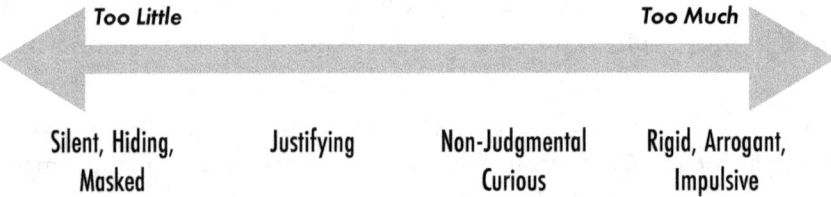

Too Little			Too Much
Silent, Hiding, Masked	Justifying	Non-Judgmental Curious	Rigid, Arrogant, Impulsive

> *Courage is fear that has said its prayers.*
> *—12 Step fellowship wisdom*

Courage: A recovery perspective

Using the Twelve Steps of recovery as a blueprint for recreating ourselves and learning how to live with our addiction, Step 4 directs us to identify the raw materials we have at our disposal. This is essentially the same idea as taking an inventory and doing an inspection for any home improvement project—looking at what we need anew as well as what we have that might be repurposed. The collection of that information would be without judgment, just fact-finding; that is exactly what's needed in our Step 4 work.

In the throes of our addictions we lose touch with our best selves and we are blind to how we hurt ourselves and others. Think of it as suffering from a form of "consumption," an archaic term for a potentially fatal wasting disease. Our addictions consume us physically, emotionally, and spiritually (and often financially). Drowning our thoughts and feelings with our craziness, illogical actions, and substances of choice, we lose touch with

Prompts for journaling or study with your *chevruta*/sponsor
- How can you get off your metaphorical rocking chair and take positive steps forward?
- Do you have the willingness to try to turn your problems over? What could help you?
- What does "let go and let God" mean to you?
- What is the God of your understanding today?
- Do you trust the God of your understanding to care for you?
- What are you reluctant to turn over to the God of your understanding right now?
- What holds you back from trusting God?
- How do you distinguish God's will from your will?
- How can you use Step 3 today?
- How can you stop yourself from taking it back after you "let go and let God"?

Playlist
- "Trust in Me"—Etta James
- "Trust in You"—Laura Daigle
- "Lean on Me"—Bill Withers
- "Bridge over Troubled Water"—Simon & Garfunkel
- "Three Little Birds"—Bob Marley

journey of recovery, we are surrounded by the loving-kindness of Program fellows and a God of our understanding who cares for us.

Daily reminders to help work Step 3

Following are some phrases that you might use as your daily reminders. Feel free to choose one or create your own.
- Trust in God but lock your car.
- It always works out for the best.
- God does not need my help today. Have a nice day.
- It is easier if I can float with the flow of the universe.
- Let go and let God.

Kabbalot to cultivate trust (*bitachon*) as you take Step 3

If you lean toward excessive bitachon you might try:
- Check your actions with your sponsor or *chevruta* to see if you have done enough footwork.
- Say the Serenity Prayer every morning and evening and think about what is in your power and what is not.
- Discuss a big decision with your sponsor or *chevruta* to discern recklessness from trusting God.
- Find safe ways of getting an adrenaline rush in new activities that don't require trust in God to avoid negative consequences.
- Find a way to avoid or get out of potentially risky situations.

If you lean toward sagging bitachon you might try:
- Check your actions with your sponsor or *chevruta* to see if you are confusing your will and God's will for you.
- Make a God box and practice making one deposit a day.
- Get a *hamsa*[119] charm and hang it on a necklace or keychain, or put it in your pocket, to remind you to raise your hand and ask for help.
- Start a practice of making a daily gratitude list.
- Go to an open A.A. or Al-Anon meeting to experience the love in the room and imagine the fellows you meet as God with skin on.

Secondary middot

For an athletic injury, we do physical therapy focused on strengthening structures that surround the area of weakness to absorb the load and restore function. In Mussar practice, we do the same thing, leaning on middot that will bring us back to balance. When I am short on bitachon, *hakarat hatov* (gratitude) gets me started on the path back to where I need to be. One useful exercise is making a daily gratitude list. I include mention of good health, a circle of supportive friends and fellows, a forgiving family, and enough money to meet my needs. Given my starting point of insecurity, anxiety, stress, manipulation of others, martyrdom, and fear, how can I not be grateful for all that I have now? The lens of gratitude helps me see that my life is bountiful and, in fact, beyond rational explanation.

In addition to gratitude, I lean on the soul traits of silence (*shtikah*) and humility (*anavah*) to quiet the voices in my head which profess to know what needs to be done. These middot help me hear the quiet voice of my *yetzer hatov* guiding me to better choices. Finally, I need patience (*savlanut*) and alacrity (*zerizut*), both of which are integral aspects of willingness. Letting go of outcomes is hard when I am not in control of the timing. Sitting with that discomfort is the essence of *savlanut*. About alacrity, our Sages said, "The trait of enthusiasm is an ornament to all the other traits and perfects all of them."[117] Alacrity is defined as energetic readiness—we need alacrity to become willing to "turn it over" and then to accept the outcome, especially if it goes against our grain. Pirkei Avot describes our task as making His will our will.[118] Equanimity (*menuchat hanefesh*) helps us create a distance from negative stimuli like anger and impatience. This serves us whether the emotions are ours or what others are sending our way.

Mussar practice is replete with tools that help us strengthen the muscle of bitachon. That work builds the wall we can lean on as we take the next steps, often referred to as "cleaning house." In the course of our personal work in the Program and in defining our spiritual curriculum, we each find the priorities for our personal focus in changing the patterns that no longer work for us. Whatever the mix, this Step 3 opens the door to the action steps which we dare to take, knowing in our hearts that as we walk our

"enemy" to my own detriment. For example, fear of scarcity, worry about the future, and frustration that others would not do what I thought they should were all self-defeating. The idea that fear, worry, and anger were not forbidden but rather were on my spiritual curriculum was transformational—it meant that I could engage with them and use them as signals that I was out of balance with God. Whatever the issue, I came to realize that I could exercise my choice to turn it over, to "let go and let God," using the tools that work for me. My toolbox includes my God box, practicing awareness and prayer (The Serenity Prayer, A.A. Third Step Prayer, the *Mi Shebeirach*) and invoking collateral, supportive middot.

The power of *bitachon*

Trusting others is difficult for most humans. We can only know if someone is trustworthy over time and acting "as if" makes us vulnerable to being hurt and disappointed. Trusting something that is intangible and uncontrollable is even harder. The experience of feeling safe amid the tumult of life is a reward that makes the idea attractive. The inclusion of God in the definition of this middah and Step 3 may offer you some help. Do you want to risk missing out on it? You can't score a goal if you don't take a shot.

Taking the action of trusting is a choice, and it is informed by Jewish wisdom which teaches that one who trusts in God will be surrounded with favor.[116] Are you willing to trust our Sages for their guidance? If so, harnessing bitachon as spiritual energy that can help you face life's challenges is a good place to start. My experience has been that trying it, even with little things, has strengthened my faith to turn the big things over. We hear so often in the Rooms that people's lives are so much better than they had ever dreamt was possible. Knowing that not everyone got what they wanted but still feel this way encouraged me.

At times when I feel lost in a world that is unstable, practicing bitachon helps me feel anchored and burden-free. Even if only fleeting, it is a needed salve and does keep me and my fellows coming back. Watching those around me reveals that faith in a God of their understanding fosters living in a frame of mind where they can make wiser choices and move forward with confidence. Just as Step 3 promises, the gift is free for the taking. I like free.

to address our problems; only after we've done our fair share will divine assistance be forthcoming. Our task is to balance human effort (*hishtadlut*) with bitachon.

We have been given judgment, intelligence, and the powers of choice and reason, as well as the free will to use them. We say in the Rooms that we must do the footwork and not succumb to laziness, despondency, or lack of faith by relying on God to do what we are meant to do ourselves. Thus, we read in sage Jewish wisdom, "Seek His will in all you do, and He will show you which path to take."[115] Bitachon is a sense of assurance that comes from our hearts and souls that the Divine is holding us and caring for us. It is the simple certainty, inner confidence, that we are not alone on our journey.

Cultivating *bitachon*

Let's turn our attention to how we cultivate bitachon. More than most middot, bitachon needs to be developed and nurtured. We constantly battle alluring and conflicting signals, and ego (showing up as our yetzer hara) tests our resolve. While we may want to trust God, wanting is not enough. We need to be willing and to take the steps necessary to discern our will from God's will for us, and to trust what we "hear." If the voice you hear is your own, it is likely that you are confusing your thoughts and God's will.

Being open to the input of others is important to protect against such self-deception. Others can frequently help us see our resistance to letting go of the outcome we desire and to letting God (or the flow of the universe) manifest His will—whatever that may look like. This is made difficult because God's presence in our lives is fleeting and not obvious, and God's role in the world is beyond our understanding. In addition, looking outside ourselves for help is almost countercultural.

Cultivating bitachon starts with emunah (faith). Faith grows when we can see the presence of the Divine (or power and flow of the universe) all around us, in us, and between us. It has been my experience that adopting an attitude of gratitude for all the goodness that surrounded and embraced me played a significant role in nurturing emunah and bitachon for me. Paradoxically, this practice also helped me realize that I was colluding with the

Along these lines, Rabbi Cantor Alison Wissot teaches that bitachon is believing that the path we are on is the right one for us.[112] Stop and think for a moment. There is peace of mind in accepting that all we have and the path our life has taken is as it should be. It makes sense, then, that addiction has been described as a spiritual disease. We steal, lie, cheat, and suffer from envy, anxiety, and stress because we do not trust that we have or will receive what we need. Our ego, at times acting as our yetzer hara, rules the roost, and at the choice point, we make decisions driven by the false belief that we are in control. It's useful to remember that in recovery-speak ego is Easing God Out, synonymous with lack of bitachon.

Alan Morinis posited in *Everyday Holiness* that our lives are our "spiritual curriculum"—the good and the bad alike. We are not entitled to like the way things are. A mindset in which we see opportunity in the full range of experiences that flow through our lives can be a source of peace—gratitude from what we learn on the one hand, and freedom from burdensome negative thinking on the other. The challenge of finding gratitude for the harsh, hard-learned lessons explains why gratitude is so often a discussion topic in the Rooms of recovery. Here is a radical thought—just maybe, our journey through addiction to recovery is the path we needed to connect with our Higher Power, aka a God of our understanding. The struggle, which is a journey toward faith and trust, ultimately yields the gift of fulfilling our Divine purpose of finding wholeness through connection with our HP and our holiness.

Powerlessness and *bitachon*

Before we leave Step 3, I think it's important to address the relationship between trusting God and the surrender and powerlessness of Steps 1 and 2. Torah can be interpreted as teaching that bitachon means trusting one's burden exclusively to God.[113] Is there such a thing as too much bitachon? I would argue that we are guided to leave the outcomes to God, but not the footwork. In other words, trusting God does not mean that we can relinquish our responsibility. The Alter of Novardok taught that one has to trust God while using intermediate experience, emphasizing that it is forbidden to rely upon miracles.[114] We must do everything in our power

that when I was trapped by the cleverness of my disease, I fully embodied these prophetic words.

Ibn Paquda identified trust in God as a path to peace of mind and tranquility of the soul, benefits he said will extend to all our affairs, religious and secular. He expressed this metaphorically, referring to peace of mind that comes from not having to travel on faraway roads, which is so physically ruinous and menacing.[110] Being trapped in addiction does often cause us to veer off the intended paths of our lives. Ruin and even death of body and spirit, as well as hopes and dreams are, in fact, what we face as a consequence of having lost our way to the obsessions that overrun our will and lives. There is hope in the idea that the individual with bitachon can turn away from all of life's problems, for they know that they will not be left wanting.

In regard to turning our will and lives over, ibn Paquda again quoted Jeremiah: "Blessed is the man who trusts in God, who makes God his refuge."[111] We can take this to mean that a life directed at good (godly) choices brings one to enjoy great comfort and reward. Someone who trusts in God is spared from human troubles such as shame, fear, and worry. There is great allure and comfort in the promise of freedom that comes from living with trust in God. Sitting opposite this rather idyllic vision is the fact that life happens and often seems very imperfect. I have come to appreciate that the ups and downs challenge our faith and trust in God by design. Viewed through a lens of healing and recovery, our challenges give us the opportunity to grab hold and lean against that proverbial wall, if we are willing.

Many of our human issues can be traced back to the lack of trust in God. The very common tendencies toward worry and fear are ailments of our inner spiritual domain that relate to trust that things are or will be as they should be. Our problems can paralyze us, distract us, push us off balance, and suck up valuable life energy. Think about it for a moment—worry and fear pull us into the future and reflect a lack of trust that things will work out as they should. We usually want what we want and suffer dis-ease about things not being in accordance with our wishes. We may be fearful of our capacity to bear what happens, we may not accept that the outcome is what should happen, or the outcome may be justified but not to our liking.

"Hmm," she responded collecting herself, and then said, "I am sure there is a force bigger than me that helps us reach toward something bigger and better and more good than we can be alone." She went on to say that she was "willing to call it God as a placeholder, although you do not need to"—in other words, it's a personal choice. They reversed roles and the rabbi asked the MC the same question. He replied that he "sometimes was sure there is a God."

This dialogue sounds charming, no? It is real, not a fable! These are real people, contemporary Jewish thought leaders with innate spirituality and a deep knowledge and love of Judaism.[106] Their views were formed by exposure to a range of Jewish teachings, as well as other spiritual thought, and reflect the spaciousness within Judaism to struggle with ideas about God and find a Higher Power of our understanding, as Step 3 invites.

If reference to God in Step 3 evokes anything that is a barrier to you, feel free to fill in the blank as it best serves you. I recall from college philosophy that God does not want to be the subject of debate, fairy tale thinking, or theory, but rather to be realized, and we are the conduits. Along the lines of the pulpit rabbi in the story above, I can share that I envision God as the positive flow of the universe, and thus I personalize Step 3 as something like …made a decision to turn my life and my will over to the care of the universe.

Making it personal: Why trust God?

As if he were writing intentionally to us addicts on this topic, Rabbi Bachya ibn Paquda[107] cited Torah which teaches, "Cursed is the man who trusts in man and makes flesh his strength, while his heart turns away from God."[108] He went on to say, "If he [man] relies on his wisdom and ingenuity, his physical strength, and his own efforts, he will labor in vain, his strength will fail, and his ingenuity will be inadequate to achieve his goal." Referencing Torah again, R. Bachya reminded readers that "God traps the clever in their own cunning."[109] In these few sentences of Torah and sage wisdom, written about a thousand years ago, ibn Paquda covered the ideas of free will run wild, our will vs. God's will, and hitting rock bottom. I will admit

wall is one analogy that might work for you: Knowing that a wall is there is faith; leaning on it to help keep your balance is trust.

Bitachon is the source of confidence that enables me to attempt to take the next step forward. In terms of organized religious teachings which assume faith in God, these concepts are often used interchangeably. In regard to taking the steps of recovery, it is useful to appreciate the difference between these middot and the opportunities they provide for us to take an active role in our Programs.

God of your understanding

Before diving further into the Step, I want to touch on some Jewish ideas related to the God of our understanding. This topic has filled countless volumes and lifetimes of study. Some ideas on the topic are pretty lofty. We need not detour into philosophy, theology, or debate to understand Step 3. Let's start with a simple, declarative statement: Judaism asserts that there is one God, the Creator. From this perspective, even atheism is not a problem, but narcissism is. The God of the Hebrew Bible and of classic interpretive rabbinic texts has more than 100 names.[105] The Hebrew Bible and older prayer books traditionally use the masculine form, referring to God as "He." This convention has been changed in many modern prayer books and much liturgy to reflect the idea that "The One Above" is beyond the limits of male or female. In fact, God is often spoken of as all existence, beyond our imagination, everywhere, all-knowing, all-powerful and in a covenantal relationship with the Jewish people. Therein lies the rub—God is often referred to as our protector, and the fact that bad things happen to good people opens the door to doubters and skeptics.

Judaism has room for doubts or questions and for a God of our understanding. Some of our most cherished wisdom, as voiced in the Midrash, reflects rabbinic debate; libraries are filled with books that reflect our ongoing human efforts to find and understand God. Because we Jews always have stories, let me tell you one that bears this out. The characters in this tale are two rabbis—the master of ceremonies (MC) is a media producer and the other is a well-known pulpit rabbi. The MC was interviewing the pulpit rabbi; his last question to her was, "Are you sure there is a God?"

writings, Nachmanides[103] separated faith (emunah) and trust (bitachon), noting that trust requires faith as its foundation. Referring to the Divine, he said that it is impossible to have trust without faith. In this paradigm, faith precedes trust, and trust cannot exist without faith.[104] Keeping in mind the discussion of belief in the previous chapter, the last link in this chain of thought is the idea that belief, which falls short of the conviction of faith, does not guarantee trust.

Letting go and letting God is a choice. We often hear a synopsis of these first three steps in the Rooms as "I can't (Step 1), He can (Step 2) and I'll let Him (Step 3)." For me, it was reasonably easy to acknowledge that letting go is a good idea, since I was not having any success; nonetheless, it was hard to put into action. Here, in Step 3, we simply need to decide that we will try to turn things over. Each opportunity is a choice point (*nekudat bechira*), and we get to revisit it over and over with each decision. Thinking for a minute of *seder*, the middah of order, Step 3 allows us to see our truth, consider our options, and set off in a direction. For most of us, belief is not a straight line; so, too, choosing [Divine] assistance when we reach a nekudat bechira is an opportunity to trust our lives and problems to someone/something outside of us.

The relationship between faith and trust

Let's explore the relationship between emunah (faith) and bitachon (trust) a bit further. Emunah reflects knowing, in our hearts and minds, that there is a power of the universe—perhaps God—that leans toward doing good for all of creation, including us. Emunah takes a long-term view, arching over our lives as a whole. This middah provides a foundation that can help us understand the hardships we experience on our journeys. Faith holds fast to the idea that God is inscrutable, and that life has to be this way for us to learn what's needed and enjoy the growth that comes from opportunities to make choices. In contrast, trust, if we embrace it, helps us handle the problems of the day by tapping into available personal support and assistance. Through the lens of trust, we know that we are not alone, that we are embraced and journeying as part of the flow of the universe. A

the Program and intend to stick to it, you've already begun—you have acquired willingness and are on the way to completing Step 3.

To think about your relationship with God, I am going to suggest that you envision standing in moving water—a flowing river or breaking ocean waves. Your actions and stance determine whether the water is punishing or supportive. Walking against the current is awkward and arduous, and what little movement you achieve can quickly sap your personal energy, even raising the possibility of being drowned in exhaustion. Each of us can choose whether to let our free will run, creating a turbulent wake that endangers our life and well-being, or to tap into the flow, moving with the current and enjoying ease, balance and grace. Step 3 offers us the support we need to turn and start walking in the direction of the flow so we can be carried by the current.

As we wrap up this piece of our exploration of Step 3, I want to acknowledge that motivation may get us going, but discipline keeps us growing. Step 3 occurs largely in our minds. Our continued growth requires that we move into the action of Steps 4 through 9. There is a saying related to our stinking thinking: *a rocking chair can be in motion, but it will get you nowhere.* I ask you to please join me in standing tall and moving forward on this journey to recover your best self and best life.

Trust (*Bitachon*): A Mussar perspective on Step 3

> *Blessed is the man who trusts in God.*
> —*Jeremiah 17:7*

Bitachon, translated as trust and usually in reference to trust in God, is the middah that is at the heart of Step 3. This middah is foundational in Mussar practice, forging another powerful connection between recovery and Mussar practice. To bridge between Step 2 and Step 3, and to complete this opening triad of steps in which we realize our limits, I want to look briefly at the relationship between emunah and bitachon with you. In his

- subject to being given a pink slip if the God of our understanding does not work for us

Suffice it to say that the reference to God in Step 3 does not refer to any single religious or personal theology, and an individual's lack of such beliefs is not a barrier to success in taking Step 3. Rather, the Step seeks to evoke the idea of tapping into something other than ourselves. Admittedly, it might get a bit thorny when we say that the entity "knows" what is best. Perhaps you can suspend a literal understanding and simply accept letting go of outcomes. Would you consider simply embracing the idea that we do not need to force everything to happen as if we were in charge?

In the course of my work on Step 3, my sponsor gave me a refrigerator magnet that says, "Good morning! This is God. I will be handling all your problems today, and I won't be needing your help—so just relax and have a nice day." As silly as this sounds, it is a great reminder to practice Step 3 and embody the slogan "let go and let God." Understanding that we are not God is a great starting point. For many, progressing to the larger problems we are facing as we take Step 3 is a process; putting our trust in the flow that is outside ourselves takes time and practice. I did so first with only small things; over time, I learned to let go of even high-stakes problems.

Coming into the Rooms with almost no relationship with any God or Higher Power, I initially sought guidance from the fellowship. I listened for what the Program said I should do. I was honestly not sure that the HP that some called God was trustworthy with my life and problems. However, I came to understand the frequently heard phrase *I'm a child of God and a person of worth*. In the context of Step 3, I learned and ultimately embraced the idea that I am cared for and can rely on the force or flow that sustains the universe. Thus, once I was open to seeing the beauty and order in the universe, l evolved to form and engage with my own concept of God as a force for good and caring in the universe of which I am a part. Trust is something that needs practice, and I still often need the reminder from that little magnet. While the journey is not necessarily a straight line, I can say that over the arc of time, things have worked out better than I ever dreamed was possible. I have built my trust and learned to value the guidance that comes from outside. You may wonder how to let it in. If you have joined

covery. We are not in the outcome business. I will venture to say that when you let go of your will and trust the voice that nudges you in the direction that your Higher Power has chosen for you, your life will become more serene and also more fulfilling. It has been my experience that doing this has allowed me to live with my disease without the drama, discord and chaos that are inherent to being taken hostage by it. All you need to do is figure out what humility and acceptance look like for you. Seems simple, but it's not easy.

The white elephant

Ideas of God, God's will and God's voice can be polarizing with a lot of personal baggage. I assure you that this need not get in the way of your recovery journey. Humans struggle to find words that adequately represent God or something Divine. We do not have universally-accepted pronouns—is God he, she, or they?—nor proper or befitting common names. We use language that humanizes God or the concept of God in an effort to comprehend and relate to it. Just the word "God" suggests an entity which has form and boundaries, the antithesis of a hidden and infinite power and knowledge. The idea of God is made more complex by the personal experiences we carry coming into the Program. The God of your understanding may fit with more conventional imagery or can be:

- the **g**ift **o**f **d**esperation
- a **g**roup **o**f **d**runks
- **g**ood **o**rderly **d**irection
- all-knowing, patient, unconditionally loving, always with you and sitting on your shoulder
- judging and punishing
- in control of everything
- permissive, allowing us to make our own decisions and to repeat the same mistakes over and over, to experience the consequences of our mistakes
- in charge and laughing at our plans
- helping us accomplish things we thought we couldn't

I was growing to trust. That said, I am imperfect at this, and I should give you a heads-up that turning it over is likely going to be an ongoing process. As I was writing this book and telling someone how I was struggling to find the words, my Program friend asked, "Are you asking [God] for help as you sit down to write?" Ah! How could I have missed that?

Letting go, whatever that may look like

Let me to tell you about a personal practice that has been useful to me in service of "letting go and letting God." This is my adaptation of a common Program tool. I start by writing on an index card whatever is weighing on my mind and heart, like worry about my qualifier (the addict I love) or something that feels like a major decision—perhaps an upcoming expense, removing the bondage of self or a relationship issue—that I need to let go of. At the end of the sentence I've written about my worry, I add a phrase without which I don't really turn the worry/fear/resentment over. For example, I might write, "Dear God [of my understanding], please keep Emma under your wing," and then I add my magic words, "whatever that may look like." Somehow, that closing phrase makes all the difference for me. I take my note and put it into a small box—often called a God box in the Program—that sits on my bookshelf. Doing so sends it into the universe for a solution that comes from outside of me. Once a year or so, I clean out my God box and my experience is that always—yes, always!—things have worked out, often differently but also better than if I had been in charge.

A primary obstacle to letting go is that we want a guaranteed outcome—we want to get what we want. And remember that our disease is lying in wait. As masters of self-deception, we need to be vigilant and do the hard work of discerning God's will from our own. Indeed, a critical part of willingness is accepting God's will for us—whatever it may look like. How do we do this? We need tools to guard ourselves against our disease and self-will: looking at our motives; sharing with fellows, our sponsor, or a therapist; and practicing patience. These strategies help whether we are dealing with our own problems or our reaction to the problems of others.

Getting our will to conform to God's will through humility and acceptance is a good use of our personal energy and an essential part of our re-

revealed that my life was quite unmanageable and that alone, I did not have the power to change the truth about what I had created. In this regard, my reality in taking Step 3 was that I had little to lose. In other words, the gift of desperation motivated me to get willing to try something else.

As previously mentioned, the *Big Book* describes us addicts as examples of self-will run riot, revealing that we are selfish and self-centered in our beliefs that we are in control and have power over our jailer, be it the bottle, the line, or the hit. Workaholism, shopping, sex, and love addiction also fit the bill. For those of us in Al-Anon, our insanity includes thinking that we can control anyone else, including the user, perhaps saving them from themselves while harming ourselves goes unnoticed. True to form, it was my experience that running my life my way brought me to a point of ruin—my relationships, career, financial security, etc., had all been destroyed.

Both the addict and the person who loves the addict suffer from distorted thinking that "the world revolves around me." We misuse our willpower and delude ourselves into believing that we can overcome our problems by bombarding them with our will. Chapter 5 of the *Big Book* notes that even though we have accepted the truths of Steps 1 and 2, we must still be convinced that a life run on self-will cannot be successful. There is a paradox hidden to us—our way was secretly focused on protecting the disease and controlling the obsession or others' perception of us, so we were, in a way, set up to fail. Surrendering control as suggested in Step 3 felt like a huge risk that others might see the truths we (our egos) were working so hard to hide.

Fear that we may not get our way can exacerbate the resistance that holds us back from change until there are no more excuses and no one else to blame for our troubles. At first, we might ask for guidance on big problems where we see that we are totally powerless, like avoiding jailtime for forging checks. We abhor the truth that doing the crime opens us to doing the time.

I was more likely to seek guidance and be willing to act on it as my recovery progressed. My ego and self-will needed the time in the Rooms to become rightsized. With some time under my belt to create a space for openness, I found myself increasingly willing to "sleep on it" before making a decision, hoping that what's right would reveal itself as that hidden voice

argue, an act of faith and hope and an inflection point in the Program as we transition to new solutions.

Step 3 entails a shift in our attitude that includes surrendering the notion that things will go our way, in addition to accepting that we are not in control. This step of our journey is sometimes described as "turning it over," referring to the idea that we will seek care and support outside ourselves. The foundation for these ideas is faith that there is help, if we are open to accepting it, from some power or force of the universe that is greater than us. For some, though by no means all, that force is named God. The slogan "let go and let God" is another way to summarize this step. If it meets your needs, substitute any name for the God of your understanding. In any case, stop trying to be God and get out of the way.

Willingness to seek and listen is the core of taking Step 3. At this stage of recovery, most people begin to get relief from the burdens of obsessive drinking and drugging or their perfectionism and control by trusting fellows and the Program. Do you sense that anxiety and worry have begun to lift away? Many say they do experience that. The fact that our best thinking got us into the messes in which we find ourselves encourages us to be willing to try anything. But giving away what we believe to be our power is not easy for most people to accept. There are some big ideas and challenges inherent in Step 3. As we have done with the previous steps, which are also very nuanced, let's break this down together.

The gift of desperation

I don't know about you, but turning anything I own and value over to someone or something else requires that I can trust that other party. Step 3 invites us to entrust our actions (our lives) and thoughts (our will) to a recipient identified as the God of our understanding. My thoughts and actions seem like all of me; these words triggered my fear that nothing of me would be left. We will get to the God part in just a bit. I am, in fact, a backseat driver; giving myself away was a tough pill for me to swallow. That's ego speaking—self-serving, trying to protect what she thinks is her job. Reflecting on what I heard among my fellow travelers exposed the truth that my way of living was not actually very successful. Steps 1 and 2

Chapter 7

Step 3: Trust

Step 3. [We] Made a decision to turn our will and our lives over to the care of God *as we understood God [him, her, them, it]*.

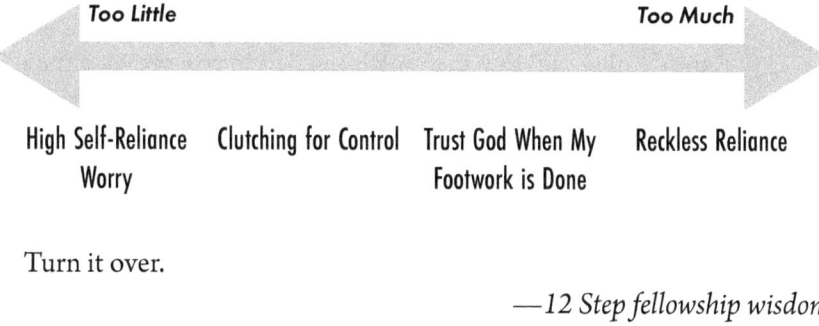

Turn it over.

—*12 Step fellowship wisdom*

Trust: A recovery perspective

We make decisions each day. Some decisions are complicated and weigh heavily on us, requiring much thought and courage; others are almost automatic. Because life keeps happening and we show up with patterns of habitual thinking and reacting, not all of which are helpful, we get to make some decisions over and over. Each decision is a link or bridge between our understanding of what is currently the case and actions we must take to create a desired change. Doing the work of Steps 1 and 2 of our Program, and revealing the truth of our reality, opens our eyes to the need for different life choices. Step 3 gives us an exit from being chased by unmanageability and is a portal to change. The key to our progress is deciding to be willing—willing to try to cut away the armor that has blocked the entry of goodness into our lives so we can tap into the hidden positive flow of the universe. Deciding to wade into the waters of recovery in Step 3 is, I would

- How does the hidden source touch your life?
- How has the addiction situation affected your sanity?
- When have you experienced a sense of wholeness in the brokenness in your life?
- How does faith figure into your understanding of your disease?
- Consider when Moses smashed the tablets. Have you ever smashed something precious to you?
- Can you describe a moment of awe?
- How do you cultivate faith?
- Where do you go to experience the presence of God? How does it affect your understanding of the universe and God as hidden or present?
- Rabbi Wolbe said that no book is needed to strengthen emunah, and that studying nature has the same results. Does this idea work for you? Explain.

Playlist
- "Anthem"—Christensen and Patalla
- "Lean on Me"—Bill Withers
- "Count on Me"—Whitney Houston
- "Emunah"—Itzik Dadya
- "I'm Your Man"—Leonard Cohen

Kabbalot to cultivate faith *(emunah)* as you work Step 2

If you lean toward excessive emunah you might try:
- Make a list of what you want to turn over to your HP. Check your motives. Is it fear of failing, laziness, or surrender?
- Identify your actions today and be sure that your to-dos outnumber the list you've made for HP. Adjust accordingly.
- Wear a rubber band on one wrist every day. Always start with the same wrist. In a situation when you've taken ownership of an action that's scary or hard, move the rubber band to your opposite wrist. When you move it, you're essentially rewarding yourself for acting on faithfulness.
- To remind yourself of your responsibilities, wait a couple days to see if your HP will cook dinner for you, wash your clothes or go food shopping for you.
- Consider whether you would let your HP drive your car.

If you lean toward sagging emunah you might try:
- Compose a gratitude list. Make a list of good things that have happened to you, focusing especially on the ones that you cannot explain.
- Commit 15 minutes daily to immersing yourself in your senses. Listen to the wind, listen to a symphony with your eyes closed and identify as many instruments as you can, see how many colors of green you can find in nature.
- Go to an open A.A./Al-Anon meeting to hear someone's story and experience the love in the room.
- Say the Serenity Prayer every morning and evening, and any time you feel overwhelmed.
- Find an image of kintsugi and use it as a screen saver.

Prompts for journaling or study with your *chevruta*/sponsor
- What does "came to believe" mean to you?
- What is the God of your understanding today?
- What might you do to heighten awareness? How might the practice affect your life?

time. Cultivating faith is also a process. We can't skip steps along the way. Faith grows throughout our lives from the struggle of living on life's terms, nurtured by flashes of experiencing the Divine. The starting point is the act of seeking our place and purpose, grounded in humility and the knowledge that there must be more to life than is readily apparent, and that there is in fact an entirely mysterious dimension to life and living. Awe of the beauty and order in the universe is an experience that feeds and nurtures emunah.

The interactions among our middot create multiple entry points to the work of recovery. We can examine what blocks us from being restored to wholeness from the perspective of each middah and find solutions that will be uniquely ours. For example, poor time management may mean that life is in such disorder that we miss meetings, which are essential tools in our recovery. Work on the middah of seder provides possible solutions to this obstacle. Alternatively, we may be rushing around so fast that we have no time to see the miracles in front of us. Here, the middah of yirah may be a valuable tool.

The key is the act of seeking. Do not be distressed if you feel imperfect or if you don't feel like you have a close confidential relationship with God. Few of us have this nailed down. As we embrace the act of seeking through work on all of these middot, faith emerges; it grows and gets stronger—albeit mysteriously—within the course of our experiences, and from that inner place it nurtures us. Call it what you will—recovery, sobriety, spiritual awareness—what a gift! Wherever you find yourself in these teachings, I pray that you will open your inner life and enjoy the blessing of faith and the serenity of living with faithfulness.

Daily reminders to help work Step 2

Following are some phrases that you might use as your daily reminders. Feel free to choose one or create your own.

- I embrace the act of seeking.
- Lift your eyes.
- I embrace my brokenness.
- The cracks reveal my light.
- The cracks embrace my imperfections.
- God [or a Higher Power/Hashem/the Shechinah] is with me.

creation.[98] It is my personal theology that the world was created to provide us the opportunity to become partners in creation. We have been given a venue and the resources to become our best selves—perhaps that is our primary human purpose. In this context, our addictions and feelings of brokenness are simply part of our incompleteness. Mishnah teaches that our brokenness (the wreckage of our past) can be a reminder of where we came from. We are taught that the Israelites gathered up broken pieces of the first set of Tablets with the Ten Commandments and kept them with the new Tablets in the ark.[99] According to Rabbi Luzzatto, humans were created for this purpose. Our spiritual work, including Twelve Step and Mussar practices, are the paths to wholeness (*shleimut*). I am comforted by the idea that the goal is taking aim for—in Program-speak—progress, not perfection. To paraphrase Morinis, Mussar is a path for becoming living embodiments of our ideals, so we can transition from our partialness—even brokenness—toward becoming more whole; in wholeness we become vessels for holiness itself.[100]

Listening closely to those further along in their journeys of sobriety revealed to me how protecting ourselves from the pain of our lives and choices had caused our hearts to harden and close. Absent emunah, life was just too scary to bear. It's important to note that in addition to blocking pain, we had also blocked out joy. Having lost hope, we allowed our hearts to rust over. Many of us arrived at the Rooms having died—emotionally and spiritually. With that perspective on my disease, I understood the teachings of Deuteronomy where the Torah describes opening the heart using the imagery of circumcision: "You shall circumcise the foreskin of your heart."[101] Unveiling the heart opens a relationship with the Divine (as well as others) and is part of being open to emunah. Rabbi Dessler's words, "arouse yourself, make a move,"[102] provided the ray of hope I needed to take Step 2 with the hope that we could be restored.

Secondary middot

Step 2 also relates to the middot of order (*seder*), humility (*anavah*), and awe (*yirah*). "Coming to believe," as was described in the first part of this chapter, is an ordered process that happens over time, one step at a

> Won't I find you
> Your glory fills the world…
> I sought your nearness:
> With all my heart I called you.
> And in my going
> Out to meet you,
> I found you coming toward me.[96]

In other words, I began to feel the presence of a God of my understanding. That God was a travel companion looking after my well-being. More than knowing, what I am describing is a feeling that transcends knowing. I would describe the internal manifestation of this as faithfulness—a dynamic, growing confidence that as a Jew, I could withstand the journey and evolve from it, and that there was hope for a better future for me. Emunah grew out of seeking.

For me, the beauty and order I found when I purposefully opened myself to and practiced awareness—when I turned my metaphorical radio on—allowed me to buy into the idea that there must be some hidden transcendent force under it all that permeates the universe and works for my benefit. My work in Step 2 opened the door to emunah, to the idea that there is this boundless and limitless force. And my work on emunah in my personal curriculum facilitated my taking Step 2. Filling my heart with faithfulness and hope allowed me to move forward.

The healing power of emunah

As I came into the Program and started Step 2, still in despair about the way things were, I felt like I was broken, incomplete, and imperfect. I was comforted by the words of Rabbi Dessler, who wrote, "do not worry, however far away you may be; arouse yourself, make a move and Hashem will bring you near. He is trustworthy to revive the dead."[97]

Like Nachshon standing at the edge of the sea, emunah allowed me to venture into the waves, toward freedom and—in my case—recovery. To take this step I embraced the Mussar teaching of Rabbi Luzzatto that we are created incomplete so that we can complete the work of our own

from my disease and the brokenness it yielded, I found comfort and internal emotional energy that ultimately supported self-acceptance even with my imperfect emunah. Lapses and engagement with emunah that I saw in our ancestors' stories allowed me to surrender to the unknown of the Steps and of sobriety in my search for freedom.

Do you see yourself here?

- Driving to the meeting, perhaps you feel as Abraham did when leaving the comfort of his home. His faith was at the root of survival of the Jewish family. You have the same opportunity.
- Trying to make it through a 24-hour period without "using" to help us cope and feel better is a contemporary version of walking between the walls of the Red Sea. Our fellows in the Rooms show us the path between the waves.
- If you feel at risk of drowning in racing thoughts, feelings, and physical unwellness, perhaps you can think of your demons as Pharoah's soldiers chasing us. The Israelites found the faith to "cross over." Harnessing our fear to keep ourselves safe is putting it to good use. The wisdom of Proverbs says, "Happy is the man who is fearful always."[95] Our fear need not keep us from the work of recovery. We can use it to propel ourselves through the steps.
- Thinking about seeking freedom from the bondage of addiction and stinking thinking, let your mind dwell on the story of the Israelites following Moses through the desert. Recall the doubt that our forebears suffered while wandering. Perhaps those we meet in the Rooms of recovery are our Moses, leading us through our personal deserts.

Connecting personally to our history became inspiring and the fellowship made it possible for me to step into the unknown feeling that I was not alone. "The Dream Poem" by Yehuda Ha-Levi [abridged] helped me get clarity on what I was feeling:

> Where, Lord will I find you:
> Your place is high and obscured.
> And where

personal relationships were deep and unwavering. They had faith in the Program and the God of their understanding and were thus committed to the Steps and fellowship.

Simply walking into a meeting or—later—sharing at a meeting were my earliest moments of acting on faith. I was surely faking it in the beginning. My faith grew out of my action, and these choices to engage even minimally were my Red Sea moments. I was afraid of standing still lest I be captured by the demons that had enslaved me, and I was equally afraid of moving forward, filled with fear of the unknown in my future. I envisioned being Nachshon, who was alone at the edge of the sea with the Israelites trying to escape Pharoah's army. He was the first to enter the water, and not until it was up to his nose did the sea split, allowing the Israelites to pass safely. Like him, despite my uncertainty, I sensed and was emboldened by something hidden.

I began to examine my own relationship with emunah by thinking about our ancestors. In our Hebrew Bible, the Israelites who were about to cross into the Promised Land were commanded to be strong and resolute "for the Eternal your God who marches with you will not fail you or forsake you."[94] Their conviction that there was a Higher Power traveling with them was engendered by open miracles for their benefit. Seeing was believing. In addition to the parting of the Red Sea, the plagues visited on Pharoah, Miriam's well, and the manna that sustained them on their journey through the desert gave our ancestors emotionally compelling reasons to believe they were not alone. Yet they still had doubts.

I'm not sure about you, but I'd say that we see fewer open miracles in the normal course of life today. My mind was opened to the possibility of miracles (albeit invisible) through an analogy I heard in the Rooms related to listening to the radio: the music is always there inside the box, but it's up to us to turn it on. In other words, perhaps the evidence of a Higher Power in the universe is here and we are blind to it because of our disease.

While I knew the stories of our heritage well from childhood, they were just that—stories. They lived in my head as inspiring parables but unlike personal memories, the stories of our ancestors did not reach my heart—until I saw myself in the struggle of addiction. In my search for freedom

is arduous and the suggestion that we "keep coming back," a slogan often shared among Program fellows, is a life jacket for those times when our faith is challenged and even slips away. Like our Jewish stories, our journeys through the Steps show that emunah is revealed through tests.[92] Faith is revealed in the seeking. Consistent with this, Chapter 5 of the *Big Book of A.A.* ("How it Works") says that God could and would relieve us of our disease if He were sought. Alan Morinis teaches that faith is dynamic and meant to grow, and that "a fully resolved faith is a dead faith."[93] We must work at faith.

Experiences through which we can cultivate emunah are available in any or every moment. Making the time and opening our hearts to the actions and experiences is a choice. Pursuing recovery opens up such choices with a benefit that is self-reinforcing. Recovery opens us to emunah, and emunah opens the path to recovery.

Making it personal

From my earliest days in the Program, I was aware that much of the talk I heard in the Rooms reflected my fellows being in relationship with a God of their understanding. The idea was foreign to me. I had a vague notion that there was a Divine power, but I had absolutely no personal relationship with that power. Over time, I saw that those who kept coming back to work the Program in various ways seemed to have what I wanted and hoped for. People around me in their disease were on the same sinking ship as I was. Returning to the Rooms and hearing people's stories was my starting point for building my personal emunah.

Their past stories included feelings and reactions that were much like mine, but their current lives were generally free of the drama, loneliness, fear, and shame that I was suffering. They had a supportive network of friends, they were able to ask for and accept help when needed, and they seemed to enjoy loving relationships with others. They seemed to have an inner peace that I envied. Their success gave me some reason to believe, and I noted that their belief had taken on the quality of absolute, rock-solid faith in the Program and in their personal understanding of a power greater than themselves. The feelings that the Program saved their lives and

ative—debt, legal issues, broken relationships, family dysfunction, job loss. It is entirely human to struggle with doubt and big questions about the meaning and context of our lives. It is interesting that the word "Israel" is translated to mean one who struggles with God.[90] In some part, the essence of being Jewish is about struggle—with ourselves and with ideas about Divine presence.

Back to emunah. As it relates to Step 2, "maybe" is a Jewishly acceptable starting point. This served me well in my early days of recovery, and I imagine that the same may hold true for you. Faith is a journey, a process that is reflected in the progression of Step 2. The knowledge and experience of those who preceded us in the Program is enough to allow some to surrender to the wisdom of the Program as the power greater than themselves. Some view their relationship with a sponsor or fellows in the Program as their Higher Power. I was slow to come to such faith in the Program and in my sponsor. Seeing that others seemed to have what I wanted (a life without chaos, and with loving relationships and joy) encouraged me to give the Program a shot. Like dating and falling in love, willingness to go through the motions of working on and talking about the Steps allowed a relationship to blossom in which I let down my barriers, began to trust, and grew to rely on the counsel of fellows. I faked it and happily made it to trust the Program.

Over time, to really go all-in, I needed something that was personally mine and more substantive. There is irony in calling faith that there is a transcendent power "substantive" since we cannot prove that this Divine source exists. Nonetheless, envy of those who were successful and described this as their "magic juice" made it worthy of consideration and a real effort to make it so for myself.

Personal experience is the gateway to the faith that takes residence in the heart of many. Shared experience, strength, and hope among fellows are seeds. Over time in the Rooms, these can yield glimpses of awareness and connection to a Higher Power. Alan Morinis describes experiencing God as "sparkling flashes."[91] Once the seeds are planted, they need to be nurtured. The seedlings of faith are fragile because faith is dynamic and subject to challenge by events of life. The journey through the Twelve Steps

Indeed, the Mussar masters taught that to cultivate faith, we only need to open our eyes to the miracles of life that are revealed by our senses. In *Parashah Lech Lecha*, God instructs Abraham to look toward heaven and count the stars.[87] Morinis says "the world is the tableau of the divine, and in looking at it and experiencing its marvelous artifacts and ways, we can perceive the physical reality and the divinity that lies within it."[88] The glimpses of beauty hidden in plain sight open the door to emunah. More than the facts of what we see, these teachers stress that the awe we feel nurtures emunah. Clearly, our notion of the Divine is not as important as our relationship with the Divine. That latter is the essence of emunah.

Emunah and Step 2

As it relates to enriching Step 2 work, Mussar practice on emunah can fill our hearts and strengthen us for the hard work of living aligned with Jewish values in our recovery. Key foundational questions might include whether there is any reason to believe that this mysterious hidden power of the universe exists and, if so, how we access it.

The first-century sage and scholar Rabbi Akiva addressed the first question over a thousand years ago:

> The heretic asked Rabbi Akiva to prove to him that G-d existed, to which Rabbi Akiva replied: "Who made your suit?" The heretic answered: "The tailor." Rabbi Akiva then asked him to prove it. The heretic then declared: "The very existence of my suit proves that it was made by a tailor." Rabbi Akiva then retorted: "In the same way that the suit testifies to a tailor, so the world testifies to the existence of a Creator."[89]

It makes sense to me that if a suit is not made by itself, it seems equally obvious that the world was not, opening the door to the idea that it may have been the work of a power greater than ourselves.

Understandably, many—especially newcomers—struggle with the idea that such a power exists. For one thing, most of the "data" we have is neg-

my faith in the Program and/or faith in a mysterious power of the universe that helped others did sustain me through the pain of withdrawal, the myriad changes necessary to make recovery my highest priority, and the ups and downs of life in sobriety. And faith continues to feed my hope of a sober future. Thus, I would argue that faith is the basis for hope. Permit me to leave you with one related thought—were it not for hope, there would be no need for faith. Do you agree?

Cultivating *emunah*

Let's explore some pathways to emunah. Along the line of "fake it till you make it" in Program jargon, taking spiritually or religiously intentional actions can give rise to faith: "good intentions will follow good actions."[84] Although I cannot explain it, my experience is that observing Shabbat (a form of doing something Jewish) was a path to faith for me. After many years of going through the motions of the Program and reading and re-reading Step 2, the consistent practice of streaming Shabbat services on Friday nights resulted in a spiritual connection and gave rise to my inner experience of emunah. This transformed my understanding of Step 2. Becoming familiar with the liturgy and music of Shabbat services allowed me to self-identify with the Jewish people and the Jewish story, and it planted the seed of a relationship with the source of our journey. Likewise, over time, attending meetings, working with a sponsor, and listening to fellows gave rise to my faith in the Program. This transition was a turning point in my commitment to the work of recovering and is entirely consistent with Jewish wisdom that faith takes work. Doing can indeed give rise to emunah.

Alternatively, as it relates to finding emunah and acquiring a relationship with a Higher Power, Rabbi Wolbe, the great 20th-century Mussar teacher, encouraged us to study nature.[85] He taught that what's revealed explains what's hidden. By extension, awareness of the hidden is crucial to cultivating emunah about a transcendent source. Soaking up a mountain vista, being warmed by the sun or human touch, or examining a flower evokes something most can feel. Rabbi Elkhanan Wasserman is quoted as explaining that "… the wonders of creation demand of every intelligent person to arrive at the conclusion that they were erected by a Divinity."[86]

to faith that relates to my sobriety or that of my loved ones? Our tradition teaches that there is one God, all-powerful and everywhere, so from a Jewish wisdom perspective the answer is, "of course."

I had no faith when I came to the Rooms. More accurately, I had no faith in anything but myself, even though that wasn't working out so well. Experiencing such doubt is frequently the case when we show up broken, in active disease. For those who are willing to open themselves to it, Step 2 opens the door to the spiritual solution contained in emunah. Nurturing this middah is an important aspect of our Step 2 work, bringing to bear this powerful mysterious resource which is at our disposal and ever ready to help us. In relation to Step 2, having emunah that there is a hidden source allows us to let go of our futile efforts to control the uncontrollable.

How faith relates to hope

Arriving at the Rooms in desperation, I fleetingly considered that if I could believe that there was some supreme or grand power, then maybe I could also believe that it could somehow help me change the course of my life. The idea that I could get better reflects hope—another concept that we need to unpack in this "word soup." Hope is often mentioned in reference to Step 2. Faith and hope are intertwined yet distinct. Please, stay with me as we dive into these ideas.

Emunah is the foundation of hope: Hope enters the picture when we project into the future. Let's take the seemingly simple hope that we can get sober. I knew that, even with my best efforts, I could not make that happen on my own. And I knew that continuing to do the same thing and expecting something different to happen was a form of insanity. On its own, my hope was nothing more than a pipedream or empty optimism. Our hope only gains substance and potential to be realized if we invest in it and take an action to create a reason to believe that what we hope for is possible.

Following the Twelve Steps to get sober was something that I knew had worked for many who had come before me. I had faith in the Program, and engaging in it was an action I was free to choose to take. Allowing yourself to feel hopeful rests simply on faith that others' history could repeat itself for you. Over time, it has been my experience that seeking and nurturing

beliefs, new facts might cause you to change your mind. From this perspective, the idea of believing as a foundation for Step 2 seems a bit tenuous. It's not an especially strong launching pad for something as arduous as getting sober and renewing ourselves in mind and body.

To tease these ideas apart, it's useful to keep digging a bit. Maimonides' use of the adjective "complete" appears to describe a quality of belief. In accord with this idea, Yeruham Levovitz[82] took the idea to a higher level: he described emunah as "a feeling of absolute certainty [where] there is no room in one's heart for any doubt whatsoever."[83] Levovitz thus referred to the level of confidence in a particular belief and also elevated it from thought to feeling. Faith, then, reflects that what we feel is the absolute truth. Think for a minute about feeling defeated and powerless and hearing from someone, "I think this may help." Compare that to hearing "I have faith that this will help." The latter provides a level of assurance—it has the power to grab our attention and engender a degree of certainty, thereby helping addicts like us, who are searching for solutions, feel like we are on solid footing.

Step 2 invites us to engage with a Jewish concept of emunah—absolute confidence in a transcendent power outside ourselves. Recognizing that faith is an entirely personal conviction, permit me to share my working definition. Feel free to borrow it or change it as best suits you. In regard to a HP, faith to me is my concretized belief that there is a hidden [re]source of the universe. I am totally confident of this view because of repeated personal experience. For example, based on my experience yesterday and the day before and every one of my preceding 25,915 days, I have faith (and know irrefutably) that my heart will beat and my body will digest food but not itself even while I sleep. Something hidden and grand engineers and powers the cells of my body, and my reliance on those truths is absolute. I do not think of it often, but I am filled with awe and gratitude when I do. I am faithful in this regard and will not try to take control of my heart rhythm or digestive function, nor do I need to know how it all works. It is as it is meant to be.

A related question is how—or if—faith in one arena extends to other aspects of our lives. For example, is faith in my cardiac function extensible

it's important to wade through such esoteric reflections. It is because emunah is pivotal to recovery. All of us show up in life as imperfect beings, some more imperfect than others. Faith provides a pathway to self-acceptance and self-love. I liken faith to the gold dust of kintsugi, the Japanese art of mending broken pottery. Integration of gold dust into a piece's brokenness results in a beautiful new whole. Serving as our gold dust, faith is the glue that makes us whole. Thus, emunah is the antidote to the despair that we addicts carry as we walk into the Rooms of the Program, and it unlocks the door to hope, which helps us forge through the work ahead. Emunah has the power to restore us and to sustain us. It is my experience that feeling or being in emunah (feeling full of faith) is fleeting, but has the potential to be infinitely renewable. The knowledge that it's always present for me—if I seek it—brings me great comfort.

Step 2 references belief, and many in the fellowship refer to hope as another principle of the step. Faith, belief, and hope are intertwined yet distinct. Let's tease them apart, and then we can get personal to see how emunah can be cultivated to fuel your ongoing journey toward recovery.

How faith relates to belief

Step 2 invites us to believe that there is a hidden power in the universe and that that power can restore us to sanity. How does faith relate? Writing about his beliefs about God, Maimonides (a great Middle Ages Jewish philosopher and scholar) wrote, "I believe with complete faith."[81] Don't let the God part distract you—we will come back to it later. Maimonides's statement is important because it reflects his thinking that belief and faith are different. Starting with the belief part: a belief is something we hold to be true, usually based on some experience or facts. It has its foundations in the past and is black and white—either you have it or you don't. Regarding a belief, we might say "I think that…" or "I believe that…" For example, based upon my vacation experiences, I believe that the best beaches in the world are in Hilton Head, South Carolina. Our beliefs are our truths—they are ideas that are essentially our opinions based on the facts we have.

Going to Hawaii and experiencing black sand brought a new perspective to my beach thinking that challenged my earlier opinions. In the case of

I feel enlivened, inspired, and hopeful when I am with fellows in the Rooms of recovery. I have experienced the Higher Power of the group and the wisdom of the Steps and my sponsor, and I am blessed to draw inspiration and courage from them. I found strength in knowing that innumerable others have come to A.A. and Al-Anon and found recovery. These are things that I feel in my heart as much as I know in my mind. New facts—for example, a fellow relapsing—do *not* have the power to dissuade me from my beliefs. I can say resolutely that the power spoken of in Step 2 has done for many of us what we could not do for ourselves. It doesn't matter whether we have any idea how this power greater than ourselves is going to help, just that we've come to think it is possible and seek it.

Faith (*Emunah*): A Mussar perspective on Step 2

> *I believe with complete faith…*
> —Maimonides

I want to bring focus to the soul trait of faith (*emunah*) as the cornerstone of Step 2. As you have already learned, Step 2 invites us to believe that there is a hidden mysterious dimension to life and living. Emunah involves seeking to relate to that mystery in our everyday lives. This soul trait may be challenging; it's a bit like understanding love. You know what love is, you know how it feels to have it, and you know what it looks like to act in a loving way. We seek love because it helps us feel whole. Now, try to describe it! The same can be said about faith.

The nature of faith (*emunah*)

Let's start with what it is not, at least in my experience. Faith/emunah is not a steady state that we achieve which then remains fixed. Faith is something sensed or experienced from encountering flashes of the Divine. Through faith, we connect to what is hidden in the universe; once you have experienced it, emunah is as real and life-giving as love is. You may ask why

us, which is restore us to sanity. Translating this to mean that I can become a responsible, caring adult and stop trying to control the uncontrollable seems like a tall order! *OK, maybe it's theoretically possible for others, but what about me?* My rational, skeptical inner voice cautions me. *After all, I have not had much going my way in a long time and my life was really messed up.* Looking carefully at the language in Step 2, we see that it does not promise that we *will* be restored; it says the power "*could* restore us…" Since stuff happens all the time for which there is no explanation, I can't reject this idea. Saying "maybe" seems the same as "could."

That brings us to the belief part of Step 2.

The believing part

By introducing the words *belief, restoration,* and *power* (greater than ourselves) together, Step 2 can get us tangled up with ego and ideas of God. While "Higher Power" is a term often used to refer to the "power that is greater than ourselves" and might connote God, that is not what's on the table here. Let's go back to look at the language of Step 2 carefully. It does not say we should believe *in* this power. We will talk more about believing in a Higher Power or God-like entity later. Rather, the Step invites us to "believe *that* a power greater than ourselves could restore us to sanity." Step 2 asks us to accept that we can get better. It offers us hope! As I described above, I came to embrace the idea that the possibility existed. My experience in the Rooms with others like myself was living proof. Something in or about the Program allowed fellows like me to recover and enjoy lives of happiness, serenity and service. If you aren't there yet, I have enough hope for you and me both, and I am happy to share mine with you until you have your own. In the meantime, "fake it until you make it."

I want to explore one final aspect of Step 2. The Step says we "came to believe." I don't think that anyone walks in the door being a believer. Belief as contemplated here grows over time; as it grows, confidence in the belief gets stronger. Engagement with Step 2 may start as blind faith or wishful thinking, but over time, the idea becomes implanted in our hearts as irrefutable.

our sponsors is often a starting point for willingness, and for some it can help them get and stay clean and sober. My best efforts and power of will alone, which included threatening, negotiating, pleading, and praying—could not get those I loved sober, nor could I fix myself. Coming into the Program did inspire us toward recovery, making the idea of a power greater than ourselves very real and rationally defensible. So on that basis, I bought into this idea that there is a power that is greater than mine.

Restoring us to sanity

Let's move on, then, to consider being restored to sanity. It's reasonable to doubt whether any force or power actually has the ability to restore people, especially me and those I love. I do know that outside the Program, people who are sick do miraculously get better. Is that luck or something else? Within the fellowship, people told me that by working the Program they were healing, and I saw it for myself. Again, was that a matter of time, just chance, or something more? I have seen fellows go from despondent to hopeful and happy. The stories we hear in open meetings provide evidence that recovery and restoration happen around us every day. Why and how was unclear—was it hidden power, human power, luck, or something else?

As for me, honestly, I was unsure. I had not "asked" for help or quieted my self-will (aka my ego) to leave room for any personal change. Becoming aware of those around me in the fellowship planted the idea that if others could find recovery here, maybe it could happen for me, too. Since my best thinking did not yield positive results, there was little downside in being willing to consider this as possible. So I accepted the idea that restoration and recovery might be possible. If you cannot get to acceptance, you might consider something that many try: acting "as if," faking it for a while, as the fellow at my first meeting advised me to do.

A promise?

Coming into the Program, I was unaware of my insanity; it was hidden under the blanket of denial I had spread over my life. Over time, listening to others helped me see my stinking thinking and unhealthy patterns of interacting and reacting. Step 2 introduces us to what the power can do for

struggled with these ideas; I was no exception. My rational self wanted data. Is there really a power greater than me that can help me and improve my life, and how can I be sure? Permit me to share my approach to these ponderous questions.

Power greater than ourselves

With the words "power greater than ourselves," Step 2 invites us to look beyond ourselves. Right off the bat, my ego fought this idea; I inferred that it meant that I can't take care of myself and my life. Then came the question of control: If I was not in control, who would be? And if something else was in control, what if I did not like its solution or answer? I did start addressing these questions in Step 1 with the begrudging admission that I was powerless. My doubts lurked in the shadows of self-will that lingered as I went on to take Step 2.

Step 2 does not focus on who or what the power is. Some might initially argue that the Step refers to a religious entity. That is not, I believe, the case—the intended idea is a nurturing power that guides us in dealing with the effects of addiction and alcoholism in ourselves and those we love.

For me, seeing is believing (except for my own truths, of course). Leaning on rational thought and ego, I was immediately skeptical of this power idea. To help us think about such powers in the universe, Program literature encourages us to look at nature and make note of its order and vast beauty. Once I became open to the possibilities, wind and gravity came to mind as forces greater than anything I could muster. I had to acknowledge that there are some forces that are stronger than me. These reminded me that there is also a life force that controls the seasonal cycle, keeps my heart beating, and allows my body to function when I am sleeping. Lo and behold, willingness to explore the idea spawned a "maybe" in my belief.

In addition to forces of nature, there are human forces to think about. For example, the collective energy of a group is visible and palpable in sports contests, especially when cheering on underdogs. My personal experience as a member of the fellowship revealed that joining and engaging unlocks a power that originates in the collective experience and wisdom of the group. Being immersed in it at meetings or when in relationship with

chaos, and how I used detachment from my feelings to protect myself from myself. Perhaps most importantly in terms of moving toward recovery from the effects of addiction, I began to develop awareness that I owned a part of my problems. I was not a passive victim. An honest self-appraisal showed me that I often resorted to dishonesty and deceit to get what I wanted. Fear, despair, and resentment controlled my thinking and decisions, and I did not like what I saw in the mirror. I became empowered through learning that I had choices.

When the time to share in the fellowship circle came around to me, I often passed, usually choking back tears. Giving my name was an accomplishment. Then, one day, the energy or power of the group gave me enough courage to speak. I began to let down my armor and open my heart. I am happy to report that I did not die from it—in fact, I felt more alive. I slowly allowed myself to feel part of "them." Awareness expanded over time—insights came slowly as I gained perspective on my misplaced blame and shame. Still constantly wary, I found comfort in looking around and realizing that everyone in the Rooms was like me and I was like them. We all had created wreckage in our lives and the lives of others, and we all came to the Program seeking hope that change was possible. Although I did not realize it at the time, claiming my seat and affirming to myself and my fellows that I was there in the Rooms of recovery where I belonged was the beginning of change and hope.

By raising our hands and giving voice to our truths, we begin participating in our own healing and become part of the solution for ourselves and for others. I came to see that those around me who were actively engaged in the work of recovery were generally happy, caring, trusting of others, and seeking to grow and be trustworthy. There was value in the seeking, which I learned was why we all kept coming back.

Belief, faith, and hope

Step 2 introduces several big ideas and challenges. First is acknowledging that a power greater than ourselves exists and—related to this—that it holds the key to recovering, to being restored. Believing these ideas took the work of Step 2 to another level of difficulty entirely. Many around me

Developing mindfulness

In addition to the aspect of togetherhood that opens the Step, it is useful to examine the order or progression of thinking built into Step 2. There are three sub-steps here: 1) I/We came; 2) We came to; and 3) We came to believe. "We came…" seems to state the obvious: we showed up. Some of us showed up voluntarily, some at the suggestion of a mental health professional, child, or spouse, and some by order of a court. These differences do not matter. Coming to the Rooms of recovery, we all had to choose whether we would stand outside the recovery circle or step into it. The decision to step into the circle and take the hand of help that was offered was much harder than bringing our bodies to the venue and must be acknowledged. It is a big deal. Fear, shame, distrust, and hopelessness were barriers we had to cross. Chasms.

Keeping the universality and power of these thoughts in mind, it is really important to note that Step 2—like the others—begins in the past tense ("we came" not "we come"). In this form, I saw that the Step conveys what worked for those who came before us. This whisper of what worked for others was the push I needed to cross the threshold. It bolstered my confidence that by harnessing my desperation and adding just a bit of willingness, I could embrace what has worked for so many others. I remember the numbness when I entered the meeting room for the first time, and for many months I was just going through the motions of showing up. But I also remember the warmth of the hand that held mine at the closing of the meeting.

I've heard my fellow recovery travelers say that over time, beyond simply bringing our bodies to the Program and mastering the logistics of how different meetings were run, we "came to." Like coming out of anesthesia, we slowly became aware. In contemporary parlance, we might refer to this as mindfulness or being present with our thoughts, feelings, bodily sensations, and surrounding environment. Personally, I could sense the communal love and compassion among fellows—especially as people shared from their hearts about their thoughts, feelings, and actions. I heard others talking about the same sorts of things I had never shared with another human soul. Slowly I opened my mind and heart to the realization of my own truths, my

Honestly, the rest was a total blur. I do recall feeling safe and accepted for that hour. That's about all I remember, except for hearing the words as the meeting closed: "Keep coming back. It works if you work it." Something made me willing to think about it.

At the time, I was in the midst of an ugly divorce, and I had some spare time when my children were with their father. Although I'm not sure why, I did go back. I will admit here that I sought meetings that were a good distance from my home to be sure that no one in my community or workplace would see me. And—following my natural tendencies as a shy, introverted person—I held myself at a distance. I was mostly closed to my own feelings and to the love of others. Essentially, I was auditing the Program.

Week after week, I was welcomed back. Clearly, none of my life circumstances or my particular craziness mattered to anyone else. I cried at meetings for the better part of a year and was filled with shame and fear. No one was trying to pry my secrets from me, but I kept being reminded that *our secrets keep us sick*. As I had throughout my schooling and professional life, I planned to study the literature and master the Program. I had no exit strategy, but I was sure that with my intelligence I could grasp what I needed, remain comfortably reclusive, gain control, and be on my way.

With the gift of time, I have discovered the depth of Step 2. Let's break it down and look more closely at what Step 2 really says.

The collective "we"

"We" runs through the steps as the unstated subject of all this work. The use of "we" reflects the thread that unites us and the fact that being part of the fellowship means that not one of us need ever again be alone in our disease. Engaging in the work of recovery with others in the fellowship makes us part of something bigger than ourselves. This is incredibly important and valuable because "we" can do together what "I" cannot do alone. Insofar as we each are inspired by what we see, hear, and feel around us in the Program, "we" can become a source of experience, strength, and hope for those who follow us into the Rooms of recovery.

the basement of a church. I was simultaneously overwhelmed and numb. How did it work, what should I say, when should I speak? Fear was my foundation—fear of death due to an overdose or stress, fear of financial insecurity, and fear of my secrets being revealed. I was a mess, my family was a mess, and I had no life. I was broken physically, financially, emotionally, and spiritually. In my mind, I was a failure by every measure.

Keep in mind that I was in my mid 40s at the time. Having been dropped off at that meeting, I was like a child on the first day of school. I wanted to cling to my mother for safety. I walked tentatively across the threshold into the meeting room. The fluorescent lighting was harsh and cold. I recall feeling as if I were a solo performer standing on the stage of life, under an intense spotlight that revealed all my warts to the audience who had me in their sights. I was quickly spotted as a newcomer, greeted (with warmth), and offered coffee. I heard the buzz of fellowship around me. There was laughing, and although some individuals looked pretty rough (as did I), it seemed that everyone else was comfortable being there. My strategy was to hide in the back, scope it out, and assure that my truth was protected—I was in a strictly "need to know" mode—and I hoped to slink away before anyone noticed me.

As the meeting started, someone referred to a large poster on the wall and read The Twelve Steps[80] aloud starting with Step 1: We admitted that we were powerless over alcohol and our lives had become unmanageable. I had to admit, "Yep, that's me, at least the unmanageable part." And then someone else read Step 2: We came to believe that a power greater than ourselves could restore us to sanity. I immediately thought, "I came; I showed up. Done." Then I said to myself, "Aha! There's that God power stuff and I'm not insane. I don't need to be restored so this isn't for me." As I got up to leave, someone met my glazed eyes and took me aside.

> "Your driver is in the meeting next door. They'll be done in an hour. Why don't you stay for just this one meeting? You don't want to leave before the miracle."
>
> I said, "I don't believe that stuff, my situation is not so bad, and I'm not crazy, so this is not for me."
>
> He responded, "That's OK. Fake it for an hour."

Chapter 6

Step 2: Faith

Step 2. [We] Came to believe that a power greater than ourselves could restore us to sanity.

⬅————————————————————➡

Too Little — **Too Much**

| Emotional & Spiritual Death | Loneliness Fearful & Controlling | God as Companion | Fanaticism |

First things first.
—12 Step fellowship wisdom

Faith: A recovery perspective

Step 1 challenged us to look under the veil of our denial regarding our addictions; we found wreckage and pain. In addition to facing the truths about our brokenness, Step 1 challenged us to surrender the delusion of control. Step 2 offers us the opportunity to take the hand of fellow Program members offering to share their experiences, strength, and hope. It points the way to serenity and opens the possibility of a different reality for those who are willing. Dr. Martin Luther King, Jr., described taking such an action as an act of faith, reaching for the next step without being able to see the whole staircase.

I cannot lay claim to taking the lifesaving step forward to Step 2 on my own. Someone who saw my pain and understood the promise of recovery picked me up and took me to my first meeting. It was nighttime and in

- What practices enable you to determine the truth within yourself?
- How might you become more truthful with yourself?

Playlist
- "It's Only Life"—The Shins
- "Your Life is Now"—John Mellencamp
- "Truth Be Told"—Carly Pearce & Matthew West
- "Honesty"—Billy Joel
- "If We're Honest"—Francesca Battistell
- "It's Been a While"—Staind

- Use the phrase *yetzer hatov* as your log-in ID or password. You become what you think.
- When washing your hands, imagine that the suds are falsehoods being cleansed away. Name one out loud each time you wash.
- Looking into the mirror each morning, admit to yourself where you have been untruthful or your life is unmanageable. Restate it truthfully out loud.

If you lean toward brutal truth you might try:

- Wear a rubber band on one wrist every day. Always start with the same wrist. In a situation when you've successfully chosen a gentle way, move the rubber band to your opposite wrist. When you move it, you're essentially rewarding yourself for choosing a compassionate action.
- Practice zip the lip.
- When washing your hands, think about the fragility of the bubbles and imagine touching another's bubbles gently, trying not to burst them. Name out loud someone with whom you want to be more gentle each time.
- Before sharing your truth, ask yourself if it will be hurtful; if so, *pause*!—**p**ostpone **a**ction **u**ntil **s**ensitivity **e**merges.
- Try screening what you are about to say using the acronym *think*: are your words **t**rue, **h**elpful, **i**nspiring, **n**ecessary, **k**ind?

Prompts for journaling or study with your *chevruta*/sponsor
- How do I keep myself sick?
- Why is it so difficult to admit my powerlessness over ____?
- What keeps me holding onto the illusion that I have the power to change someone else?
- Do I allow anything to pass my lips that I am not certain is completely true?
- How do I know when my life is unmanageable?
- Who have I hurt with falsehoods?
- By answering these questions, what have I learned about myself?
- What lies am I telling myself? Why?

addicts; just as he described, truth could help us turn away and distance ourselves from our hurtful choices.

One aspect of lying and being habitually deceptive to protect our disease is that we are stealing trust, often from those we love. How does it feel being a thief in addition to being a liar? Striving to free ourselves from such ugly labels provides strong motivation to choose truthful speech. Mussar teachers advise us to say nothing that we do not know is true. Working on the soul trait of silence (*shtikah*) can help us make our way back to the middle, being honest, trustworthy, and a pillar of the world. Another way to think of this from a Mussar perspective is to embrace the soul trait of honor (*kavod*) which drives us to treat others with respect. Falsehoods reflect a failure to respect someone enough to tell them the truth.

Such is the victory we can enjoy in taking Step 1, embracing truth and working to distance ourselves from falsehood, one day at a time. With the guidance of Steps 2-12 and a God of our understanding, we can ascend the mountain of wreckage of our past and stand in the place of honor and light, becoming a light to others.

Daily reminders to help work Step 1

Following are some phrases that you might use as your daily reminders. Feel free to choose one of these or create your own.
- Be distant from falsehood.
- Keep your motives clean.
- Guard the world with Truth.
- Weigh your words on the scale of truth before you speak.
- **Wait** (acronym)—**W**hy **a**m **I** **t**alking?

Kabbalot to cultivate Truth (*emet*) as you take Step 1

If you lean toward excessive falsehood, you might try:
- Wear a rubber band on one wrist every day. Always start with the same wrist. In a situation when you've successfully chosen the truth, move the rubber band to your opposite wrist. By switching wrists, you're essentially rewarding yourself for taking a good action.

can hurt others, failure to self-regulate suggests that we do not value the other enough to be truthful; we can choose whether to be more respectful.

With such an approach, we can transform our choices and cultivate the character strengths that will allow us to show up as our best selves. The Talmud[78] tells of a place named Truth. The residents would not deviate from the truth in their statements, and no person from there would die prematurely. Truth protected them from the Angel of Death. I contrast that with Falsehood. It leaves us isolated and closed off from the connections that bring us the life energy of love and acceptance. So, before moving on, take a few moments to reflect on what causes you to lie. Perhaps you can identify some issues related to resentment, anger, fear, shame, or pride. Do these feed your yetzer hara? Maybe you are holding onto fear of disappointing someone (or yourself), fear of shame, or fear of loss (financial or other). As we move on through the Steps and middot, we will come back to this question, looking for soul traits in your inner world that are out of the middle range.

Secondary middot

There is *never* one way to refine ourselves. Our Mussar curriculum is unique to each individual. While teachings related to truth (*emet*) might suffice for someone working Step 1, it could be beautiful to work Step 1 with the added perspective of the middah of humility to bolster cultivating the trait of truth. Think for a moment about the arrogance of believing that "I can change someone else" (such as making them stop drinking). This lie we might tell ourselves clearly comes from having a bloated sense of self-importance. In essence, such thinking and related actions would reflect a belief that I am God—not exactly humble.

Rightsizing ourselves relates to humility, and its applicability here is an example of how our middot intertwine. Humility (the middah of *anavah*) is foundational; it's said that all our virtues depend on humility, so you will see it come up again and again. Such an interaction between middot is reflected in the teachings of Rabbi Luzzatto, who wrote that arrogance blinds us to our own defects and decline.[79] This looks like denial for us

Cultivating truth

In a general sense, working toward recovery and self-refinement involves focusing on soul traits that are in play when we are at the *bechira* point, the place of making choices. In the case of falsehoods, the bechira point is at the choice between a difficult truth or an easy lie. Rabbi Luzzatto offered many invaluable ideas about refining our middot so that we remain on a good path. He dealt head-on with the need to address traits that reflect activity of our yetzer hara (he referred to them as evil inclinations), such as stealing, fraud, and promiscuity. Some traits are clearly recognizable; others emerge when the heart has been seduced into rationalizing poor choices as permissible. Consider denial, a hallmark of our disease. Telling lies to ourselves and others was clearly within his scope of concern.

Luzzatto's writings on the virtue of cleanliness[73] connect strongly to the ideas of truth in our lives. Clean motives, he said, are a pathway to good action and good action is a pathway to good living. For support, he cites Psalm 24 in which David says, "Who may ascend the mountain of the Eternal and who may stand in the Place of His holiness? [Only] one with clean hands and a pure heart."[74] Luzzatto described the challenge we face as an intense war. Step 1 frames the battlefield as our minds and hearts. The enemy is an aspect of our own nature. In Luzzatto's words, "...man's nature is weak, his heart surrenders easily to temptation, and he permits himself those things [whose faults] he can rationalize."[75] I hate it that he described me to a tee!

Keeping our hands and hearts clean is a matter of vigilance and choice. Life is filled with tests. Our disease (addiction) is not a matter of choice but learning to live with it is. *Orchot Tzaddikim*[76] (originally published in the 15th century) teaches that we need to remove unbalanced soul traits so they do not sway us from our center. Rabbi Levin, in the classic Mussar text *Cheshbon HaNefesh*, got more specific. He taught that "...a person must first carefully inspect and dig deeply for the cause of his malady [i.e., falsehood]..."[77] explaining that we can uproot it through work on counterbalancing soul traits. For example, since many of our lies are spoken, we are advised to look at our speech, taking care to say nothing that we do not know with absolute certainty to be true. Insofar as our words and actions

and speech becomes just a tool to manipulate and conquer. Such speech is not only untrue; it also mirrors a crooked spirit and a soiled heart. In other words, we suffer spiritual death. It is with this emptiness that many of us show up at the doors of Twelve Step meetings.

The agent of falsehood: the malevolent inclination (*yetzer hara*)

We spoke earlier, in reference to self-restraint, about the choice point (*bechira* point—*nekudot bechira*) at which we can make an effort to avert a bad choice by engaging with our inner selves. There is a concept in Jewish thinking that may be helpful in explaining our addictive tendencies and, more importantly, in marshalling the hidden inner resources we can call on when challenged to choose the next right action. I am specifically referring to the inborn forces named *yetzer hatov* and *yetzer hara*. Think of them as inclinations that are in tension with one another. Our yetzer hatov pulls us toward altruism and helping others; our yetzer hara pulls us toward self-preservation. Jewish thinking is that through free will, we can choose which path to take. For example, leaning toward good and listening to our yetzer hatov, we can overcome a lustful urge that could lead us into an affair, or we can visit someone who is dying even though it makes us sad or uncomfortable. In contrast, the whisper of our yetzer hara can pull us away from good to make choices that are more self-satisfying. Building a home, having children and making money are motivated by our yetzer hara. The yetzer hara can lead us to choices that benefit the world; however, it can also tempt us to give into self-satisfying desire and what is unwise or hurtful to others or ourselves. Having an affair or neglecting the sick and homeless because of our selfishness or discomfort are examples. God wants us to pick the good; our lives are rich with the near-constant opportunity of choice.

Alcoholism, addiction, and their related obsessive thinking and feelings enslave our yetzer hatov. That leaves the yetzer hara free to lead us away from the moderate middle of our middot. The patterns common to addicts, such as lying, cheating, controlling, stealing, manipulating, managing, mothering and martyring, all reflect our yetzer hara as an agent of poor choices, pulling us off-center. It cajoles us to think that our dalliance isn't so terrible, even though we know we should not succumb.

a job loss as being the result of a reorganization rather than a decline in our work quality or our unreliable attendance is another example. Denial, closed-mindedness, and an unwillingness to consider the facts are other forms of falsehood common to addicts and their loved ones. A teaching of Rav Dessler on truth and falsehood applies here.[68] He taught that anyone whose perceptions are colored by self-interest will never see the truth in any area in which his bias operates. Only when one's bias is removed will he be able to understand the truth. From a personal perspective, as long as I am in denial [biased that my loved one (or myself) is not an addict], I can never see the truth. Let's tie this back to Step 1. For the addict, surrendering to the truth of powerlessness removes our own bias and unlocks the possibility of seeing our unmanageability for what it is. Truth is an admirable trait to cultivate, providing strong support for taking Step 1.

The why

So, why do we lie? In *Cheshbon HaNefesh*,[69] Torah scholar Rabbi Levin taught that lying is a dreadful spiritual illness.[70] At first it stems from the pursuit of permitted pleasure, money, prestige, or seeking the honor of others. It then progresses toward the pursuit of prohibited pleasures. In the end it takes on its own life, lying for the sake of lying! To me this smells a lot like my ego trying to be in charge. My Program friends talk about ego as Easing God Out; perhaps this explains why falsehoods are a spiritual illness.

Rambam[71] addressed the habit of falsehoods over a thousand years ago in his writings on virtues. I take comfort in knowing that this is a long-standing human issue. He was focusing on the importance of mindset in our choices and noted that being habitually distant from truth makes us numb.[72] The habit of lying is common to us addicts. Our hearts harden to accommodate the uneasiness (dis-ease) that we feel deep inside from being liars; we know the truth. We become closed to love and loving under such circumstances. This does, in fact, mirror the isolation in which many addicts find themselves.

Maimonides wrote that in such individuals, truth is valued so little that a person no longer even realizes the difference between the true and the false

is not a negative; the key is how we use it. Indeed, Jewish thought teaches that deviating from the truth is permissible under certain conditions. These include for the sake of peace or to avoid hurting another person. Saying how much you appreciate a gift even if you don't like it would be an example of a falsehood that would be acceptable. And, of course, there is the talmudic parable of the ugly bride. We must find something beautiful about which to comment. But, I'm sorry to say, using falsehood to avoid an argument about someone's obsessive thinking or addictive behavior is not a legitimate reason to lie to a loved one or to ourselves. Addicts may be quick to invoke the exceptions (e.g., blame, unfairness, bad luck, victimhood) as devices to avoid confrontations and arguments related to their behaviors and justify their diseased thinking. The price is high; doing so can result in death—physical, emotional and/or spiritual.

In regard to damaging choices, everyone involved must remain committed to truth. That said, we cannot force our truth on another. My telling an addict what I think about them for the purpose of motivating them to change is outside the boundaries of practicing truth. Taking Step 1 is about seeing our own truths.

Telling lies is part of our human nature. Everyone is susceptible to the misuse of truth or to falsehood. This truth may be why the Torah directs us to distance ourselves from falsehood[64] rather than teaching the absolute of "do not lie." No one can hit the mark all the time. While Rabbi Luzzatto noted that lying is a harmful sickness, he acknowledged that it is widespread among people.[65] Like our talmudic Sages,[66] he acknowledged that it is man's nature to desire theft and promiscuity. Our falsehoods, which steal trust at the very least, are part of being human.

That said, both truth and falsehood are active choices. Let's go back to the lies we tell in the course of our addiction. Torah's reference to falsehood was based on the words spoken, the message being conveyed, and our motives. This takes us back to that Program ideal of keeping our motives clean. Our Sages have said it is forbidden to deceive people.[67] Being intentionally misleading and overtly deceptive are forbidden: we are not to bend reality to serve our own purposes. Despite the best of intentions, lying to cover up for an addict falls within this zone of unacceptable behavior. Explaining

ships? What experience have you had with stories you told yourself? What is the difference if you are the giver or receiver of untruths?

Rabbi Yisrael Salanter was credited with teaching that truth is present when something follows the path for which it is intended without veering to the side.[61] Jewish tradition teaches that our intended path is acquiring Torah and living its values. The challenge is that our soul, which is designed to steer us to do what's right and is derived from Divine Truth, lives in a body that is driven by human ego and is seeking self-satisfaction and self-protection. To the extent that our addictions (chemical or psychological) sway us from serving God (following our intended path), we are not living in truth. It has also been taught that truth leads to good and the fulfillment of God's will.[62] Insofar as our focus is self-serving and we are preoccupied with reacting to the chaos of unmanageability with our own interests in the driver's seat, most addicts miss the mark of doing what God wants—doing what is good and right. The wreckage and chaos of our lives generally preclude our living with positive intention, consistency, and integrity.

A contemporary Mussar master gives us another way to think about this that is more digestible for me. Rabbi Wolbe (1914-2005) wrote that truth exists when nothing contradicts from objective reality.[63] To the extent that we mask the reality of our addictive choices and their consequences with deception and denial, we are not in the domain of truth. Such is my truth. What is your truth?

When we look at the middah this way, it appears that the factual accuracy of our words is not the core issue. The harm we cause (to ourselves, others, and the world) by undermining the ability to trust one another is the measure we must focus on in cultivating this soul trait. Failure results in constriction of the heart, a means to numb ourselves to survive the pain of life without trust. Our growth and the freedom to experience the joy possible from loving and being loved is lost.

The nature of falsehood

If we are not in truth, where are we? Although nothing is as clear as black and white, the simple answer is that we are in falsehood. Falsehood itself

and deceptions are what keep the addictions alive. Thus, we say, you are only as sick as your secrets. Step 1 is about accepting that our secrets and lies keep us trapped and sick—emotionally, spiritually, and perhaps even physically. Truth-telling is an essential ingredient of recovery. When we stop lying to ourselves (and those we love) in the course of taking Step 1, we find ourselves standing at the gateway to freedom and serenity.

Truth (*Emet*): A Mussar perspective on Step 1

> *Distance yourself from falsehood.*
> —*Exodus 23:7*

Emet is the soul trait referred to as truth. We are not going down the rabbit hole of debating *Big T* Truth and *little t* truth; that is the domain of philosophers and theologians. Rather, it's useful here to bring focus to our attitude about truthfulness and how we exercise choices in our actions, speech and thoughts that relate to ourselves. Step 1 is all about surrendering to the undeniable truths of our reality (that our lives are unmanageable) due to our disease and perhaps the disease of another; we are responsible only to step into self-management.

The nature of truth

The human struggle with truth has been a central theme in Jewish text going back to Adam and Eve in the Garden of Eden and our Sages who sought to help us find meaning. Truth was viewed as a pillar on which the world stands[60] and it follows that untruth destabilizes the world. I think about my own choices and how the lack of truth (from my addict, for example) affected our relationship and my well-being. It is my experience that untruth causes relationships to falter; fear and anger seep in unconsciously and our hearts harden when we cannot trust another to speak or act in truth. How do you feel without the foundation of truth in your relation-

and simply accepting the truth of our reality opens us to the possibility of change and healing.

Step 1 is about getting honest

The action called for in Step 1 comes from getting real and honest with ourselves about ourselves. The capacity to be honest is considered critical to recovering. In practicing truth, we must discern between rigorous honesty, loving honesty, and brutal honesty. Surrender here refers to rigorous honesty, and it is so very hard to do. The *Big Book* says that anything less than a wholehearted commitment to the Program will create poor chances of success from our work. We cannot learn to swim with one foot on the ground; we must be totally immersed. Ergo, not just honesty, but rigorous honesty, is the key.

In general, this Step does not itself invite us to share our truths about the choices of others. There are cases when we love an addict and we are asked to share our truths. As it relates to others, we may be drawn to brutal honesty to drive home a point or simply because of the anger and resentment about the destruction we believe they cause in our lives. Brutal honesty may be rationalized; for example, we might call it tough love. In truth, trying to force a change in someone else (like getting them to stop drinking) by telling them the brutal truth of everything we see them doing wrong is not likely to yield success and, in fact, might foster resentment and discord. From a Program perspective, our focus must be on ourselves and our Program work. Even with good intentions, the poor choices of others are not our business. When it relates to sharing my truth about someone else and their habits, I can convey my concern out of love, recognizing that I am not in charge of the outcome and that "our person" may not change anything. At such a point, we must remember to love ourselves with honesty and compassion regarding our feelings about the situation.

Our bodies just are the way they are; we have a disease that requires management. In fact, we likely suffer from interdependent issues of body, mind (emotional wounds), and spiritual emptiness, all of which need to be addressed in our work to heal. We don't have to like those truths, but pretending they are falsehoods risks that we will kill ourselves. The secrets

us vulnerable to ever-deepening cycles of shame, guilt, fear, frustration, and more irrational actions to relieve our pain. Everything suffers: career, health, relationships, finances, and our emotional well-being. We dare not let anyone know; keeping this nightmare a secret becomes our highest goal.

Our motives are logical; we want to be seen as competent and valuable, as lovable and loving. We obsess to be or feel in control; and ultimately, we run ourselves ragged putting out the fires that are visible and threaten our secrets and the lies we tell to protect ourselves. There is nothing logical or admirable about our thinking. Our motives are misguided; we grow sicker and sicker, and often it is our own stinking thinking that keeps us sick.

During periods like this, our best weapons are our human defense mechanisms: control, manipulation, denial, deflection, rationalizing, blaming, and avoidance. Lying, cheating, and stealing are also available to us. We adopt tactics to hide the truth about ourselves from ourselves and avoid the discomfort of facing our reality and revealing it to others.

The problem is that our human tools don't necessarily work in fighting lizards, allergies, or misperceptions which appear real to us. Fixing what's wrong requires a combination of cleaning toxins from our bodies and cleaning toxic thinking from our psyche. Taking away the booze, sex, drugs, or efforts of obsessive control can deal with physical aspects of our disease. The emotional/spiritual holes that we are trying to fill in the first place still need attention.

Within the Rooms of Twelve Step meetings, we hear our stories come from the lips of others. And it is there that we learn that we sabotage ourselves and about the power we can gain by admitting that we are powerless over the habits that make our lives unmanageable. We also learn that we are not unique or alone.

The action being called for in Step 1 is often called surrendering. It is important to clarify that surrender does not mean submission. Nor does it mean failure. Surrendering does mean that we are willing to stop fighting. What opponent? Call it what you will—that darn lizard, our disease, our stinking thinking, our allergy to alcohol, our ego or id or, as the *Big Book* describes it, "self-will run riot."[59] Letting go of the need to blame something

my own lizard. In other words, we [addicts] cannot, by willpower or reasoning, fix ourselves because the compulsion to seek relief (via attempted control or chemicals) is stronger than everything, including the desire to change. I am powerless over my own addiction and, surely, I lack the ability to change anyone else.

The idea of a physical allergy [to alcohol] is another approach for understanding our disease.

The "Big Book" of A.A. says that alcoholics can't drink in moderation the way most people can because alcoholics are allergic to alcohol, and this is a basis for calling alcoholism a disease. The word "allergy" may be a bit confusing because we typically think of allergies as an inappropriate immune response that causes swelling, sneezing, itchy eyes, runny nose, and general misery. Those are symptoms we are more likely to associate with cat hair and shellfish than with alcohol addiction. ...

The use of "allergy" in the Big Book is idiosyncratic. It seems to be used more generally to mean an abnormal reaction to a substance. Whereas most people are satisfied with two or three drinks, alcoholics want to drink more the more they drink.

Although it isn't medically or technically accurate, the notion of alcoholism as allergy may persist because people find it useful. For one thing, people typically have no idea what you're talking about when you tell them about GABA, glutamate, dopamine, down-regulation, and the prefrontal cortex. People do understand allergies and in particular they understand that an allergy is a reaction to a substance that only affects some people and may have life-threatening consequences. Furthermore, an allergy is not your fault. While it isn't your fault, you still have to do whatever is necessary to avoid your particular "allergen."[58]

While this idea of our idiosyncratic hyperreactivity to stimuli is described in terms of alcoholism, it is generalizable to people, places and things out of our control. Left untreated, the cycle of this disease simply feeds on itself. We continue to fall short of what we expect of ourselves and what others expect of us, despite our best intentions. Our insides surely don't match what we want others to see. Our diseased thinking and feelings of low self-worth (which may be masquerading as egotism) make

SECTION II: A TREASURE MAP

bling, Overeaters, etc.) for a reason, and it is our surrender to that fact that opens the door to infinite possibility.

Finally, we are not intended to do this alone. The opposite of addiction is not sobriety, it is connection. Join us, please. Onward and upward we go!

Knowing that this is part of your day enhances your awareness. What you write need not be long. You can briefly capture your experience that day—describe the situation, your behavior, and the outcome. How did the trait come up and how did you apply your Mussar learning in the situation? To help you get started, we provide some prompts.

Intentional Exercises (*Kabbalot*). These are deliberate actions we take that are intended to leave an internal impression and reinforce the refinement we are seeking. As an example, an individual who has too much humility (and tends to shrink or hide) might wear brightly colored clothes in an effort to practice being less recessive. To help, we have provided some suggested actions that fit whether you find yourself experiencing an excess or shortage of the trait you are working on.

Playlist. Listening to music is not conventionally part of Mussar practice. Rabbi Naomi Levy (*Einstein and the Rabbi*) points out that music does penetrate to the soul. Music itself facilitates learning for some. For others, it is simply a beautiful carrier of a message. We share the playlist as an additional path to developing and refining a trait.

Final notes

While there is no one way to approach either Mussar or the Twelve Steps, there is one concept that applies: they are *programs of action* and they require *practice*. The elements of personal practice work together. For example, journaling, kabbalot, and the daily inventory combine to bring purposeful focus and reinforce an individual's efforts for self-refinement, one day at a time.

It takes effort over time to grow and to change; no one is expected to get it right all the time. Give yourself permission to strive for progress, not perfection. But beware, it is easy to confuse activity with progress. Talking and thinking about change makes us feel better; working the steps and middot helps us *get* better.

Your supply list for this journey has two essential items: surrender and engagement. We hear in the Rooms that it is not the Program according to you. It is the Twelve Steps of A.A. (or Al-Anon, ACOA, Debtors, Gam-

for each Step are an important place to start. They create a bridge to the principles on which we focus for the perspective that Mussar offers. Then, go back and reread each Step in turn, working the practices. Please refer to the glossaries in the back of the book to help with terminology. And keep in mind that in recovery work, actions speak louder than words.

Both Mussar and Twelve Steps are programs of action. The details of your Step work are between you and your sponsor. Our Mussar sages identified practices they saw as integral to the inner changes people seek; we have adapted them and present suggestions for each Step. Mussar is traditionally practiced with a study partner (*chevruta*) or a study group (*va'ad*). You might think of your sponsor and home group in this framework. In classic teachings, Mussar practice had rhythm.[57] Since your Step work dictates your rhythm, we share these as daily practices while you are on each Step. We encourage you to try them with learning partners. Feel free to expand on the practices to make them work for you. Feel free to read ahead about other soul traits if you think that one may better fit your needs at the time. We do caution against simply dismissing the work because it seems boring, you feel you've mastered it, or you decide it's not relevant to your recovery. That might be the voice of your disease or your trickster (*yetzer hara*) resisting change (More on the *yetzer hara* in Chapter 5). Growth from Mussar practice is gentle and slow. The practices of journaling, kabbalot, and daily reminders all work together to reinforce our learning. Like Twelve Step work, it does require some surrender to those who have wisdom that we lack. We encourage you to trust the Sages. Our experience and observations are that it works if you work it.

An outline of suggested practices

A Daily Reminder. This is a short, positive affirmation that is a gentle reminder of the trait you are working on. Several suggestions are provided. Feel free to create your own. We suggest writing it on a sticky note and placing it where you will see it over the course of the day. Simply writing it down is positive action that reinforces awareness of the desired change.

Journaling. Writing about your experience with the soul trait is an important daily practice. The action of writing brings focus and clarity.

practice and Twelve Steps invaluable for anyone who yearns to reach their highest human potential.

Our goal is to explore the interactions between a set of soul traits and the Steps, to give those who seek to live in recovery additional tools that come from the Mussar tradition. In the chapters that follow, the starting point is the Step. There is repeated reference to a Higher Power in the Steps. A Higher Power doesn't have to be God; it could be nature, the universe, fate, karma, your support system, a recovery home group itself, medical professionals, or whatever you feel is outside of and greater than yourself/your ego. What you believe to be your Higher Power is a very personal thing.

Drawing on Twelve Step Program Conference-Approved Literature, personal experience, and stories of addicts from the Rooms of recovery, key ideas in each step are explained. If you are a newcomer, this will help you learn the major points of each step. If you are just walking into the Rooms for the first time, we do recommend reading this in parallel with your Step work because the Steps are designed to work in order. If you have already spent time in the Rooms, we hope you will find here a fresh way to see what may be familiar. We then introduce a Mussar soul trait that is foundational to that particular Step and a related principle. Core Mussar ideas underlying work on that trait are introduced and applied to the Step work, bringing the voices of Jewish sages to the work of recovering.

For each Step, the primary soul trait is represented by an arrow that captures the range of ways it might be expressed in each of us. The ends of the arrow represent extremes of too much and too little of the trait. The area in the center is where we are our best selves and closest to [Divine] perfection. The pulling away from the center represents inner forces of good and poor choices that are in tension with one another. No one ever reaches perfection; it's better to think of that center area as a zone in which we are our best selves. Where we are on the continuum varies from moment to moment and situation to situation. The goal is to spend less time in the extremes and use the tools of the Program and Mussar practice to move toward the center where we are our balanced selves.

We suggest that you read the book once through to get a sense of the Steps and Mussar practices as we understand them. The recovery readings

we cover truth, faith, trust, courage, shame, alacrity, humility, responsibility, compassion, loving-kindness, holiness and generosity.

Mussar trait terminology

We caution you that within a Mussar framework, even those traits with names you recognize are defined differently than is common. They offer an important benefit of broadening our thinking and self-understanding. Let's take humility as an example. From a recovery perspective, humility refers to rightsizing ourselves. For most people, this entails thinking of ourselves less. Let's start by describing becoming more humble as taking up less space. Mussar teachings on humility include the idea of taking up less space, but go further to teach that in some instances we may have too much humility, causing us to shrink too much. In such situations, we may need to extend ourselves and reduce our humility to take up our rightful space. In addition to such expansive views, Mussar soul traits encompass the role of our hearts in our soul traits. We'll come back to this in more detail in the pages that follow.

Mussar teaches us to focus on working the traits, while in Twelve Steps we work the Steps. The Steps are linear, while the soul traits are interdependent. The Steps offer relatively fixed assumptions about what drives our distorted thinking, while Mussar traits are nuanced, living dynamically on a continuum that ranges from excess to scarcity (e.g., too much or too little humility as described above). It is my experience that Mussar's unconventional description of a middah can open new perspectives on a Step. As you read the Mussar perspectives presented here for each Step, you will likely see applications of the trait to other facets of your life as well as in the Program. This suggests that you are doing the work correctly. Undoubtedly you will identify a body of work (your spiritual curriculum) and lean into it as you need to in all aspects of life. Perhaps most important, the Steps are largely head-driven (do what you *know* is right) while Mussar focuses on "teaching the heart what the mind already knows"[56] and acting from the *heart*. Notwithstanding such differences, the work of recovery and Mussar share a common goal of developing the capacity and desire to be of service to others. The universality of that aspiration makes Mussar

So, is this book for you? Yes. Whether you are a Jew or non-Jew, newcomer or old-timer, religious, spiritual, atheist, or agnostic—please join us on this adventure and embark on the wonderful journey to yourself and your beautiful life.

How to use this book

In Chapter 3 we described structural and conceptual parallels between Twelve Step and Mussar approaches to personal refinement and growth. Beyond the common structural backbone, both Mussar and Twelve Steps are spiritual programs; they offer a blueprint for living with purpose. Both challenge us to attempt, albeit imperfectly, positive behavioral change and spiritual mindfulness. The goal is to find emotional well-being and make meaningful connections with others and with a God of your understanding, in the world in which you live. My personal experience is that those who choose to embrace such directions for living with purpose, meaning, and fulfillment really do enjoy enriched lives. While each program can be viewed narrowly, perhaps just as a tool for recovering from addiction or living Jewishly, when the Twelve Steps and Mussar are woven together, they can turbocharge recovery. Our goal here in Chapter 4 is to show how these two systems complement each other.

In the evolution of the Twelve Steps of A.A., each Step was associated with a guiding principle that reflected the personal qualities required at that stage of recovery. These are referred to as the Twelve Principles; they are values related to personal responsibility and include honesty, hope, surrender, courage, integrity, willingness, humility, love, responsibility, discipline, spiritual awareness, and service. Beginning about 1,000 years ago, Mussar sages espoused a practice centered on self-refinement in these same areas. Such personal attributes were thought of as traits of our soul; refinement of them was considered an aspect of actualizing our Divine purpose. There are hundreds of soul traits (middot). They include many of the same values that are codified as the Twelve Principles of A.A. and go further to include other important traits for learning to live with ourselves. For example, our Mussar sages addressed anger, laziness and worry. Our focus here is on 12 middot that align with the goals of living in recovery. Going step-by-step,

daily living for exploring your core values, loving others and yourself, and enjoying happiness and deeply meaningful relationships? We encourage you to give yourself the gift of making the time now.

Mussar itself provides a path to uncover what stands in the way of being our best selves and living our best lives. It enables us to uncover and recover our core values and inner human beauty in a world that pulls at them and throws up mud that can dim our inner light. Through the sage wisdom of Mussar teachings, provocative questions, and simple activities for you to try, we will help you grow self-awareness—a starting point for change. Join with us to practice making choices that can help unlock your best self and best life.

Again, we ask, is this book for you?

If you are seeking to uncover or recover life with your best self, whether a newcomer or seasoned veteran, Jew, Christian, Hindu, Muslim, agnostic or atheist, each chapter brings you a fresh perspective on the Twelve Steps. *Mussar in Recovery* is born out of personal experience, learned strength and hope, and shared with authenticity, love and gratitude. You will see how the principles underpinning recovery can work at a deeper level on all aspects of our personal lives. The more we learn, the more we realize how much there is yet to learn. This book will feed your yearning to learn more and go deeper.

If you are a Jewish addict working on your recovery, Mussar wisdom brings a Jewish voice to enrich your work, helping you erase feelings that you are uniquely flawed and alone. You will discover that you can walk your human journey with dignity, taking your place as a link in a chain that traces back more than 5,000 years. Like our ancestors, you can be free and enjoy the happiness that your life and the universe offer.

If you are curious about what the Sages had to say about how to be your best self and live your best life, Mussar wisdom will bring you new insights on the human condition and help you forge a path to heights you likely never thought possible, walking you through trails of personal refinement and growth.

Chapter 4

Putting it to work

It works if you work it...
—Fellowship wisdom

Is this book for you? Yes.

While this book is written with those in recovery from addiction in mind, the teachings have universal application for anyone seeking to live a life that is fulfilling at the deepest levels. This is a book to help anyone create serenity and joy while living out this challenge we know as the human condition. That sounds bold, yes? We offer it with deepest humility. We believe that it can be true for you because of our lived experience.

Please, don't be put off by the fact that we use the Twelve Steps of recovery as a framework. The Twelve Step programs are blueprints for living a deeply fulfilling life, as is Mussar practice. They guide a journey to knowledge, understanding, love and compassion for ourselves and others. And they help us reveal our beauty and find awe in living by removing obstructions that we mistakenly thought were protective, by pointing us toward a relationship with a power greater than ourselves. By opening our eyes to the inner forces that influence how we show up for life, the wisdom in these programs can affect our choices and help us refine ourselves and our lives.

Living with a recovery mindset (in the broadest sense of the term), being guided by Twelve Step and Mussar thinking, fosters authenticity, balance, beauty, and wonder in our lives. Who among us has mastered those? Think about what's on your plate. We may try to balance relationships, parenting, caring for older parents, school, work, shopping, money, sex, an array of feelings, the state of the world, and our physical health. And the list goes on and on because life is complicated. Have you had time in the morass of

cause less suffering for others. Then you will make the contribution to the world that is your unique and highest potential."[54]

"…If not now, when?"[55]

Example: Recovery through a *Mussar* lens

Permit me to provide an example of how *Mussar* and Twelve Step practices (aka spiritual tools) work together. Sensitivity allows us to notice that we are critical of others—an addict or spouse or child, for example. This might reflect that we fail to see the good in them, focusing on the negatives only. Insofar as we all are creatures of the Divine, our negative judgment might reflect some self-hate or past hurt. It also reflects a lack of honor for ourselves or others.

A corollary is that if we practice the soul trait of honor (*kavod*), we can refine our negative patterns of thought and action. A reminder mantra might be "If I don't have anything nice to say, don't say anything." For the period in which I am working on my practice of honor (of others or myself), I can hold and reinforce this thought by using a screensaver reminder on my computer, by journaling about successes (and failures), and by sharing my experience and study of resources such as *Everyday Holiness* with my *chevruta*. Together, these practices, including *tikkun middot* and *cheshbon hanefesh*, are all aspects of cleaning my side of the street and keeping it clean during daily living. The tools help me refrain from harsh judgment. The payoff is that I become more spiritual (attuned to my place in the flow of the universe) and my relationships with myself, others, and God improve. That's what living in recovery with a Jewish voice can look like.

Getting on with our work

Each of the Twelve Steps is explored and reimagined within the frame of Mussar in the chapters that follow. For each Step, we introduce Mussar teachings on a foundational middah, linking it to recovery practice. The Mussar tools for each Step will also include suggested reminder phrases, journaling prompts, and kabbalot.

Living life on life's terms is no easy task. While it can be frustrating, we own a part in the complexity and challenges. Both Mussar and Twelve Steps help us identify our own patterns as stepping stones to mastering what lies underneath and controls us. Alan Morinis teaches "…the sooner you become familiar with it and get on to mastering it, the faster you will be free of these habitual patterns. Then you will suffer less. Then you will

ing thinking and behavior. Being free means that we do not need to use self-restraint to control ourselves. In the Mussar realm it reflects that we are not even enticed by what's in the windows on the other side of the street.

Alan Morinis describes the path to Stage 3 as a focused practice on what is underneath or motivating a middah. In the scenario above, hearing about the problems of others (listening to gossip) may soothe our own low self-worth (lack of self-honor). In the reverse, talking about the financial problems created by our addicts may be a way that we convey that we are a victim (they are the bad guy), reflecting too much humility.

Healing my sense of being inadequate and accepting myself as "enough" frees me of the need for external validation. If I could achieve Stage 3, in the ideal, I would not gossip for two reasons. First, my balanced sense of self would not require that I measure myself against anyone else. Second, my honor of others as inherently good would make gossip a form of defacing God's work, antithetical to living spiritually.

Transformation is a high bar. Our tradition teaches that "in all toil there is profit, but mere talk tends only to poverty."[52] In the Rooms we hear that talking in the Program makes us feel better and working it makes us get better. Mussar practice, like recovery work, is not a destination, it is a life journey. Pirkei Avot teaches "you are not required to finish the work, yet neither are you permitted to desist from it."[53] It's important that the journey is about progress, not perfection. It is notable that there are no perfect people in the Torah. Judaism doesn't espouse perfection as our purpose. Ironically, the focus is on human imperfection, addiction being one example. Programs for living such as Mussar and Twelve Steps enrich our spiritual lives by teaching us to appreciate the gift of imperfection and how to be our best selves by engaging with it.

Time has proven the value of Twelve Step programs. The ability of Mussar practice to enrich Twelve Step work has, until now, gone largely unnoticed. Exploiting the parallels and synergies between Mussar and Twelve Step programs can enhance the recovery practices of non-Jews and Jews alike. For Jews, the voice of Jewish wisdom can help overcome a barrier of feeling different and excluded. We can even feel pride in the thousand-year-old tradition that informs Program thinking and practices.

es lose their power over us and subside. This is invoking the middah of equanimity rather than succumbing to our own indifference or agitation.

Mussar, like Twelve Step programs, suggests tools to use in our work. Mussar practice includes study of primary and interpretive literature/teachings; a daily reminder phrase; a journal or diary for our accounting of the soul; meditation and prayer; and sharing with our learning partners. The steps, slogans, literature, meditation practice, prayer, sponsors, etc. are corresponding Program tools.

An important point of difference between Mussar and Twelve Steps is the Mussar practice involving *kabbalot*. *Kabbalot* are exercises or intentions that we commit to that relate to the desired change in a soul trait. This is a "contract" with ourselves, perhaps our *chevruta* or *va'ad* partners (and, depending on your belief system, with God), expressing what our desired change will look like. It doesn't have to be a radical change. And we need to accept that we will never do it perfectly. Small steps represent real and important progress on our journey toward our Divine purity. In this way, Mussar is gentle.

Transformation (Stage 3 Mussar Practice)

In Stage 1, the discipline of Mussar practice brings focus to our personal strengths (and weaknesses). In Stage 2, we use the tools to go beyond our inventory of "present or absent" and excess or scarcity, and make a conscious effort to control the behavior that arises from that middah. The Psalms[51] describe this as turning from evil and doing good. In recovery terms, self-restraint might be described as staying on my side of the street.

These are simple ideas on the surface, but they're not always easy to put into action. Using gossip as an example, Stage 1 is an awareness that we listen to, maybe enjoy, and spread gossip about others. Imagine whining about what our addict or spouse is or is not doing. Being aware that the tongue is a weapon creates a bechira point and we can, in Stage 2, decide to refrain from spreading gossip; even harder, we could ask others to refrain from gossiping in our presence.

Harder yet is what is recognized as the third stage of Mussar practice: transformation. Transformation happens when we are freed of an offend-

can result in my falling short of my aims. When in the state of dis-ease it is fair to say that our free will has run wild. My failure of sensitivity lands me in that place. Most important, the practice of tuning into myself provides me with opportunities to choose which version of me is going to show up.

Self-restraint (Stage 2 Mussar Practice)

Self-restraint refers to the efforts we can make to avert acting out a bad choice. Recovery is a program of action and so, too, is Mussar. The late, great contemporary scholar Rabbi Jonathan Sacks taught that Judaism is unique as a religion of action rather than merely contemplation and thought. A mitzvah or good deed is not complete until an action is taken.

In the Mussar tradition, positive action starts when we engage with our inner selves. Jewish tradition teaches that we must act once we see our truths. Rabbi Eliyahu Eliezer Dessler was an Orthodox rabbi and one of the main leaders of the Mussar movement. He used the Hebrew word *bechira*, meaning choice, to describe this inflection.[50] It's here at the *bechira* point (*nekudot bechira*) that we can give in to, or resist, free will and choose to pursue a spiritual solution, cultivating those revealed inner virtues that bring us closer to our Divinely given goodness.

The starting point for such change is identifying the trait that is out of balance. At the bechira point, we can develop choices of what action to take. Specific actions arise when we envision a middah which counters the imbalance. Referring to the continuum described above, for example, fear and worry may reflect lack of faith, an important middah. If we are low on faith, we might pull ourselves back to center by engaging with the middah of trust in our Higher Power. Another example might be when we are struggling with lack of patience. This may be countered by practicing the middah of silence rather than engaging in an argument. As it relates to an addiction, for example, rather than avoid or repress powerful urges, we are instructed to "surf" the accompanying thoughts and feelings, "riding the waves" without acting upon them. It's not about numbing ourselves; it's about "making room" for these impulses and being present with them with compassion, curiosity, and reliance on God (or something outside ourselves, such as a sponsor or the Program) for strength so that the urg-

Alan Morinis helps make this idea of centering or moderating on the continuum actionable.[48] Metaphorically, balance, reflecting the Divine ideal and our inherent beauty, is found in the middle. An excess of humility on the continuum may enslave us in shame and isolation (too much humility, self-rejection); on the other end of the spectrum, our own arrogance and oppression of others may reflect too little humility and trap others in our attempted control. Ponder that a moment; the ideas are not obvious, but they are foundational to rightsizing ourselves, which is integral to recovery and living as our best selves.

As mentioned previously, leading teachers have identified three stages in the practice of Mussar: Sensitivity, Self-Restraint, and Transformation.[49] To hear the Jewish voice in recovery it is helpful, perhaps, to think about the parallels between these ideas and the 3 A's (Awareness, Acceptance, and Action) described earlier. The teachings and practice of Mussar correspond directly to the work of recovery. Through rigorous practice, these ideas collectively help us close the gap between who we think we are, who we really are, and who we want to be.

Sensitivity (Stage 1 Mussar Practice)

Sensitivity is awareness of what's true about ourselves. We seek to know what's working well and what needs attention. We are vessels containing a full range of Divine attributes (soul traits). To simplify our thinking and work, we can focus on these traits as if they are distinct and separate; in reality, they are interdependent. Nonetheless, bringing focus, even in isolation, allows us to engage in the work of repair.

The goal in Mussar is to become aware of the sensations that arise when we are triggered and our middot go off-center. Here are some examples of how my soul curriculum (and related middot) come into play in my everyday life. I feel a hardening in my chest when my ego is challenged (humility), and I feel an uneasiness in my gut before I call a help desk for support (impatience). Also, I crave sweets when I feel badly for harshly judging my addict (silence, honor) and my skin gets tingly when I tell a lie (truth). These sensations are flags or signals that rise up before I find myself in trouble. Failure to meet the warnings with some healthy behavior

It is easy to see within ourselves positive qualities of the Divine, such as humility, loving-kindness, and generosity. The so-called negative traits such as shame (*boshet*), anger (*ka'as*), envy (*kinah*), and judgment (*shifut*) may also be in our inventory; while they can be unattractive, it is important to remember that these also have their origin with the Divine. Most of our traits serve us well until we find ourselves at an extreme, when they can become destructive. Even the so-called negative middot can have positive outcomes. For example, getting angry at injustice drives us to *tikkun olam*, healing the world, which is an inherently worthy Jewish value. We can use jealousy of others' knowledge to stimulate our own commitment to learning, and we can use judgment to discern danger and safety.

Example: The importance of the center
Let's return to the Soul Trait Framework that was described earlier, and delve deeper here into humility to illustrate how a soul trait that is out of whack might relate to our character defects. This connection is at the root of how Mussar practice can enrich our recovery work.

Humility sounds like something [good] to strive for, yes? But, at the extreme of too much humility, one might be so humble as to be cowardly. The Talmud tells a story during Roman times when the failure of Rabbi Z. ben Avkulas to act resulted in the destruction of the Temple and the Jews' exile from the land. Not helpful. When there is addiction in the family, such thinking might cause us to accept unacceptable behavior from the addict. There is a cascade of hurt among those involved.

On the flip side, managing and mothering someone to protect them might be done out of love or the misplaced idea that we know what's best for them. Such lack of humility denies others the honor of self-expression and, in the case of an addict, enables them to be irresponsible and dependent rather than experience the consequences of their actions. Looking at a more obvious negative trait such as anger gives us another view. Feeling anger might be justified when we see social injustice. The key is channeling emotional and spiritual energy to create solutions that are healthy for us and those we love.

essence, prescribed in the course of our creation, I reject the idea that soul traits are defects of character, as they are referred to in Program lingo. My perspective is, I believe, a simple extension of the uniquely Jewish thought that we are inherently good, having been made in the image of God.[44]

These virtues or aspects of our inner selves are identifiable with self-awareness. Many are our strengths, and some are unproductive patterns. Through a Mussar lens, think of those aspects that are not working for us as simply out of balance. Alan Morinis describes Mussar as "helping you identify your spiritual curriculum (the traits you would benefit from bringing into balance) and giving you the tools to engage with the inner work of recalibrating those traits that obstruct your soul's light from shining into your life."[45]

Thus, in our work, we do not have to become good; we need to find our inherent goodness that is veiled by old, unproductive patterns so that our light can once again shine on the world. Permit me to restate this; it is important and you may not have heard this in a long time. We addicts are not bad, defective people. We are not weak of character or losers. We have a soul sickness. Since our soul or life energy (whatever idea works for you here) is of Divine origin we can think of addiction as a spiritual disease. Repairing our souls, one trait at a time, as is our Jewish tradition, is a path to healing. In line with this, Tanya (a Chasidic text) teaches that the soul's descent into this world is for the purpose of our ascent.[46] In other words, we are the vehicle for our souls to achieve God's purpose of love and compassion in his creation.

That goal is a tall order, given that owing to our human nature, our middot can migrate to extremes of useful and not useful. Nonetheless, repairing them (*tikkun middot*) through study and practice of Mussar is a spiritual path to restore our divine beauty that can give us life purpose. The promise of Twelve Step programs and Mussar are the same: Through disciplined practice, we can remove the veils that cover our innermost selves and let our Divine light shine brightly for all to see. Through these actions of working our spiritual curricula, we fulfill the inherently Jewish commandment "you shall be holy."[47]

with the struggle of making changes in themselves to recover lives of joy and purpose gives us hope that we can do the same. Over time, through these actions we can transform our lives.

As we embark on the Steps, we learn to keep the focus on our right-sized selves and do the next right thing. For some, this means stepping into their full potential; for others, it means stepping away from the imposter they embodied as a smokescreen to their true feelings. Inevitably, we form intimate relationships with those to whom we entrust the secrets of our crazy choices and stinking thinking. Shedding our secrets liberates us from the personal prison we constructed and uncovers the inner light that had been hidden by our disease. The service of helping others by sharing our experience, strength, and hope allows us to be a light unto others. Not to be grandiose, but serving others this way, by refining ourselves, improves the beauty of the universe; it's a gift that keeps on giving as grateful recipients pass it on. These are actions that we can take in everyday living. They are applicable in interactions with the addict and with our children; with our bus driver and with a judge adjudicating a DUI. It's spiritual work. It's a blueprint for living and millions in the fellowship who came before us maintain that this mode of living holds the key to recovery.

The Mussar inner journey: *tikkun middot*

Refining ourselves is familiar to Jews. You may recognize the idea as part of our High Holiday practices. During the month of *Elul*, we search inward, taking stock (called *cheshbon hanefesh*), literally an accounting of the soul. During Elul, we strive to address what's out of alignment in our soul traits and repair any damage we have done as a result. Mussar practice extends the work of Elul to be a perpetual process of taking stock, accruing self-knowledge and attempting refinement. *Tikkun middot* is the practice of repairing what's not working in our inner selves.

Middot are part of our unique and inherent inner beauty. We each are unique in our mix of these inner qualities. Our middot, or soul traits, are not inherently good or bad, they are simply characteristics of our humanity. Torah describes the energy or spirit of life, which includes these traits of our soul, as the breath of God.[43] Insofar as these qualities are part of our

to develop an awareness of, and tap into (accept and rely on), something greater than ourselves in the universe. This Higher Power is of our own understanding, and it is the foundation of the spiritual aspect of recovery. At its core, the concept of HP is that there is some invisible aspect of the universe that looks out for our welfare and that is available to us personally. It may take the form of a sponsor, the steps, our meeting group, or something Divine which many refer to as God. You choose.

Accepting the concept of something bigger outside of us opens the door to thinking about our place in the natural order of things. For many, this is comforting and provides a feeling of wholeness and safety that we are not alone. This realization is described in the Twelve Steps as a spiritual awakening. Letting go of the idea that we are in control, that we know all the answers, that we are God and can fix whatever is broken is hardest of all, but it is also a great liberator. Accepting this idea that we are not in control and not responsible for everything and everyone (rightsizing ourselves) is captured in the Serenity Prayer,[41] which might be called a Program theme song. It opens the space for us to focus on our ourselves and our own program for living. This is, in fact, a full-time job.

A#3: Action

Maya Angelou is attributed as saying that you can't really know where you are going until you know where you have been.[42] Living differently, according to the Program, includes the action of processing the inventory of the traits or our patterns mentioned above. The inventory work is a means to learn about ourselves (where we have been), including what drives our behaviors (our character defects). This exploration is without judgment and is a starting point for embracing our past and learning how to see it in a new way. Most important, with this frame of reference, we can forge a vision of where we are going—how we want to show up in life.

The action aspect of recovery is about owning our power to choose how we intend to act or react with the objective of closing the gap between our current ineffective patterns and a desired state, even though the process is uncomfortable. I've heard this described as acting our way into right thinking. Seeing fellow addicts let go of denial and resistance and engage

A#1: Awareness

Our starting point on the 12 Step journey is awareness—self-awareness particularly. Seeing your part in the drama of your life is an early stage in our recovery work. Do you lie to hide your truths or failings? Do you drown feelings in substances to blunt discomfort? Are you reactive, fearful, resentful, selfish, and angry? Do you cover up for others? I am referring here to the facts about our lives, revealed in everyday events of living life on life's terms. The truths reveal themselves at every turn. Perhaps the most blatant and unwelcome truth is that we are imperfect.

The foundation for change is an inventory of the inner traits that drive our behaviors (called our character defects in Twelve Step lingo). The process of taking our inventory forces us to look at how, when and where our life experiences and natural desires have warped us. Overcoming denial and becoming aware of our patterns and the unhappiness we have caused others and ourselves is hard to do, but necessary to move toward correction.

A#2: Acceptance

Accepting the imperfection revealed in our inventory work is a choice. It can be liberating when viewed from a healthy perspective. There is comfort in knowing that "we are perfectly human and humanly imperfect."[39] Hearing fellow travelers describe how they feel as they tell their stories allows us to see that we are not unique. Being seen by others with empathy and without judgment (feeling accepted) rids us of the need for isolation and gives us permission to practice self-acceptance. Acceptance can also mean that we see other addicts through a lens of humility and compassion, freeing them of the burden to meet our expectations of perfection.

It is said in the Rooms of recovery that pain comes from resistance. Much of the pain we experience as addicts comes from resisting acceptance. Accepting our imperfections and those of others is a loving action that we can learn to embrace.[40] Please understand that acceptance is not an excuse that frees us or others from responsibility, nor does it condone anything. Rather, it creates an opportunity to get back on our own track and change our choices, so we minimize future damage to ourselves and others.

In addition to the revealed aspect of our awareness and acceptance, there is a concealed dimension. Our work may include the opportunity

guidance.[36] Like many who enter the Rooms of recovery, he was seeking relief from life's unmanageability. (This parallel is not intended to suggest that Morinis has any connection to addiction or the Twelve Steps.) He found a personal teacher—akin to a sponsor—and stepped into Jewish learning, ultimately discovering healing and meaning through Mussar practice.

Inspired by his journey, Morinis founded The Mussar Institute (TMI) to share this path toward wholeness, personal purpose, and spiritual connection. His book, *Everyday Holiness*, serves as a foundational guide to modern Mussar practice and could be considered its "Big Book." Another important voice in this renewed landscape is Rabbi Ira Stone, whose Center for Contemporary Mussar and book, *A Responsible Life*, add depth and perspective to contemporary Mussar study.

As do people in the Program, students of Mussar all over the world have bonded in working their practice, enjoying transformation guided by Jewish ethics and values and grounded in a relationship with God as they understand a Higher Power. Adding Mussar into our Twelve Step toolbox imbues recovery with a valuable Jewish voice.

The Twelve Step journey: inward and upward

Looking inward to see our true selves and "our part" of our problems is integral to the recovery journey. We speak of this in terms of taking our personal inventory. Most come into the Rooms on their knees, struggling with job and relationship problems, issues related to physical health, and/or emotional distress. Hopelessness, fear, shame, and guilt are barriers to acknowledging the truth about ourselves. Hiding from the disease turns most into liars, cheats, and thieves. The victim may be someone else or ourselves. At this stage, we are usually in denial…it ain't just a river in Egypt.

Awareness, Acceptance and Action, referred to as the 3 *A's*, describe actions that foster healthy change and growth that feed recovery.[37] The corresponding Mussar triad is Sensitivity, Self-Restraint, and Transformation.[38] While the terms suggest differences, these frameworks for Mussar and Twelve Step work are an aspect of how the practices align. Let's explore these.

A bit of historical context: How did we get here?
(adapted from *Everyday Holiness*)

Mussar is a tradition of Jewish wisdom that draws on ideas found in Torah and Talmud, the "Big Books" of Judaism. Reference to Mussar appears in the Bible 51 times, largely in the book of Proverbs.[34] It connotes ethical instruction and is a guidance system for living to our highest potential (serving God) by practicing Torah values. Sound familiar? A.A., Al-Anon, and any other Twelve Step program is a blueprint for living to our highest potential by practicing the Steps, Traditions and Principles of that Program. The end goals of recovery and Mussar are aligned—uncovering our light and living to our personal best, guided by a set of values that help us make good choices.

Early writings (~10th-11th centuries) positioned Mussar originally as an individual practice; Rabbi Israel Salanter[35] transformed it to be a community practice, perhaps because he saw the relationship between Mussar and the idea of *tikkun olam* (repair of the world). Although we will never know for sure, Salanter and his disciples expanded Mussar practice by innovating within the *yeshiva* (Orthodox Jewish college/seminary) curricula, taking time away from Talmud study to allow the student community to focus on Mussar study, supporting their individual development.

By 1939, Mussar (as a holistic spiritual program) had gained traction across Eastern Europe. Mussar was taught and practiced widely under the supervision of a teacher and within a community of fellow students. Even today, students seek guidance from teachers and fellow students to understand and overcome their challenges, just as addicts actively seek the experience of others in their community to grow in how they apply the teachings.

Absent the internet and seamless global connectivity, Mussar remained largely concentrated in Europe. Tragically, most of its practitioners and teachers were murdered in the Holocaust, and the tradition was nearly lost, outside of a small subset of Orthodox yeshivas. At the start of the 21st century, a revival began outside the traditional yeshivah world, sparked by independent educational efforts. One key figure in this revival is Alan Morinis, a Canadian TV and film producer turned spiritual seeker. Facing a personal crisis in his business life, Morinis turned to Mussar for spiritual

ing the joy of connection, purpose and reward. Across the Jewish denominational spectrum there has been pressure to revisit the tension between compliance with externally imposed rules (many of which seem irrelevant today) and fulfillment from within. Whether the agent of gathering is a synagogue or independent institution of learning, many people have found that they can enjoy meaningful connectivity as a small group (*chavurah*; pl. *chavurot*) of like-minded Jews who assemble for the purpose of sharing ritual practices and communal experiences such as lifecycle events and Jewish learning. The *chavurah* is a circle of Jewish adults who meet periodically (often in members' homes) to talk, study, socialize, and share the challenges of living life, grounded in a Jewish perspective on their humanness, relationship to God, and place in the universe. The parallels to Twelve Step meetings are clear.

Other structures of Jewish learning also bear a striking resemblance to the structures and systems that are common in Twelve Step recovery programs. The *chavurot* described above are examples of one form of congregating (meeting). A *va'ad* (council) is a Jewish study group that is traditional to Mussar. Like Twelve Step program meetings, both a *chavurah* and *va'ad* provide Jewish seekers with settings in which members gather to unpack the wisdom of text and wrestle together with how the ideas can be applied to life experiences.

Beyond the *va'ad*, Mussar practice also commonly involves two students studying text together, debating each other and connecting their lived experience with Jewish ideas to find meaning together. The term *chevruta* is used to refer to learning with a partner/friend. This resembles the sponsor-sponsee relationship within the Program. Mussar one-on-one study partners (pl. *chevrutot*) push one another to get honest and to think more deeply. Learning together from text, they support and challenge each other to refine their collective understanding and chosen approach to showing up in life.

While we learn a great deal on our own, we learn differently with a partner who brings additional experience and perspectives to an issue. The Program tells us to talk to each other and reason things out. The Talmud states that scholars who try to learn [Torah] alone will become stupid.[33] It goes on to declare that "two scholars learning together sharpen one another."

Members of the Program gather in a variety of settings to work on their recovery—uncovering their best selves. Group meetings are at the core. These vary in size from two to hundreds of fellow seekers (aka fellows) and include face-to-face gatherings and virtual meetings online. Program meetings may take several forms, but at any Program meeting you will find addicts talking about what obsessive thinking and behaviors such as drinking or controlling others did to their lives, personalities and relationships, what actions they took to help themselves, and how they are living their lives today. In addition to personal sharing, members study Program books and pamphlets which provide detailed guidance to inform personal recovery and the organization of the groups. Drawing on Program history and individuals' stories, the *Big Book of A.A.* is intended to show those interested precisely how others have recovered. The book *How Al-Anon Works* serves the same purpose for those in the sister Program. Guided by common language and principles, these "ragtag groups of misfits" (of which I am a grateful member) the world over are able to work together and help one another learn how to live using the solutions they learn through one another.

Members of the fellowships are encouraged to work closely with one other person, a sponsor, who is a confidant and personal resource. A sponsor is an A.A. or Al-Anon member who has made some progress in the recovery Program and shares that experience one-on-one over time with another person who is attempting to attain or maintain sobriety (living with integrity and authenticity) through a recovery fellowship. The relationship is intimate, mutual, and often longlasting. Based on confidentiality and trust that most sponsees have not experienced for a long, long time, a sponsor is both a guide and a mirror. Listening without judgment, a sponsor helps the sponsee use the Steps as a framework for making different choices as together they process the experiences of the past through a lens of togetherness, love, acceptance and hopefulness.

Organizing togetherhood: some Jewish ideas

The Jewish community at large has been challenged to evolve how it serves the desire for personal engagement with texts and the sense of seek-

Treating others as worthy is a thread woven through the Program. This is a tall order, considering how flawed most of us are. Jewish wisdom holds the key; Rabbi Moshe Cordovero[31] taught that we must not focus on the faults of others. He wrote that we must extend prayers, good favor and mercy to others, even those who might be presently unworthy because of their bad actions.[32] Along these lines, the Program teaches that as kindred spirits (who were undoubtedly in the same position not long before), we can be worthy by extending kindness to our fellows, withholding judgment and expecting nothing in return. Such is the magic of the Program and fellowship—extending kindness to others by sharing our experience and strength to create hope that change is possible. A solution to many of our problems, including the self-centeredness we all suffer, comes from taking right action supported by right thinking. By treating others as worthy, we become worthy. This is reinforcing for both parties; the Program itself and the fellows in the community are sustained with lives that are re-created.

Organizing togetherhood—the Twelve Step way

Taken together, the members of A.A. (or Al-Anon), collectively, are citizens of a worldwide community of addicts who unite to practice fellowship by sharing their common interests and a bond that is cemented by pain, empathy, compassion, and shared goals of creating a new way of living. The rooms of people that create Twelve Step meetings provide a venue for these individuals to congregate, where they can learn from one another how to organize, structure, and implement the work of living with their disease without being slaves to it. There is no ruling body in the Program; to navigate together, members of Twelve Step recovery communities are guided by **principles** for making personal choices, **traditions** of interacting with others, and philosophies of **service** for sustaining the Programs. These are spelled out in books and pamphlets that are published and distributed by each Program. Notwithstanding minor differences, at its core, each Program is the same across the globe. These tenets are the common denominator. They provide guardrails respected by all that allow those gathered anytime, in any place, to explore and share their experiences and to support one another in learning to live with their dis-eases.

built synagogues, established communal organizations, and created systems to help serve the array of needs that arise in navigating their lives. There are many practices that Jews do collectively as a community. For example, the language of Jewish prayer conveys the idea of connectivity into community within the whole of the universe. In parallel with Program teaching, Jewish prayer is dominated by *we* and *our*. We gather into groups for much of Jewish ritual practice.

Our liturgy teaches that, on the individual level, we are part of something bigger and we are to focus on those around us. Jews are called to use their abilities to offer encouragement and support when someone is struggling.[26] More than just doing good actions (*mitzvot*), we are taught to bring an attitude of love and compassion to our actions on behalf of others. A classic example of kindness extended to others in the spirit of generosity is the requirement that the farmer must leave the corner of his fields unharvested to provide for neighbors in need ("…you shall leave them for the poor and the stranger").[27] The idea of community extends from Jewish congregations to embrace us as individuals. Rabbi Jill Jacobs notes that Jewish people call themselves *Am Yisrael*, the people of Israel, rather than *Dat Yisrael*, the religion of Israel.[28] We each are part of this whole and it helps us feel complete.

In this regard it is useful to think, for a moment, about the A.A. vision through a Jewish lens. Struggling with addiction was a point of commonality. Dr. Bob and Bill transcended that singular fact about themselves and were moved to ask, in Rabbi Hillel's terms, "if I am only for myself, what am I?"[29]

Focus on the other/another reflects a core Jewish belief in the power of lovingkindness. The Program holds that regardless of someone's history, they deserve a chance to set their lives straight. With a Mussar lens, this embraces the teachings of Psalms that the world is built on *chesed* (lovingkindness).[30] Although they were certainly not gods, without sounding inflated, you might say that Dr. Bob and Bill offered the possibility of personal re-creation for those who acquire the Program teachings and practice fellowship.

parallel program and was an outgrowth of A.A. The Al-Anon fellowship was formed by Anne Smith and Lois Wilson among the wives of those in A.A.

The connection between A.A. and Al-Anon reflects our common human nature that our "tribes" give us identity and help us feel whole. The recovery community does foster a sense of belonging at a time when many of us feel we have been cast aside. The benefit of being part of the Twelve Step recovery community goes beyond feeling "part of." Seeing others like ourselves navigate life successfully gives us hope and purpose. Our newfound sense of self and self-worth propels us forward, back into the stream of life.

The first word of the first step of the Twelve Steps is *We*. Recovery is a "we" program. A key Program message is that you/we never need to be alone again. The fellowship among those who are together in the Rooms of recovery helps those who suffer from addiction to break the isolation and the bonds of shame that stifle their spirit and lives. The Program narrative says that we will each get better by sharing our stories and working the Steps in collaboration with others; change comes from taking action. Hearing how others like us manage life helps us appreciate our patterns and helps us see different choices. What we learn opens the door to thinking of others rather than just ourselves; we begin to practice kindness with our compatriots in the Rooms. The collective energy and personal connections ultimately give members of the community the courage to change. About this the *Big Book of A.A.* says:

> The feeling of having shared in a common peril is one element in the powerful cement which binds us. But that in itself, would never have held us together as we are now joined.
>
> The tremendous fact for every one of us is that we have discovered a common solution. We have a way out on which we can absolutely agree, and upon which we can join in brotherly and harmonious action.[25]

The idea of community is also core to Judaism and has been pivotal to sustaining the global family of Jews. Wherever Jews have lived, they have

Chapter 3

How Mussar practice aligns with recovery

Learning together we sharpen one another.
—Talmud Ta'anit 7a

We are excited to meet you here on this page! We will take it as a signal that you want to know more about how Mussar practice relates to the work of recovery. This chapter provides high-level overviews of the Twelve Step framework and corresponding Mussar ideas so you, our reader, can begin to appreciate their remarkable similarities and synergies. More will be revealed when you work the programs. It is our experience, and that of friends in our circles, that Mussar clearly provides a Jewish foundation for recovery which can be integrated into your personal recovery toolbox.

Community & fellowship—principles of engagement

Community and fellowship provide the foundation for both Twelve Step recovery and Judaism, including Mussar practice. Let's focus first on the 12 Step Program. As the story goes, Alcoholics Anonymous grew out of the relationship that developed between a stockbroker and a surgeon, William (Bill) Wilson, and Robert (Dr. Bob) Smith. Both struggled with their alcohol use and they met with each other for mutual support. After a long conversation and several interactions, Bill and Dr. Bob realized that support from other recovering alcoholics was a valuable tool in helping one another stay sober. This led to the eventual founding of A.A. for individuals with a common willingness to share their experiences and carry the message of hope and collective strength to other struggling alcoholics. Al-Anon, the Twelve Step program for those who love addicts and alcoholics, is a

balance. Permit me to illustrate how this works with the trait of humility (*anavah*). Humility is foundational in Mussar thought and is often out of whack among addicts.

Self-criticism or "being a doormat" lives on the side of excess humility. This may look like hopelessness. Accepting unacceptable behavior from others or thinking of ourselves as unworthy because we fail to control the addict (which might be ourselves) are other forms of low self-esteem. At the other extreme (too little humility) is arrogance or an exaggerated sense of self-worth. Addiction is often associated with inflated self-perception. Believing that we can control the world or others also sits on this end of the continuum. The middle zone is the place of balance; in this example, it is a place of being rightsized or in balance relative to the extremes. It's where we know and accept that we are human, not God. We cannot control what others do, maybe not even what we do—and we alone cannot fix anyone.

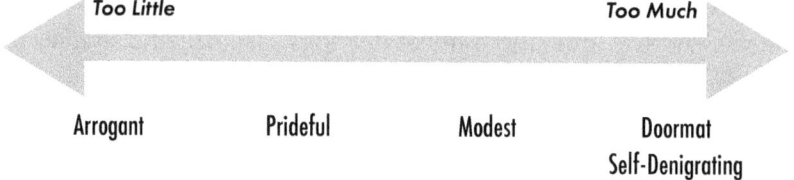

Too Little			Too Much
Arrogant	Prideful	Modest	Doormat
			Self-Denigrating

In this example, the work of recovery would be rightsizing our sense of self. Rightsizing is thinking of yourself less rather than thinking less of yourself. Mussar provides a pragmatic, accessible framework by suggesting that we visualize where we are on the continuum of too much or too little; Mussar offers tools to refine our spiritual malady and bring us closer to a healthy balance where we are more likely to take right action. This aligns with an ideal in Jewish thought that we are measured by what we do, not merely what we think. It also fits Program thinking that recovery is all about the action we take to create new solutions. Mussar shows what that looks like and gives us tools for daily living to make it so. Healing comes gently from the action of striving for change. It's about progress, not perfection. It is our hope that *Mussar in Recovery* will lay the foundation for your right action, right thinking, and ongoing healing.

identity, is a source of comfort for many. In fact, I have observed it restore a sense of pride to Jews in their Twelve Step journeys that is a springboard to self-acceptance. Acquiring Mussar allows us to make deliberate changes in self-perception and self-expression. When we miss the mark, we only need to try again and slowly we will become our best selves.

How it works

Mussar and Twelve Step programs live at the intersection of spirituality and ethical living. They are pragmatic approaches to manage the tension between our natural human inclinations toward both doing good and causing harm. Both focus on cleaning house of what's no longer useful, to open a space to be occupied by goodness (aka the Divine). In this way we discover, or perhaps recover, our Divine spiritual qualities.

Alan Morinis explains that man has a physical body and an ephemeral spirit; that everything that exists in our inner world (spirit) is an aspect of our soul. This includes our personality, emotions, talents, desires, conscience, and wisdom. The traits of our soul, also called character traits or *middot* (*middah*, singular) are the drivers of our thinking and chosen actions. Jewish wisdom teaches that soul traits include qualities such as humility (*avanah*), patience (*savlanut*), gratitude (*hakarat hatov*), compassion (*rachamim*), honor (*kavod*), trust (*bitachon*), and faith (*emunah*). Morinis invites us to think of each trait on a continuum, with excesses on the ends—too much of the trait on one end and too little on the other.

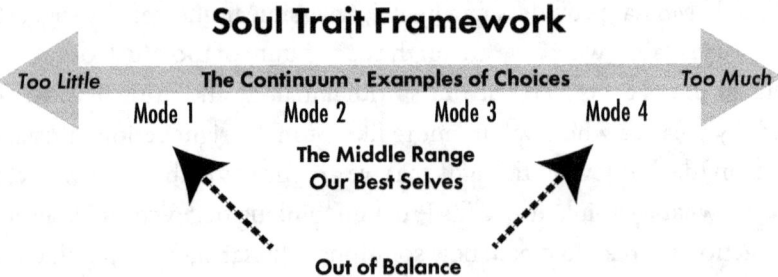

The middle range on the continuum represents a healthy balance and is the space where we are our best selves. Stinking thinking is a casual term often heard in the Rooms as a way of referring to soul traits that are out of

may not even realize that these were missing until we begin to enjoy them as byproducts of our recovery efforts. While we focus here on utility in regard to those who seek recovery from the effects of addiction, we all have some obsessions: work, food, cleaning, shopping, how others see us, or social media are examples. The ideas for finding and refining ourselves are applicable to all of these. "Because Mussar's purpose is to provide guidance on how to live, and because it addresses the fundamental way human beings are put together and function, its teachings have universal application. The fact is that you don't have to be Jewish to benefit from Mussar. Its insightful teachings are applicable to all souls—men and women, young and old, Jew and non-Jew—without exception."[23] The good news is that it includes us addicts.

Adding the vibrant Jewish voice embedded in Mussar practice to the individual's work in Twelve Step programs enriches the self-awareness, refinement and self-acceptance that are at the core of healing. The framework of Mussar and the parallels with Twelve Steps are described here in Chapter 3; discrete practices specific to Mussar are introduced in Chapter 4. Like the Twelve Steps, Mussar provides a blueprint for living. The benefits come from taking action: "Mussar is something you do, not simply something you learn."[24] Mussar ideas and practices are coupled to each of the Twelve Steps in the remaining chapters of *Mussar in Recovery*. To start, each step is unpacked and a key spiritual principle identified. For each step, Mussar teachings on related character traits and restorative practices are provided to bring a Jewish voice to the work of recovery.

Mussar provides tangible goals and tools to mark our own progress in the work we are doing. Integrating Jewish culture and spiritual beliefs into the work of recovery can help Jews overcome a sense of difference and feel at home in the Program. When we view ourselves through a Mussar lens, we see that we are simply human, not uniquely "bad," as Jews are often made to feel. Through Mussar practices, hope becomes tangible. The progress we make helps break through the shame we all carry. This can be especially meaningful for Jews who feel alone and targeted just for being Jewish. Drawing on wisdom that has its origins in Jewish history and teachings, with which Jews have a positive sense of connection and

is good. However, for a Jew, such an experience can be counterproductive because it puts a veil over the client's authentic sense of self and reinforces feelings of being odd/different. It is critical that such an experience robs the Jewish addict of "...two antidotes we have for treating all the conditions we suffer from—community and prayer."[21] This highlights the importance of finding the right resources for a Jew seeking recovery services. Respect for rituals such as dietary laws, keeping Shabbat, and access to a Jewish congregational community are all possible. It's usually just a matter of logistics. Such service providers do exist and, thanks to the web, are now easy to find.

Introducing Mussar: A Jewish spiritual pathway to recovery

Mussar is a treasure trove of wisdom that was long hidden within the Orthodox Jewish community and, until recently, remained unknown to many in the mainstream Jewish world. The word *Mussar* is translated from Hebrew to mean correction or instruction. It refers to a spiritual attitude for living and a reinforcing set of practices. Mussar connects our heart and head.

Like the Twelve Steps and living in recovery, Mussar is a spiritual practice that brings attention to knowing and refining the inner forces that animate us. Mussar guides us in cultivating our inner selves with ideas and practices that fit hand in glove with those that form the Twelve Step program teachings. Both Programs are blueprints for living as the best version of ourselves so we can enjoy lives filled with happiness, serenity, and joy. Alan Morinis, a contemporary teacher of Mussar, explains in his seminal text *Everyday Holiness* that Mussar "offers us a map of the inner life and a body of practices we can employ to transform our inner ways."[22] Transforming our inner ways—how we think and make choices—drives changes in our actions and affects how we show up in the world. Mussar and recovery are practices that help us close the gap between who we are today and who we want to become by showing us how to create change.

Why it's important

Mussar practice is an important resource that addresses the spiritual needs of anyone seeking wholeness, hope, comfort and connection. We

energy of the universe, your spiritual advisor, sponsor, or best friend. This opens the door to our being aware that *it* resides in us as well.

Like any feeling, the connection with something or someone outside us is entirely individual. It's not important that this be the same for us all; it's simply important that we know how it feels for us as individuals. (I would describe it as fleeting, flooding, powerful, elevating and also humbling; I am most likely to feel it when in nature or immersed in music, including Jewish ritual music, or studying with my *chevruta* (learning partner). So, my spirituality refers to the self-knowledge and feeling inside that I am connected by an invisible thread to the universe outside of me. Doing spiritual things refers to actions I take that are in harmony with the positive flow of the universe. For Jews, fulfilling *mitzvot* (biblical commandments) is spirituality in action. For those who believe that that flow emanates from a Divine source, spirituality involves a connection to the Divine in which we are drawn to do the work that enhances the world around us.

And now for a complication. Religious groups do have shared ritual practices (such as worship services) that are intended to open the door to our spirituality—to sensing that we are part of a larger universe and that the energy or spirit is part of us. Since we often practice rituals as a group/community in our houses of worship, it is easy to blur the line between religion and the spiritual experience. Some do have a spiritual experience while worshiping in their congregation; for others it happens at the ocean or atop a mountain, having nothing to do with religious systems and obvious links to God. For still others, it may come from the intimacy of letting another person see inside them or having someone trust them with their secrets. Again, the differences in how it happens do not matter. For addicts or anyone who has isolated and withdrawn from their vitality, the spiritual experience has the power to draw us back into the flow of life. Rami Shapiro writes that "growing spiritually does not eliminate suffering, it only puts it in a greater context."[20]

The means of unlocking spiritual capacity can be especially important to Jews seeking recovery at drug treatment centers. Many treatment centers require clients to attend church with the idea of tapping into a community and spiritual engagement that can be sustained after treatment. The motive

begin to see that if we have a Higher Power, so do our loved ones. A saying commonly heard in the Rooms of recovery is *let go and let God* (or HP). This HP talk tells us that we can rely on HP to help us handle life. The recent study by the Pew Research Center found that American Jews are more likely than non-Jewish US Adults in general to say that they believe in some spiritual force or Higher Power (50% for US Jews; 33% for non-Jewish US Adults). These ideas of a Higher Power are indeed complex and confusing, and they are, at the same time, very aligned with Jewish wisdom.

Myth #7: Recovery is a spiritual program. Jews don't do spiritual.

Psychiatrist Rabbi Abraham Twerski observed that the Twelve Step program is entirely "compatible with Jewishness," noting that much of the content seems derived from classic Jewish texts.[18] Noting that spirituality was the "backbone of recovery from addiction via the Twelve Step program," Twerski endorsed membership for those who could not overcome their addiction through their own Jewish observance.[19] Creating a path for Jews without compromising their Judaism saved lives. Let's explore some ideas that might explain his position.

Spirituality starts with the idea that there is something bigger/other than what we can see and understand. Stop a moment and think about standing amid a congregation or atop a beautiful mountain. Breathe in the feeling that you are a part of it. When touched by such a connection, we are bathed in and nourished by the energy of the universe. Where does it resonate in your body? That sense of oneness is a spiritual connection to something bigger than ourselves. It is a bridge to becoming part of the flow of the universe.

As it relates to recovery, the idea that such a transcendent force does exist or may exist opens the possibility that we can tap into it and that doing so can empower us. Beyond thinking abstractly that it's "out there," we can know it personally by tapping into the sensations we experience when we feel connected to *it*. This is where the term *spiritual* comes in. Spirituality starts with the personal experience of feeling connected to *it*, whatever the label—God, the Divine Source, Higher Power, *Shekhinah* (dwelling) or

tice. Moses, the great Jewish sage, struggled with this very problem. Even he asked for proof; he asked to see God.

> And [God] answered, "I will make all My goodness pass before you, and I will proclaim before you the name YHWH, and the grace that I grant and the compassion that I show...But you cannot see My face, for a human being may not see Me and live."[17]

Putting ourselves in the role of God is guaranteed to yield failure. Ironically, the willingness to let go of the false sense of control is a gift for those who are seeking a solution to their suffering. The Jewish prayer for healing, *Mi Shebeirach*, puts our seeking into action. Even if we are only maybe-believers, who wants to risk missing any means of healing for someone we love, including ourselves? Our *Mi Shebeirach* prayer guides us to turn to One outside us as the source of healing for mind, body, and spirit. Whether that One is God, a doctor, a spiritual healer, or Mother Nature, accepting that it is not us is freeing. It brings serenity—and that is a reward of recovery. Our Jewish heritage thus teaches that by embracing the Program we can receive such miracles in our lives.

Myth #6: The Higher Power of recovery is not Jewish.

Another term commonly heard in the Program is Higher Power. To the extent that one believes in a God that is in charge, the terms Higher Power or HP are synonyms for God. Setting aside the God piece, the idea of Higher Power is that there is something bigger than we are that powers the universe of which we are a part. HP may account for gravity or prevent the sun and moon from falling out of the sky. And perhaps HP explains how an acorn dissolves into nothing and grows into a giant oak, or that the thought of a word in our brain can be transformed into a sound that we utter that someone else can sense and comprehend.

As with the concept of God, HP can be a confusing and grandiose concept of the force that governs the universe and it can, simultaneously, be personal, relating to you or me. As we get better at working the Program, we

first consideration for us all. Let us not, therefore, pressure anyone with our individual or even our collective views…[15]

Whether we believe in one, many, or no God, there is no conflict between the Program and any specific religious dogma or personal belief system. The Program concept of God is not filtered through any group and is not limited to any teaching or any concept of God. To the extent that any members of the fellowship have a belief, such as Jesus as the son of God or the transcendent yet personal God of the covenant in Jewish thinking, they can evoke it as part of their thinking about the source of their solutions without forcing it on anyone else.

Beyond believing that there is a God, trusting God is another matter. We bump up against this when faced with the need to rely on some outside force: for example, to protect our loved ones from an overdose, fix our relationship problems, or solve our money problems. Sometimes, we intervene in another's situation under the misguided notion that we know what's good for that person better than they do. Honestly, stepping in to take charge often feels safer than risking that God might be too busy, might be angry or frustrated, or that anyone may suffer an undesired outcome.

So, let me tell you a secret. The most important part of the God-talk of recovery is that **we are not God**. Rabbi Rami Shapiro echoes the words of Bill W. and describes the heart of Twelve Step recovery: "First of all we had to quit playing God."[16] Regrettably, we cannot control people or situations to obtain the outcomes we want. We can try and, for many, this folly is the source of our irrational thinking and choices (aka our crazy thinking). Admitting and then accepting that we are powerless is very, very hard. Letting go of someone we are trying to protect or control can feel like abandonment or amputation. Letting go of the control of our own lives is also anathema. How can we be sure that we'll get what we want or that bad things won't happen?

Trusting in God without proof is difficult. Some characterize this leap as a definition of faith. The language of God in the Twelve Steps reflects the ideas that we can have faith and rely on something outside ourselves. These are simple concepts on paper, but they're not easy to put into prac-

rationally accept the white-haired, benevolent, commanding, and punishing image of God depicted in prayer books.[13] The suffering of innocent people is not a storyline that is easy to reconcile with the loving and protective imagery described in Jewish sacred text. The Pew Research Center study, which looked across the Jewish denominational spectrum, reported that the vast majority of Jews struggle with the idea of God. About a quarter of Jews do not believe in any concept of God; another 50% think of God as some spiritual force other than God as depicted in the Bible.[14] The bottom line here is that your ideas and questions about God are common to most in the Jewish community, and from personal experience I can attest that that includes those in recovery.

This particular rationale to resist the Program is not specifically a Jewish issue. Again, the only requirement for membership is the desire to stop doing what is making our lives unmanageable. In the case of A.A., this is drinking; the desire to stop drinking is the only requirement for membership. This idea extends to any unhealthy excessive behavior that makes life unmanageable for ourselves or others. The Rooms where fellow addicts meet to work on their recovery and support one another in any Twelve Step program are welcoming spaces for all, including those with defined theologies and those with none.

Myth #5: Their God is not my God (of the Hebrew Bible).

God is mentioned several times in the Twelve Steps. The exact words are "…God *as we understood Him*." The "we" means each of us. All Twelve Step programs defer to an individual's conception of a divine force, spirit or entity, according to each individual's vision. Quoting A.A. co-founder Bill W.:

> We have atheists and agnostics. We have people of nearly every race, culture and religion. In A.A. we are supposed to be bound together in the kinship of a common suffering. Consequently, the full individual liberty to practice any creed or principle or therapy whatever should be a

Chapter 2 / Opening the door to Jewish solutions

Beyond these theological links the simple fact is that in a general sense the Program only requires that we must stop doing what we do obsessively—what makes our lives unmanageable—whether it be alcohol, eating, worrying or wanting to control others and their choices. "The only requirement for A.A. membership is the desire to stop drinking."[12] While the *A.A. Big Book* reflects that we must be willing to go to any lengths to follow the Twelve Steps, no Program makes you do anything—including reciting the Lord's Prayer.

Myth #3: It's a Christian cult.

As the story goes, A.A. grew out of the relationship that developed between a stockbroker, Bill (William) Wilson, and a surgeon, Dr. Bob (Robert Smith). Both were struggling with their alcohol use and they met with each other for mutual support. It is true that both gentlemen were Christian. It is also true that the Twelve Steps were inspired by their belief that their willpower alone could not get them sober and keep them sober. They originated the concept that sobriety required surrender of their will to some Higher Power (HP) of the universe. Their ideas of how to help one another included no religious icons, beliefs, or religious ritual practices. They simply leaned into their belief of a power greater than themselves for help. Twelve Steps encourages you to define that Higher Power in whatever way works for you, leaving it to each individual to choose based on personal experience.

Because some addicts say they owe their lives, jobs, well-being or relationships to the Program, there is a disciplined devotion to following it, but it is *not* a religion. Other Twelve Step programs adopted and adapted A.A.'s Steps and Program to address a broad range of compulsive and obsessive behaviors that fit their members' focus. None include any Christian rituals or any particular concept of God, and members do not have to be religious to benefit from them.

Myth #4: They talk about God and I don't believe in God.

First, let me say that questioning beliefs in or about God is inherent to Judaism. You have a lot of company. Most modern liberal Jews today don't

Myth #1: Jews can't enter a church to attend meetings.

It is true that many 12 Step meetings are in churches. And, some say we Jews are precluded from attending them. Sources on this topic are most concerned with the appearance of impropriety and not with the spiritual or religious impact a Christian space would have on a Jew who was in a church building.[10] Long, long ago, some rabbis discouraged Jews from entering a church because they considered Christian beliefs to foster idolatry. That does not generally apply today. Many rabbis in positions of authority have not only been in church buildings but have attended functions in churches, including a full mass. There is no clear *halakhic* basis (Jewish legal standard) for this concern.

In general, A.A. or Al-Anon meetings in churches are held in classrooms and have nothing to do with worship spaces, religious services, or religious content. There may be images or other Christian symbols in a meeting room. If that were an issue (e.g., for some Orthodox Jews), solutions might include seeking out a meeting in a neutral space or synagogue. The options are plentiful: Between A.A. and Al-Anon, there are thousands of groups hosting meetings all around the world. Online meetings are also an option, although the extemporaneous fellowship that is such a valuable aspect of the Program is quite different in a virtual setting.

Myth #2: They make you say the Lord's Prayer, which is Christian.

At some meetings they do recite the Lord's Prayer. In and of itself, that is not a valid reason to reject the 12 Steps.

On the one hand, the language of the Lord's Prayer has Jewish elements. Dr. Eli Lizorkin-Eyzenberg, an Israeli scholar in Biblical Studies and early Christianity, concluded that the Lord's Prayer has Jewish liturgical roots.[11] He notes both conceptual and word-by-word parallels in Jewish liturgy and the Lord's Prayer. For example, the concept of God our father is the basis of the *Avinu Malkenu* prayer, translated as Our Father, Our King. There are other parallels in common Jewish prayer. For example, in reciting the Jewish morning prayer, *Modeh Ani,* we sanctify the name of God in this world which parallels the Lord's prayer language, "Our father, Who art in heaven, hallowed be thy name…"

Chapter 2

Opening the door to Jewish solutions

Circumcise your heart and stiffen your necks no more.
—Deuteronomy 10:16

Busting Jewish myths about recovery

Twelve Step programs (often simply referred to as Programs) offer a time-tested path to recovery. At the very least, the Rooms of recovery are filled with like-minded people who are suffering, willing to surrender to the truths about their lives and help one another seek a different way to live, moving from being trapped in their problems to discovering the freedom of solutions.

Focusing on our differences rather than what we have in common, Jews often resist joining organized recovery groups such as Alcoholics Anonymous and Al-Anon. This resistance persists despite the fact that there is widespread rabbinic support for Twelve Step programs.[9] Common reasons for rejecting Twelve Step programs include:

- I can't go to recovery meetings because they are in churches
- They make you say the Lord's Prayer and it's not Jewish
- It's a Christian cult
- They talk about God and I do not believe in God
- Their God is not my God (of the Hebrew Bible)
- They talk about a spiritual program and the Judaism I know does not include spirituality

None of these are true. Let's take it from the top.

of the Twelve Steps in a uniquely Jewish way. To the extent that Jews have unmet needs in classic Twelve Step program teachings, it is our goal here to show you how Mussar can meet those needs and strengthen the bridge leading to a spiritual experience and a life in recovery. To open the door to what Mussar has to offer, let's start by breaking down some barriers.

first, willingness becomes the fuel of change. It is fragile, being in tension with lies and denial. The old way was easier, and we are subject to being diverted at any moment. Walking into the Rooms of Twelve Step meetings adds hope to the mix; the Program can become a starting place for new beginnings.

There is a solution

Pain is inevitable in life; suffering is optional. We suffer in our addictions and illusions of control; Twelve Step programs like Alcoholics Anonymous (A.A.) and Al-Anon provide safe places for people of all beliefs to reveal their secrets, see their reality, discover choices, and acquire tools and strategies to heal. Willingness opens the door to the Rooms of recovery where we can start reframing our self-perception and acquire tools for living more healthy lives. In the Rooms, where we meet others like ourselves, we are reminded that *we are children of God and persons of worth*. This idea conforms to Jewish thought that we are good by virtue of having been created in the image of God.[8] An important Jewish message for those seeking recovery is that we do not have to change ourselves to become someone else; our work is to reveal (uncover and recover) our inherent beauty and goodness. The ravages of our disease, the wake of chaos, hurt and other damage done to ourselves and others, are veils over our inner light, and they are ours to lift.

The Twelve Steps offer a gentle program of change, one step at a time. The path is simple, but not easy. Recovery is a "we" program and is a journey, not a destination. Time after time I hear people say that the support and companionship of others who have traveled the road before us can help us achieve a reprieve one day at a time, and show us that sustained change is within our reach. As we apply the Steps to our lives, the burden of chaos that results from our own distorted thinking begins to lift; the daily reprieve allows us to feel free. By some mystery, we work the Steps, and they work on us. Over time, we find that our lives get better as we learn to cope with life by applying the solutions suggested by the Program, enabled by a strong spiritual core.

As you will see in just a bit, Mussar is a spiritual practice within Judaism, derived from thousand-year-old Jewish wisdom, that can enrich the work

Hitting bottom

The active addict is trapped in craving. I have heard this described as being stuck in LAVA: seeking Love, Acceptance, Validation, and Approval. These needs escalate. Some may be satisfied by higher-stakes gambling, more booze or higher potency drugs, or deepening entanglement with a love target, all to change how we feel—and at the expense of other relationships and responsibilities. And those who love addicts get more obsessed with protecting or controlling them. The "high" that is being chased is, in fact, elusive. Connections to what is really important are fractured or severed.

All those involved share a disease of distorted perceptions and control. Rabbi Rami Shapiro, whose personal experience was with Overeaters Anonymous, explains that it is the obsessive quest for control that defines addiction.[6] The substance abuser in this drama is trying to protect their own disease and the others in the drama are trying to protect the substance abuser from themself. Do you have a role in this play? Over time, the disease takes hold of our spirit, as well as our moral character and rational thinking, and we start to die, one bit at a time—physically, emotionally, and spiritually. Taking action to learn how to live with the disease can be lifesaving because addiction is a progressive sinkhole. Twelve Step programs live at the intersection of our spirit and choices about how we will show up to live our lives differently.

Hitting a bottom in the descent of our lives is the wakeup call that can spur us to see our truths and seek help, saving ourselves from certain death. This is what is meant by the gift of desperation. Surrendering to the reality that we cannot continue to numb the pain or fill the void inside is the only hope for survival. Paulo Coelho described what many of us experience as follows: "The eyes are the mirror of the soul and reflect everything that seems to be hidden; and like a mirror, they also reflect the person looking into them."[7] At the height of our disease, the eyes that stare back at us addicts from our mirrors are dull and empty. Our faces are likely drawn with exhaustion and frustration.

While the solution is unknown to us as we hit this bottom, some lucky ones transform the fear and self-loathing into a desire to get better. At

and/or manipulating others frequently fills us unfortunates with fear, self-hate, and self-doubt. We addicts are blind to the anger and resentments we harbor and, locked in our disease, often see no choices. None of us are simply mean or evil. Our patterns generally stem from distorted thinking which evolves over time to become illogical and downright irrational, perpetuating whatever lies we tell ourselves and others to avoid the truths we are trying to numb, hide, and/or escape. We addicts understand one another's reference to ourselves as crazy. It's a loving shorthand for the chaos and illogic with which we identify. It is important to acknowledge that in our human complexity there is a spectrum of underlying experiences and disorders of brain chemistry that may have a role in our reactions and reactivity. Some may need to be processed with outside help before the addiction can be addressed. In that regard, the process of recovery is not an alternative to professional therapy.

Whether for fear of judgment within our social and professional circles, cultural norms, or because of personal shame and guilt, Jewish families commonly hold the truths about addiction among loved ones as their "dirty little secret." The idea of admitting our darkest truths to someone is understandably frightening. Perhaps we are ashamed, convincing ourselves that we are deficient or the cause of all the problems. We naturally feel that our wrongs are worse than anyone else's.

But feelings aren't facts. We do not cause, we cannot control, and we cannot cure addiction—our own or in those we love. Our (supposed) best thinking got us where we find ourselves: living in unmanageability. It does not have to be this way. At any time, we can decide to chart a different course.

The good news is that owning the reality and our feelings can make us desperate and unlock a willingness to seek solutions and create change. Based on my personal experience, I can tell you that while you cannot go back and create a different beginning to your story, you can create a different ending.

also applies. Being the "chosen people" does not exempt Jews from our fair share of substance abuse or addiction.

About a quarter of respondents in a study of the Jewish community had a family history of drug or alcohol abuse[4] and approximately 40% of (Jewish) individuals indicated that they knew someone who currently battled substance abuse.[5] But Jews hide it. My earliest experience related to drugs within the Jewish community was seeing my parents help friends whose children "got into trouble" (did drugs). I heard that "these things necessitate discretion;" we are to keep this secret within the walls of our homes. One of my early learnings that relates to this is that we are only as sick as our secrets.

This is what it's like

The American Society of Addiction Medicine defines addiction as a disease of physiological, psychological, and spiritual symptoms that derive from a compulsive urge to engage in behaviors that are somehow rewarding but also destructive. The harmful effects are profound and far-reaching. Being an addict is not a personal choice any more than high blood pressure, depression or cancer are. It is a disease, and those who suffer experience "dis-ease" in almost all areas of their lives.

One of the hidden aspects of addiction is that people's insides often don't match their outsides. Some addicts are fully functional by outward appearances. They hold good jobs, coach neighborhood soccer, and are admired members of their community. Others show more visible signs of the disease. Looking inward reveals that addicts (me included) feel less-than—less funny, less attractive, less wealthy, less intelligent, less effective. Trying to numb the pain ultimately leads us addicts to lie, steal trust, fall short on commitments to employers and let down people we love, including ourselves.

Many addicts explain their hardships as them being the victims of bad luck or that God is punishing them, justifying their defensive, judgmental, impatient and vindictive attitudes. From personal experience, I can attest that we often do not see that we own any part of our problems. Living in unmanageability that follows excessive drinking, drugging, sex, gambling,

sex, race, religion, education, income: no one is exempt; young adults are especially vulnerable.[1] Alcohol and drugs are abused with similar incidence. It's been said that the addict affects the lives of 10 people on average, so the numbers get big very quickly. The next time you find yourself in a crowd, look around; about one in every 10 people there with you is an addict of one kind or another.

In addition to suffering from my own addiction (to my addict), I identify as Jewish. My family of origin (parents & grandparents) was actively involved and well known in their local Jewish community. Ritual practice was sporadic in my home, but the Jewish experiences of my youth implanted a sense of identity that is important to me.

Within the community, I grew up believing that Jewish parents can't possibly be addicts or have kids who are, and that nice Jewish boys or girls don't do drugs. Myths that Jews are immune to substance abuse or other excessive, self-harming behaviors are pervasive in the Jewish community. This is especially true among the ultra-Orthodox. Considering sex and gambling addictions which are more easily hidden, the problem is even bigger than the numbers suggest. Disinformation, combined with the silence on the topic, makes Jews especially vulnerable to being taken hostage by guilt and shame when facing the realities of the disease. As we become more isolated by the disease in ourselves or those we love, perceptions of normalcy get distorted within the stories we tell ourselves. In the context of addiction and recovery, secrets, shame, and guilt are referred to as our *stinking thinking*; it destroys feelings of self-worth and hopefulness, distorts truth and creates senseless barriers to seeking help.

Regarding religion, much research has been done to explore the relationship between religion and the risk of substance abuse. In general, this research indicates that across the spectrum of denominations, active engagement in religious ritual may have some benefit in reducing the risk of substance use.[2]

According to the Pew Research Center, Jews in the US attend religious services infrequently.[3] Using this as a barometer of engagement with Jewish ritual practice suggests that we Jews are at risk of substance abuse. In addition, the naturally occurring incidence of addiction in the population

Chapter 1

I am my problem

> *"Hello, my name is Hannah and I'm an addict."*
> *—Standard A.A. meeting greeting*

I'm Hannah. I love someone whose use of (fill in the blank) is a problem for me. I obsess with fear and worry as they are chasing their perfect high. I am also chasing a high; mine is fixing them. I call that other person my sibling, child, spouse, and/or friend. They are addicted to something, and I am addicted to them. Although the details may vary, our overarching problems do not differ, and our lives have become unmanageable.

I've cried, threatened, pleaded, bartered, and negotiated terms for their abstinence. They have done the same—mostly to get me off their back. We both have promised, threatened, rationalized, and blamed to explain our thinking and behavior. We are similarly unsuccessful in getting the other to stop and in changing our patterned reactions. We are both harming ourselves and others. We are trapped, in lockstep, walking through the misery of our addictions, both of us living in denial and trying to control the uncontrollable.

Can you see yourself in any of these scenarios? If so, the stories on these pages convey our experience, strength and hope for the purpose of showing you how you too can escape the shroud of darkness that accompanies addiction.

There are lots of people like us

We are not alone or unique in our disease. It is estimated that 5%-10% of the population at large suffers from the disease of addiction. Substance use disorder is an equal opportunity disease. Consider variables such as

SECTION I: THE LANDSCAPE

to relish the serenity that comes with your newfound ability to live life on life's terms and open yourself to joy.

This is not a book to simply sit on your coffee table. It is a blueprint for living; its value comes from the actions of acquiring and engaging in a personal practice as suggested on the pages that follow. May your journey be fulfilling and bring you renewed purpose and days filled with serenity and joy.

Words of Caution

The work of seeking is arduous and requires a level of fitness to assure personal safety. It is important to note that for some of us in A.A. and Al-Anon, mental illness, including trauma, may be a key part of our makeup; if left untreated, it can overwhelm our ability to recover in the Program. Twelve Step program work is never a substitute for psychotherapy or medical treatment.

Mental illness may, for example, affect our ability to remember—and to do so safely, accurately and without judgment—to see through our confusion, to discern our role in situations, and to reason things out with others. Addiction may reflect self-medicating behaviors to silence our mental chatter or the committee that lives in our head; without appropriate support, sobriety can feel like a double-edged sword at the outset. Digging through old memories can be destabilizing and is an important risk factor for some.

We encourage you to seek the help of professionals when there is any question about personal safety and well-being and the readiness to do this work. Resistance to professional help is self-defeating. The insights and perhaps medications or other therapies that normalize brain function, neurochemistry, and emotional stability can help sufferers find a stable foundation on which to rebuild and recover. If you have been in the Rooms (of recovery) for a time and find that you are stuck or not resonating with the Program, please consult a professional; perhaps they have a resource that can help you find the recovery you deserve.

— *Hannah L. and Rabbi Harvey J. Winokur*

Chapter 1 helps the reader understand themselves and where they fit in the world around them.

Chapter 2 addresses and helps overcome barriers that stand in the way of Jews seeking recovery and introduces Mussar for consideration as a resource to enrich the work of recovery.

Chapter 3 introduces some language of Mussar and shows the commonalities with Twelve Step thinking and structure. This chapter is intended to build a bridge from the platform of Twelve Steps to the teachings and practices of Mussar that will be detailed in Section 2.

Chapter 4 explains how to put the practices into action.

Section II: A Treasure Map is the meat of the book. Here, a core principle for each of the Twelve Steps is connected to Jewish thinking about related soul traits (*middot*)—the internal territory where we can nurture solutions to our problems of thinking and living.

Chapters 5-16 cover each of the Twelve Steps. We have distilled what we see as ideas to focus on in each Step and linked them to a core principle which is explored in such a way that readers can see how the Step might apply to them. Drawing on inspiring gems found in Jewish texts, we offer Mussar wisdom on a soul trait that connects to the principle of that particular Step, bringing a Jewish voice to recovery. Briefly referencing secondary middot for each Step will show how middot intertwine and can be applied to meet readers' individual needs. To make the ideas actionable, the teachings on each soul trait include:

- a suggested framework (continuum) for imagining the goal and mapping progress
- suggested daily reminder phrases
- suggested actions (*kabbalot*)
- probing questions for journaling or learning with a partner
- a playlist of music to reinforce the teachings

Section III: The Treasure Found brings it all together. Threads from these disparate thought systems are woven together to reveal five concepts that are essential to living in the solutions you discovered, leaving you free

authors have put a Jewish lens on recovery, *Mussar in Recovery* is intended to uniquely fill several needs:

1) **Actionability**: Recovery is ultimately about taking action to make changes in choices and thinking that are off-balance. Drawing on personal experience, recognized principles of the Twelve Steps, and Mussar teachings, the essence of each Step is summarized for you and connected to related soul traits (*middot*) for each Step. *Mussar in Recovery* provides perspective on the imbalances in these inborn traits (your *middot*) that cause hardship and pain, and outlines paths to correction. Commentary and deeply personal reflections are provided to reinforce self-awareness and provide discrete practices to help readers move toward positive change.

2) **Deepen Spiritual and Twelve-Step Insights for All**: While the primary focus is on Jews who are seeking recovery (think of uncovering and recovering our best selves), Mussar wisdom provides spiritual insights for anyone of any religion or of none. The Twelve Step programs of recovery (Programs) and Mussar are blueprints for living; the principles they embody are applicable to all aspects of everyone's life. Thus, this book has potential appeal beyond the Jewish community to all seeking recovery, as well as to those who are spiritual seekers simply striving to become their best selves.

3) **Connectivity**: Bringing Jewish wisdom to solve problems of living with the crazy thinking that goes along with the disease of addiction provides a connection to our heritage, traditions and the Jewish community. This can reinforce a sense of pride in identity that is important to addicts and others, who are often marginalized and feel isolated and disconnected. For many, Mussar may also provide a potential path back into ritual Jewish practice within their local community.

4) **Multisensory learning**: Most individuals learn best when using more than one sense. To help readers acquire the teachings with deep resonance, we present practices that are designed to stimulate sight (reading), touch (writing) and hearing (listening/music).

Overall, **Section I: The Landscape** frames the problems of addiction and introduces the reader to Mussar, a body of teachings and practices that history has shown enriches the personal journey to wholeness.

tools of these programs to change course from living under the influence of their own distorted thinking to enjoying lives with personal meaning, fulfillment, and joy. You will see that it is a problem in thinking that explains how we humans can make seemingly irrational choices and be pulled off course, chasing illusory solutions to the challenges of our lives. Addicts often describe themselves as crazy or insane. We are not literally crazy or insane, but our *stinking thinking* makes us look as if we are. Teachings of Jewish sages reveal that addicts are not hopeless freaks—we are just human. For some, the drug of choice is a chemical; others of us are addicted to the addicts we love or to sex, gambling, work or another person. The differences are, for our purposes here, irrelevant. We are alike in being blind to our truths; crazy thinking leads us to make choices that defy logic, and we wind up harming ourselves and others. Assuming that you too are human and imperfect, this book will teach you how to connect with your truth and uncover or recover your best self and live your best life.

Pillars of this work include refining aspects of our character and spirit that are out of alignment and cultivating a personal relationship with a Power of the Universe that is bigger than we can fathom. Character, spirit and the universe are the domain of sage Jewish wisdom and rabbinic teaching. Locating and interpreting related texts of Jewish sages with the input of Hannah's teacher helped in the birth of *Mussar in Recovery*. While the voice that you will hear when reading this book is Hannah's, *Mussar in Recovery* is the result of a shared passion of student and teacher for learning, spiritual living and service to the communities they love.

It's important to note that recovery and Mussar are often spoken about as if they are end-states; they are not. They are pathways to living with intention and purpose. The 12 Steps of Recovery is a roadmap that guides seekers one day at a time. Mussar is a disciplined pathway to uncover our divine beauty, implemented iteratively over time. When woven together, these programs for living provide complementary tools for thinking about and choosing who we want to be. They help us gain perspective on how we fit in the universe and make us aware of choices about how we will show up in our lives. The journey is about progress, not perfection. While other

Introduction

Mussar in Recovery: A Jewish Spiritual Path to Serenity and Joy connects Jewish wisdom and practices to the principles of spiritual living that guide Twelve Step recovery work. Mussar is a deeply personal Jewish spiritual practice that includes practical and actionable teachings that enable imperfect people to change the course of their lives by engaging with spiritual purpose. The Twelve Steps offer the same promise. This is a book for addicts and those who love addicts, written by an addict who weaves this ancient and contemporary wisdom together with the support and guidance of her rabbinic teacher.

As you read, think of addiction broadly: It may be chasing a substance, a person, an experience or a self-image—at the expense of physical, emotional, financial or spiritual well-being. We all have someone or something that makes our lives difficult, pulling us off balance. Both Mussar and Twelve Step programs address such challenges and suffering—they are common to humankind. With this in mind, the ideas shared here have near universal utility.

The content of these pages is not based on abstract theory or theology but rather on the real experiences of addicts with differing addictions—through Hannah's eyes. *Mussar in Recovery* shares how real people use the

Like A.A., Al-Anon is a spiritual program, and also like A.A., it is not a religious program. Thus, Al-Anon is not affiliated or allied with any sect, denomination, or specific religious belief.

On Repentance and Repair by Danya Ruttenberg, Copyright ©2022. Reprinted by permission of Beacon Press, Boston.

This Is Real And You Are Completely Unprepared by Alan Lew, Copyright ©2003. Reprinted by permission of Little, Brown, an imprint of Hachette Book Group, Inc.

Copyright permissions

The excerpts from *Alcoholics Anonymous* and *Twelve Steps and Twelve Traditions* are reprinted with permission of Alcoholics Anonymous World Services, Inc. ("A.A.W.S."). Permission to reprint these excerpts does not mean that A.A.W.S. has reviewed or approved the contents of this publication, or that A.A.W.S. necessarily agrees with the views expressed herein. A.A. is a program of recovery from alcoholism only; use of these excerpts in connection with programs and activities which are patterned after A.A., but which address other problems, or in any other non-A.A. context, does not imply otherwise.

Additionally, while A.A. is a spiritual program, A.A. is not a religious program. Thus, A.A. is not affiliated or allied with any sect, denomination, or specific religious belief.

The excerpts from *Al-Anon's Twelve Steps & Twelve Traditions, Courage to Change, Hope for Today, How Al-Anon Works, One Day at a Time in Al-Anon,* and *Reaching for Personal Freedom* are reprinted with permission of Al-Anon Family Group Headquarters, Inc. (AFG) and does not mean that AFG reviewed or approved the contents of this publication, or that AFG necessarily agrees with the views expressed herein.

Contents

Introduction ix

SECTION I: THE LANDSCAPE

I am my problem 2
Opening the door to Jewish solutions 9
How Mussar practice aligns with recovery 21
Putting it to work 40

SECTION II: A TREASURE MAP

Step 1: Truth 50
Step 2: Faith 65
Step 3: Trust 88
Step 4: Courage 105
Step 5: Shame 126
Step 6: Alacrity 149
Step 7: Humility 167
Step 8: Responsibility 184
Step 9: Compassion 202
Step 10: Loving-kindness 226
Step 11: Holiness 243
Step 12: Generosity/Heart-Willingness 263

SECTION III. THE TREASURE FOUND

New Beginnings 280

Mussar Glossary 289
Recovery Terminology 292
Endnotes 295

Acknowledgements 305
About the Authors 307

To my teachers,
who help me find meaning in the white spaces

www.ingramcontent.com/pod-product-compliance
Lightning Source LLC
Chambersburg PA
CBHW050202240426
43671CB00013B/2224